SPEAK AND GET RESULTS

THE COMPLETE GUIDE TO SPEECHES AND PRESENTATIONS THAT WORK IN ANY BUSINESS SITUATION

by Sandy Linver

with Nick Taylor

SUMMIT BOOKS NEW YORK

Copyright © 1983 by Speakeasy, Inc.
All rights reserved
including the right of reproduction
in whole or in part in any form
Published by SUMMIT BOOKS
A Simon & Schuster Division of Gulf & Western Corporation
Simon & Schuster Building
Rockefeller Center
1230 Avenue of the Americas
New York, New York 10020

SUMMIT BOOKS and colophon are trademarks of Simon & Schuster
Designed by Irving Perkins Associates
Manufactured in the United States of America

10 9 8 7 6 5
First Edition
Library of Congress Cataloging in Publication Data

Linver, Sandy.
  Speak and get results.

  1. Communication in management.   2. Public speaking.
3. Oral communication.   I. Taylor, Nick.   II. Title.
HF5718.L56   1983   808.5′1′024658   82-16827

ISBN 0-671-44204-X

Thank You

To my staff, who believe in the Speakeasy philosophy and whose strong support and professionalism have enabled me to do more with my business than I ever thought possible.

To my clients, whose speaking needs and experiences continue to stimulate, challenge and inspire me.

To my friends in the business community, who have always had time to listen and ideas to share.

To the people who have made a major contribution to this book: Jim Silberman for his continued support; Caroline Harkleroad, my agent, who knows when to push and when to listen; Peggy Tsuka-hira, whose commitment and attention to detail make her a very special editor; Wendy Nicholson, whose expertise as a publicist is matched by her ability to see the writers she works with; Doris Bucher, Speakeasy's voice coach, who worked with me on the voice chapter and is responsible for many of the voice exercises; Frederic Wiedemann, Barbara Brightman and Danny Slomoff, whose invaluable contributions in the Speakeasy classroom are reflected throughout the style section of this book; and especially to Jim Mengert, who was always able to see the forest in spite of the trees, and whose Unstated Objective is for any work to be the best that it can be.

FOR EVERY SPEAKER WHO FEELS THAT
THE CONNECTION IS WORTH THE
EFFORT.

Contents

An Overview

I wrote my first book after ten years of teaching executives how to become better speakers. *Speak Easy,* subtitled "How to Talk Your Way to the Top," grew out of the classes and seminars I conduct at Speakeasy, my consulting firm. Working in a classroom comes more naturally to me than working on a book. When *Speak Easy* was finished, I heaved a big sigh of relief. "Thank goodness that's over," I said. "Now, let's get back to teaching."

But just four years later, here I am again. Knowing how relieved I was to finish the first book, my friends and associates have asked, "Why write another book? Didn't you say it all the first time?"

Well, I did and I didn't.

Speak Easy focused on what I call the "spoken image." This is more than the words we say. It's how we use the words, the sound of our voices, the way we use our bodies as we speak. Having a strong spoken image means feeling relaxed and in control in front of an audience. A person with a strong spoken image conveys authority and energy, and demonstrates an awareness of the people to whom he is speaking. Most important, he reaches out across the invisible line separating him from the audience and works to make something happen in their encounter. Watching speakers develop that ability to get results gives me a great feeling!

But what about the other side of speaking? A speaker brings his spoken image—his style—to any speaking situation. But he also brings his content—the information he is to present. And that information must be organized so the audience can understand and receive it.

Most of my students are business people and professionals. Their work demands that they know their content. *What* they have to say in their speeches and presentations is contained in their briefcases, law books, marketing plans, and production forecasts.

So I always saw learning *how* to deliver a message as the biggest need for people in business and the professions. Since they had their content at their fingertips, my clients need only develop effective styles to be able to make things happen in all their speaking situations.

But while I was working with clients on style, the organization of content in business presentations became an issue for me. Asked to watch the rehearsal of a presentation or a manuscript speech, I found it difficult not to get involved in critiquing the content. I came to realize that knowing your content—in other words, having something to say—is not the same as presenting it so others get the message. How can you be sure other people will receive your information? Just as speakers should reach out physically to the audience, they should also reach out intellectually to overcome barriers to their content. In content as in style, the speaker should not assume a battle line exists between him and his audience. I realized there were things to show business speakers about making their content more effective that were just as exciting as helping them with style.

Communicating in business life is never just an intellectual exercise. Business people and professionals want to make things happen. Their careers demand it, so they must be effective when they speak. The people I'm talking about have to make presentations on the progress of complex engineering projects; they have to sell clients on expensive ad campaigns; they have to convince the chief executive that the company has to change directions to avoid financial trouble; they have to persuade reluctant distributors to sell a new product; they have to persuade the rest of the board to make a new acquisition. The bottom line in every case is effective communication, presenting information to your audience in a way that makes things happen.

Some people are "naturals" at these everyday business situations. A natural inspires confidence with his relaxed, easy presence before an audience. A natural's message is clear and to-the-point. When a natural has finished speaking, people in the audience somehow know what is expected of them and they do it.

The naturals I spoke with all assured me of one thing—they didn't just stand up and start talking. Their presentations were as good as the amount of time and thought they put into them. They always approached a speaking assignment or a presentation as an integral part of their jobs. A talk was never something to be taken lightly or a bothersome chore to be left till the last minute. Don Keough, in addition to being president of the Coca-Cola Company, is one of the finest speakers I've ever heard. He put it this way: "Anybody who tells you that making a speech is an easy exercise is kidding himself. When you're preparing for a speech, a tough presentation, or a negotiating session, if you're going to do it well you have to think a lot about the people who are going to be there, and about what you really want to say. You can't do that by sitting down and writing notes on a piece of paper five minutes before you go in to speak."

So the naturals understood the importance of careful planning. I began to wonder about their other secrets. How are some speakers able to present information more effectively than others? How do they focus their messages clearly? How do they make their points easy to remember? How do they avoid getting bogged down in confusing facts and figures? How do they know what attitudes their audiences bring into the room? Does all this really come naturally to them? Or are there steps that any speaker can take to become as effective as the naturals?

The books I read on the subject were no help. They didn't have anything to do with what business executives and professionals face every day.

So I began developing a content workshop to supplement the seminars on style offered at Speakeasy. My aim was to provide the business speaker with practical tools he or she can apply in a business situation. I wanted to share the secrets of the naturals with business and professional people who can use them every day. The ideas I gathered for the content workshop have evolved into a set of simple guidelines. The result is a planning process that can be easily used by any speaker, including those who have no idea where to start in planning a presentation.

I haven't forgotten about style. Your spoken image is still there every time you open your mouth. My basic philosophy about what makes an effective style hasn't changed, and I continue to watch clients in Speakeasy's seminars struggling to improve, taking risks, really opening themselves up in order to find a spoken image that's right for them. But I've pinpointed some new factors in developing a speaking style that can help business speakers become more effective more quickly. Discussions of the stress that speakers feel, the resistance that is present to some degree in every audience, and techniques for handling these feelings that can help you most when you're on your feet in front of an audience —these are some of the things about style that are new in this book.

Style and content are separate issues. You can have a terrific grasp of how to arrange and present your content, but that doesn't guarantee an effective style. You can have a great style, but that doesn't mean you have something to say.

Style and content need to be approached separately, considered separately, learned separately. They form separate sections in this book. But they come together at the moment of presentation, when you open your mouth to speak. And they interact and influence one another. If you're shrill or visibly nervous, your well-organized content won't make much of an impact on your audience. And if your style is superb but you're just rattling off disorganized details, that's not going to work, either.

The really complete speaker, the natural, deals with both style and content and excels at both. The natural brings speaker and audience together on intellectual, emotional, and physical common ground.

I want you to be a natural when you finish this book. I want you to feel in control of the total speaking situation, from planning through delivery. I want you to be able to use these lessons every day to get the results you want from your speeches and presentations. Whether you're negotiating, leading a meeting, making a speech, or presenting, and whether you have an audience of one, fifty, or a thousand, the lessons are the same. The whole process is important; each step must be done carefully if the result is to be really effective.

This book, then, is dedicated to the proposition that naturals are made, not born.

PART I

ORGANIZE YOUR CONTENT TO GET THE RESULTS YOU WANT

MANY PEOPLE IN business make things harder than they have to be by seeing a speaking situation as a win-lose situation—me against them, speaker against audience. They see themselves in one world and the audience in another, and feel that in order to be successful, they have to bring the audience completely into their world, kicking and screaming if necessary.

But our word "communication" comes from the Latin word for "common." Sharing common ground, a common understanding or goal, is the basis of all communication. Although the speaker and the audience may occupy different worlds, there is always some part of the speaker's world that touches that of the audience. There is always a piece of the audience's world that is shared with the speaker. This is the common ground that exists in every speaking situation. The objective of any presentation is to expand the common ground shared by you and your audience. A diagram of common ground looks like this:

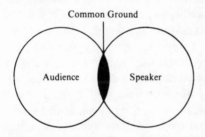

Common ground is always there, and it is the key to successfully planning and organizing the content of every speech and presentation. Speakers who reach out intellectually into the world of their audience can always bring their audience further into their world, because by reaching out they expand the common ground between themselves and their audience. They recognize that they and their ideas are important, but that to make something happen they must also consider the needs and ideas of their audience. Common ground is a central concept in the discussion of content planning and organization that follows.

Speakers make things hard for themselves in other ways, too. They apply different rules to the different forms of communication they use. In Speakeasy's workshop on content organization, clients have a tendency to assume that teaching aids illustrating one type of presentation apply to that type of presentation and no other. I hear comments such as: "This is fine for a speech. But my requirements are different. I have to make a presentation with slides." People look at manuscript speeches, slide presentations, informal talks, meetings, and negotiating sessions as if they were all different, as if each situation had its own unique set of rules. Negotiation, for example, is a form of communication that seems to have taken on a life of its own. It has become a popular subject for books and courses, and a set of rules has grown up around it. So people tend to think of negotiation as a different form of communication with unique rules that must be learned.

If you think this way you are making life too complicated. Every time you speak you're negotiating, presenting, persuading, informing. No matter what you call it, communication is communication. You communicate in a variety of ways and in different forms, but no matter which form you use it is the clarity of your ideas and your ability to persuade the audience that are important.

As you look at content organization in the section to follow, you will be looking at ways to organize your thinking for any speaking situation. There are some basic principles that apply no matter what type of presentation is involved. These principles evolve from the nature of communication itself. You may make adjustments or modifications to fit your particular type of presentation, but you still start from the same basics. A jeep is very different from a luxury sedan, but they are both meant to provide transportation and both are powered by the same basic internal combustion engine. The principles of arranging and writing a presentation that you will read here are, in effect, the internal combustion engine of communication.

Speakers who organize content well often consider their work something creative that "just happens." But effective content organization is not magic; underlying every work of art is a technique, and behind successful speeches and presentations is a planning process that involves a series of discernible steps.

Successful speakers spend a lot of time thinking well in advance about each presentation, so they are never scrambling for ideas at the last minute. They ask themselves a lot of questions, so they aren't surprised by developments they haven't anticipated. Their process of thought and questioning leads them to carefully defined objectives that incorporate their own needs and the needs of the audience, so both parties come away satisfied.

Successful speakers are sensitive to the potential for resistance in their audiences, and they use their knowledge of each audience to make sure their objectives are realistic. They test their objectives further by taking their "unstated objectives"—their personal emotional concerns—into account. They think in big ideas, big pictures that each audience can remember, and combine these main ideas into messages that they want the audience to be able to repeat when a presentation is over. They present their ideas creatively and use visual aids and resources only where necessary.

This section is devoted to exploring the components of effective content development:

— The underlying concept of reaching out intellectually into common ground.
— The objective, which is what you want your audience to do.
— The message, which is what you want them to remember and say.
— The selection and organization of content to support your message and reach your objective.

Knowing your objective in clear, unambiguous terms is the first step to a successful presentation. Happily, thinking about your objective is not something you have to do while sitting at your desk; you can just as easily think about it while you're jogging, driving to work, or engaged in any other activity that affords you time to think. It's not where or when, but the amount and quality of time you spend thinking about your objective that counts. But you have to find the right objective, because, as the saying goes, "If you don't know where you are going, you will end up somewhere else."

Finding the Right Objective

1

BUSINESSES BECOME successful because the people running them know what they want to do and make it happen. Every business has an objective that is its controlling purpose. It is a business truism that time is money, and no business gets off the ground or improves its position by marking time.

It follows that as a successful business makes things happen, business speeches and presentations must also make things happen. They, too, must have objectives that control their direction. They have to move their audiences, whether the movement is the flourish of a pen on a lucrative contract or a tiny nudge closer to the speaker's point of view. An effective speaker makes something happen.

Yet most business people, when they're faced with a speaking assignment, whether it's pitching a new client or reporting on quarterly sales, immediately start thinking about filling time. Their moments on the program loom like some uncharted ocean, and their biggest worry is how to get to the other side. So facts become their oars. They want to give the audience enough facts to carry them through to the end of the speech and to show how much they know about the subject, so that they can sit down without being embarrassed. The problem is, they don't think about organizing their facts to accomplish anything specific—they try only to amass enough facts to fill the time.

I'm amazed that people who make things happen every day in business suddenly stop trying to get results and start worrying about how long they have to talk. They don't seem to apply the same requirements to speaking that they apply to the rest of their business lives. They see a presentation as a chore, not an opportunity.

But a presentation is an opportunity, and its objective targets whatever opportunity exists for the speaker in that particular situation. An objective is necessary because if you don't know what you want to happen when you finish your presentation, you can't make sure it is going to happen. You can't take advantage of the opportunity. It is as simple as that.

If you were going in to review quarterly sales performance with your boss, you wouldn't walk into his office and dump the contents of your briefcase all over his desk. You would review the material in your briefcase and select what has to do with quarterly performance and what doesn't. You would locate the positive factors that improved performance and the factors that were negative, and make recommendations to keep what worked and change what didn't. In other words, you would begin a process of sorting out and evaluating. The end result of that process should be a clear picture of quarterly performance and what to do about it. Sales should improve as a result.

The facts at your disposal for a speech or presentation correspond to the material in your briefcase; there's always more available than you'll be able to use. Before you lay your information out before an audience, some weighing and sifting is required; some facts support your case, others detract, still others are irrelevant. Sales people, for example, would find it hard to do the job of one-on-one selling without organizing and presenting information about their products in a certain way. Yet the same people who are excellent at one-on-one selling start thinking "speech" and not "sale" when they have to make a presentation to a larger audience. Every speaker must not only get through a speaking situation, he must get something out of it.

DETERMINING YOUR NEEDS AS A SPEAKER

Laura was a successful saleswoman who attended one of my seminars. Her boss had asked her to review the company's line of restaurant and bar equipment for the members of a city's restaurant association. She would have had no trouble selling her products to any one of them; one reason was an array of energy-saving features that buyers found attractive. But faced with a group, Laura forgot about selling. Rehearsing her presentation with me beforehand, she brought in a trayful of slides that she planned to show the restaurant owners. The slides showed restaurants and bars where the equipment was used: I saw attractive neon graphics and smiling maître d's and bartenders welcoming people to lovely, well-designed places. Laura gave a successful travelogue for people who might want to eat and drink in the restaurants she showed, but in the presentation she outlined she never told her audience what her equipment could do for them. Laura had decided that somehow this presentation required something different from what she did so well every day. She was so distracted by her visual aids that she forgot her objective.

Frederick worked for a large consumer products company that had invested a lot of time and money in promotions identifying the company with a major annual sports event. His assignment was to make a presentation to marketing people from around the world. His aim was to convince them that they, too, should use promotions related to this event; the visibility would sell their products, of course, but it would also benefit his company because of its association with the event.

Before an advance review of his presentation, Frederick told me exactly what it was all about, who was in the audience, what he needed to have happen, and the sad fate that would befall him if he didn't meet his objective. But when he got up and went through the presentation, Frederick spent most of his time giving a dramatic monologue about the sports action. He recapped the event's history and all the hoopla surrounding it. In trying to convey its glamour as a marketing attraction, he got caught up in the event itself.

When Frederick finished talking, I said, "Well, what happens now?" He said, "What do you mean?" I said, "Where are we going with all this? Why do you want me to know all this sports history? What do you want to happen? What is the audience supposed to do now?"

And he thought a minute and said, "Gee. I never did ask for the order, did I?"

"Right!" I said. "In the five minutes when you and I discussed this presentation, you told me exactly what you wanted to happen and why, and how you were going to get to your objective. But then you stood up and gave me a dramatic recitation of sports highlights. It was exciting, but nowhere in your presentation was it clear what you wanted to happen. You lost track of your objective."

Laura and Frederick both needed to make something happen with their presentations, and both knew what their objectives were, but when they sat down to plan the presentation, they forgot them. Why? Because each had made a "good" speech the objective, and in the process they had lost track of the results they really needed. Both were effective one-on-one sales people, and in any easily identified sales situation found their objectives clear and easy to remember. But when they thought about talking to a group, their objectives suddenly became fuzzy and elusive.

Making something happen—capitalizing on the opportunity that a presentation represents—is what communication in the business and professional world is all about. Giving a presentation without recognizing, focusing on, and remembering your objective is the equivalent of dumping the contents of your briefcase all over your boss's desk. You don't speak to fill time by reeling off fact after unorganized fact, nor to show beautiful pictures that take the breath away, nor to impress the audience with your wit and skill as a dramatic speaker. You don't give speeches to win speech-making awards. You are there to make the best of an opportunity, just as you do in every other aspect of your business activities.

The information available to you, then, should always be geared toward meeting that objective. Your ideas and information cannot be scattered randomly on the wind; they must be pointed in the direction of your objective.

The first concern in identifying your objective is what you, the speaker, need to achieve from the presentation. You must be very clear about what you want to happen as the result of your presentation. If you don't know what you want to happen, you can hardly direct your presentation to achieve that result. In other words, why are you speaking? What must happen in order for you to feel professionally satisfied when your presentation is over? What do you want your audience to do when they leave that meeting room or auditorium? State your objective as an action verb describing the audience response you want:

"When I'm finished speaking I want the audience to:

". . . buy my product."
". . . think about investing."
". . . support my candidacy."
". . . approve my recommendation."
"I want them to like my speech" is not a legitimate objective. The speaker in every business situation, whether it's a meeting with one person, a presentation to fifty, or a speech to five hundred, has a need to go beyond entertainment to move his audience to action, to make something happen.

But identifying only your objective leaves someone out. A business must make something happen if it is to be successful, but it can't be successful without considering the needs of its customers. In much the same way, a successful speech or presentation must consider the needs of its audience, because what you want to happen isn't all there is.

DETERMINING THE NEEDS OF THE AUDIENCE

Not only do you, the speaker, bring certain needs to your speaking situation, but your audience needs to get something out of it, too. What does your audience need? Whether it's information, incentive, or assurance, the need of the audience can usually be best expressed as a question:

— "What are the costs and benefits of his product?"
— "How long will my money be tied up, and is it worth the return?"
— "Does this candidate favor tax breaks for small businesses?"
— "What will happen to profits if I accept his recommendation?"

Your audience's needs—to know, to be inspired, to be assured —are vital in determining your objective, so much so that the presentation itself should give some clue to the identity of the audience. You should be able to tell from reading or hearing a speech, without knowing the title or other information, who the audience is. Many presentations have objectives that consider only the needs of the speaker, leaving the audience completely obscured. A few months ago, I had a chance to read, after the fact, several speeches that an executive had delivered. His subjects were similar, although his audiences were not. Outside of the title pages, there wasn't a clue in any of those half-dozen speeches to tell me who the audiences were. When you hear a presentation and there is absolutely no clue in the content to help you identify the audience, it means that the speaker considered only his own needs and did not focus at all on the needs or concerns of his audience. The danger of overlooking the audience's needs is particularly acute in some of the slick, canned presentations that many professional firms use to pitch new clients.

Larry was a certified public accountant. He had taken the Speakeasy seminar, and he called me for help with the content of a speech on professional corporations he was to give to about one hundred lawyers and accountants. Larry came to my office carrying a lengthy draft that contained every conceivable piece of information about professional corporations. His speech could have been titled "Everything You Ever Wanted to Know About Professional Corporations and a Lot You Didn't." He quoted specific sections of the Internal Revenue Code verbatim. He cited cases at length and in great detail; thirteen tax cases and Tax Court rulings were contained in the twenty-two-page draft.

Larry was planning to tell his audience as much as he knew about the current law covering professional corporations. But his audience of lawyers and accountants needed more than a recitation of tax facts and rulings; these they already knew. Larry's problem was not how much information he could give them, but how he could make certain information relevant to them. The big question, for his audience, was "Should I consider a professional corporation?"

Concentrating on the needs of his audience, Larry came up with a talk that anticipated—that is, omitted—what the lawyers and accountants already knew. He threw out irrelevant information and gave his audience information that they needed most.

I was called upon recently to give a speech to a meeting of about five hundred association executives. Their jobs as heads of associations had taken them to all kinds of conventions, meetings, and seminars. My topic was "Making Effective Presentations." But in analyzing my audience, I learned they had been to many meetings at which they were likely to have heard talks on effective presentations. I also looked at some of the magazines and professional journals they read. These publications were full of tips on making presentations and using audiovisual aids. I saw story titles like "How to Use Slides Effectively," "When to Use a Slide Tape," "Videotape in Marketing Can Increase Sales," "Overhead Transparencies Can Make Your Point."

It was clear to me in glancing through their trade magazines that they had plenty of information about the use of visual aids in their presentations. I didn't want to give them more of the same. By being aware of the audience, I was able to avoid reinventing the wheel with these association executives.

Considering your audience's needs in addition to your own brings you closer to your objective than if you focus only on what you need to accomplish. Recently, my search for a new lawyer brought me in contact with attorneys from two law firms. The first lawyer invited me to his office and gave me a tour of the firm, which occupied two floors of a downtown office tower. He introduced me to the trust specialists and pointed out the litigation wing, the boardroom, and the offices of the clerks and paralegals.

The second lawyer, instead of inviting me to his office, asked if he could come to mine. Miles asked me about Speakeasy and let me give him a brief tour. He spent less than ten minutes telling me about his firm. But at the end of his visit, he knew enough about Speakeasy to tell me what his firm could do for me. Miles was shaping the content of his presentation by considering the needs of his audience.

An effective objective is a balance between the speaker's needs and the needs of the audience. What do you want to happen? And, based on what you can find out about your audience, what do you think they need from you? What must they get out of the presentation in order to be satisfied? You must always consider the needs of your audience and your own needs, and attempt to satisfy both sets of needs with your presentation. These overlapping needs—the mutual interests of speaker and audience that exist in every speaking situation—form the all-important concept of common ground. You should never take common ground for granted, even in an "in-house" situation, because although your overall goals may coincide with your colleagues', your plans for reaching them may differ drastically. Thinking about the needs of your audience isn't something to be saved for "special" speaking situations, but something that effective business people do every day even when the audience is the boss or a group of employees.

HOW TO FIND THE COMMON GROUND

Common ground is something that we take for granted every day. Communication is more difficult with strangers than it is with old friends, because new people present no predetermined common ground from which to work. We meet a stranger on the elevator and we say, "Nice day," or "We've had a lot of rain." That's trivia, of course, but what are we trying to do? We're trying to connect on a basis that both parties recognize. We're trying to make contact.

You walk into the office of someone you haven't seen for a while and you say, "How was the trip to Bermuda?" You see a client or someone from another division whom you don't see on a regular basis and you say, "How is the restoration going on that old home you bought?" Or you might ask him about his golf or tennis game.

Granted, these are all examples of small talk, but they all establish a functional basis for communication at their particular levels. The less you know a person the more you'll talk about things that everybody has in common, like the weather, sports, or events of the day. We use small talk to establish those first tentative bridges of communication at cocktail receptions and dinner parties, and we certainly do it in business. It's an attempt to establish rapport, to connect with the other person across the gulf of our initial ignorance of one another. It is a first step toward discovering the many opportunities that surely exist for relating on more meaningful levels.

Since seeking out common ground is almost second nature in social situations, we often forget about it in planning a presentation. Instead of looking for that common ground, which we would do automatically in a dinner-table conversation, we try to tell people only what we want to tell them.

Common ground in a business situation, as in a personal one, consists of similar experiences and interests. If you're asked to speak to a group, they must have some interest in what they think you have to say. If you're a brand manager talking to marketing personnel, you have a similar interest in sales. If you're the chairman of the board speaking at a stockholders' meeting, both you and your audience are likely to have an interest in year-end profits. If you're the public affairs director at a television station and your audience is composed of public relations interns, your shared interest is getting quality public service announcements on the air.

In a business presentation, the speaker and the audience can always be presumed to have shared interests that bring them together. The simplest construction of this relationship is that the speaker needs to sell—his product, his program, his ideas—and the audience needs to buy—a better product, the right program, some new ideas. Your objective must identify these shared interests and overlapping needs. Where does the speaker's knowledge touch the audience's need to know? Once you identify the common ground, you can move toward expanding it and satisfying the needs of both parties.

You don't need a secret file on your audience to identify the common ground you share walking into a speaking situation; there's a lot you won't know about them and a lot they'll never know about you. All that's necessary is to find out where your priorities, interests, and needs overlap in your given situation. Often, finding the common ground is just a matter of stopping to think about your audience. Other times it is not quite so apparent, and to find it you must ask a lot of questions.

Larry, the accountant who was speaking about professional corporations, determined that he could give his audience of professionals valuable advice that could help them decide whether to incorporate their practices. By asking questions like "What are the advantages, disadvantages, and potential pitfalls of professional corporations for my audience?" he brought his tax facts into focus and gave his audience a useful talk that met both their needs.

In my talk to the association executives, I gave them information about presenting themselves effectively to an audience rather than effective ways to use visual aids. I met my need as a speaker to give them a professional, informative presentation, as well as the need of those association heads to hear something new about a well-worn topic.

When I had finished talking with the two attorneys whose firms I was considering to represent Speakeasy, I decided to retain Miles's firm. By taking the time to identify my needs and integrate them with his own, he met his objective—winning a new client for his law firm. In each of these cases, the speakers found the common ground they shared with their audiences and built upon it to reach their objectives.

The area of common ground shared by you and your audience may be only a minute part of your total existence. But it's important that you find it, because if you don't, you're not going to connect at any time in your presentation, and as a result, nothing will happen.

Disagreement Can Form Common Ground

Many people make the assumption that you must agree with your audience in order to have common ground. But even when you know that you and your audience disagree, you can build your presentation on negative common ground. Stating a point of view that you know your audience will disagree with is a perfectly acceptable way of establishing common ground. It legitimizes the difference of opinion and brings it into the open, providing a starting point for discussion that could open the way to eventual agreement. Sharing common ground—an area of similar interest—by no means implies that you must share an opinion about it.

The president of a utility company, for example, can speak to a group of utility consumers without agreeing with them about the need for strict regulation of public utilities. They need only share a concern about regulation and the regulatory process to establish a functional basis for communication. The utility executive talking to business managers about the high cost of regulation will find quick agreement, and stands a good chance of persuading his audience to protest overregulation if that is his objective; the common ground in this case is broad and firm. The consumers' group may be just as interested in the issue of regulation, but they probably want more regulation, not less. The common ground is narrower, but nonetheless the same; the executive's objective here must be less ambitious: to convince his audience that his point of view—say, that regulation can be costly to the consumer—is at least worth considering.

Another example of negative common ground might occur between departments of the same company, when a new computer system is purchased that fits the needs of inventory and production but means more work for personnel. If you're from personnel and you're making a presentation to top management, you could attempt to establish common ground by pointing out that the system may be good for the entire company, but has created special problems for your department.

Once you identify the essence of what you want and need to happen and what the audience wants and needs, it's time to take your first step toward common ground—identifying the circumstances you and the audience share simply by being together.

SIZING UP THE SPEAKING CIRCUMSTANCES

Before planning the first word of your speech or presentation, you must systematically assess *who* is involved, *what* is involved, and *why, where, when,* and *how* the speech is going to be delivered. These questions are asked by every reporter who goes out to cover a news event, and the answers provide the reader with the full story, the best and most thorough assessment of the situation. You need the full story on your speech or presentation in order to locate your common ground and plan an objective that satisfies the needs of both you and your audience.

These circumstances, or what I sometimes call the mechanics, of the speaking situation are one piece of common ground that the speaker and the audience undoubtedly share. This circumstantial common ground can be as straightforward as in your regular weekly meeting with your boss—you know with whom you're meeting, what you're going to talk about, and the purpose of the meeting. You certainly know the location of his office and the time and day of the meeting. And you know how you will make the points that you need to make in the meeting. If you know your boss has just been chewed out by his boss, you'll factor that into your approach. If he's facing deadlines, you'll try to keep your presentation brief.

A similar knowledge of the circumstances prepares you to build upon common ground in all your speaking situations. You certainly can't make contact if you don't know who your audience is;

you might try to sell a side of beef to an audience of vegetarians. If you are making a presentation as part of a tightly scheduled, day-long seminar, you share that rigorous schedule with the entire audience, and it becomes a point of common ground that helps you determine your objective. So if you are the last speaker on the program, you know both you and the audience will be tired when you speak. That knowledge helps you decide to scale down your forty-five-minute speech to make allowance for weariness and a shorter attention span. If you are planning a slide presentation on your company's new magazine ad campaign, it will affect your objective if vision in a third of the room is obstructed by pillars. You and your audience share the format of the program, so if you have ten minutes to speak and five minutes to answer questions, you know to fit your objective to the time limit that forms part of your common ground.

It is important to think about your place on the program, not only to avoid overtaxing the audience, but also because following other speakers means you may have to consider your objective in light of what has already been said. Martin, the head of a large division of a national company, shared the dais with other executives of the same company during a two-day national meeting. Martin's speech was scheduled last; he knew that by the time it was his turn other speakers would have covered most of the possible topics. Although Martin thought about his presentation for weeks ahead of time, one of the realities he had to consider was that he could not totally prepare his presentation in advance. He was going to have to remain flexible, because he knew others were likely to cover much of what he would have said had he been first on the agenda.

Martin's wrap-up spot on the program was well situated for him to send the audience away happy about the company's accomplishments of the past year and enthusiastic about the year to come, so that became his objective. But he knew other speakers would dwell on the past year's success, so Martin looked elsewhere and found in the meeting itself examples of accomplishment and cooperation that supported his objective. Even something as simple as your place on the program can have a profound effect on your objective and on the choice of information that goes into a presentation satisfying the needs of both parties.

Knowing what mood your audience will be in can save you the

embarrassment of a speaker I know who insisted on giving his formal address at ten-thirty in the evening to a work- and cocktail-weary audience and then found them conspicuously uninterested and nodding off before he finished.

Your mutual presence—the fact that you and your audience are together—is common ground that has a significant bearing on your objective. The circumstances in which you and your audience are brought together should be very much a part of the information that goes into the planning of your objective.

Because these circumstances appear at first glance to be obvious, it is often easy to overlook them in your planning. The last thing you want as a speaker, however, is to be surprised, and a thorough assessment of every speaking situation will forestall this. In addition, most speakers sit down to work on their presentations with either an overload of information to sort out—like the material in your briefcase—or with a blank page. In either case, the process of inquiry—asking questions—stimulates your thinking and gets you started toward finding the right objective.

The Speakeasy Presentation Planning System © includes a number of important questions about your audience that can help you plan your objective with confidence. Questions like these should always be part of your planning process; don't leave anything to assumption or imagination when you consider all the circumstances which bring you and the audience together:

1. Why is this group assembled on this occasion?
2. Why has the group invited you, or why have you called the meeting?
3. Will they attend by choice or by obligation?
4. When do you appear on the program—at the beginning, middle, or end? Or are you the only speaker?
5. If you are not the only speaker, are you the keynote speaker, the main speaker, a panel member, or one of many speakers?
6. Will you be presented as an honored guest, a reputable authority, or a trustworthy colleague? Are you a stranger, about whom the audience has no preconceptions, or are you mildly disliked or distrusted, a member of the opposition? In other words, what preconceived notions, if any, might your audience have about you?
7. How much time do you have to make your presentation?

8. How much time do you have to prepare your presentation?
9. Will the audience have just eaten, be waiting to eat, be ready to adjourn? Have they had cocktails, been working all day? What other factors might affect their attention level?
10. How will the audience be dressed? What is the general tone of the meeting?
11. Is the seating arrangement classroom/auditorium, restaurant/ banquet, conference table, or some other?
12. What is the composition of the group? Include here whether they are male or female; white, black, or other minority; have high school, college, or postgraduate educations; are lower, middle or upper management.
13. What is their income average and life-style?
14. Who are the key members of the audience?
15. If the topic has been left up to you, have any suggestions been made or implied?
16. Who has spoken to this group previously in similar situations? With what results and reactions from the group?

Many of these questions may seem aimed at public speaking situations in which you can't be expected to know much about the audience in advance. But even when you're preparing for an in-house presentation, you should make it a point to ask similar questions. Exploring variations on this theme—the circumstances of your speaking situation—will always stimulate your thinking and give you information that can help you know how to reach your objective.

Demographics is the term pollsters and rating services use to describe population groups—what kind of people, for example, will vote for certain candidates or watch certain TV shows. You are doing much the same thing when you try to learn about your audience in preparing a presentation—you are trying in a basic way to predict behavior. Getting this information is the best way of assuring that when you stand up before an audience, you will accomplish what you want to do.

Thorough planning that incorporates a good, hard look at your speaking situation is important in every case, no matter how well acquainted you believe you are with your audience and the circumstances that bring you together. Develop the habit of leaving no consideration unexamined in your presentation planning.

Avoid stereotypes and assumptions in looking at the "who" of your audience. You are likely to pay less attention to your audience when you are speaking "close to home," to an audience of business colleagues, employees, or other groups you think you know quite well. When the information you seek about your audience is so readily accessible that you tend to take it for granted, you forget to ask the questions. You are inclined to say, "I know these people. We speak each other's language and I know they're on my side, so I'll be able to take this right off the top of my head."

Craig, who was taking a Speakeasy seminar, told me, "All these questions about the audience are fine for people who go around the country making speeches to strangers. But if it's people you work with, you really don't have to do it."

"What?" I answered. "Not give the people you work with, your bosses and employees, the same attention you'd give to strangers around the country?"

He reflected and said, "I guess you're right. They deserve attention, too."

They not only deserve your attention; your effectiveness as a speaker demands that they get it. Chris, an employee of a food products distributor, was asked to give a presentation about the various transportation methods considered for distribution of a new product. She outlined several types of transportation that she said wouldn't work, and then recommended a method that would. A colleague questioned her approach, asking if she shouldn't have gone straight to the recommended method without bothering to explain the methods she'd rejected. But Chris was using her audience analysis; in this case, she knew her boss liked to have a lot of background information and would want to know which other possibilities had been eliminated and why.

At a budget meeting, it may seem clear that the objective shared by you and your in-house audience is better sales projections and profit margins. But assuming that your audience will automatically agree with your proposal to increase sales can get you in trouble. You must always look deeper.

Suppose that at this meeting, the people in marketing promise increased sales by offering customers several additional color options on the product. Here, they're treading on common ground with the production staff, for whom adding several new colors could necessitate major plant adjustments that are not included in their budget. To enter the meeting with a brainstorm presentation about how you're going to increase sales by offering new colors is one thing, but to do it without becoming aware of the production department's concerns would be professional suicide. You should always confirm your assumptions by asking the right questions, no matter how well you think you know your audience.

All of these questions illustrate the fact that you don't operate in a vacuum when you plan any presentation. The questions are simply devices to help you reach out and make contact with your audience by finding the right objective. The information they generate will keep your objective in focus. Each piece of information, each detail, can help form the foundation of an effective presentation that does what you want it to do.

Getting the Answers

Now that you have some of the questions, you must figure out a way to get the answers. But who has the time to do all this research? It's not as difficult as you might think. Usually, the best way of getting what you want is to ask for it.

If your speech is to a group outside your company or association, you can learn about your audience by asking the person who contacts you some of the same basic questions you saw above. Let's say the program chairman of a downtown civic club in Houston has called or written you about speaking on wealth management in times of inflation. Members of this club are likely to fit a certain profile. But remember, don't rely on stereotypes. You can and should confirm your assumptions with the person who contacts you.

You won't always be speaking to a civic club which has someone as convenient as a program chairman, of course. It is more likely that you will be making presentations to clients or colleagues. The same rule of thumb applies: If you don't know, ask. I think you'll be pleasantly surprised at how willingly people will give you the answers. Clients, for example, want to give all the information that's necessary to assure that a presentation, product, or service meets their needs. If your presentation is to a group of people in your company, everyone from department heads to secretaries will be glad to supply the information that can make what you say more interesting and attuned to them. Business colleagues have a similar interest in letting you know as much as possible about the situation, since your increased knowledge benefits them by permitting a more thorough and better-focused presentation.

A careful look at the common ground provided by the circumstances of your speaking situation will provide a surprising amount of valuable information. What you now know about your needs, your audience's needs, and your surroundings is information that gives you confidence and a sense of control. As your presentation takes shape, it moves toward filling needs and making something happen. Aiming for your objective is a lot more exciting than just filling time.

Right now, you think you've got the right objective. But before you go further in planning your presentation, there are some vital tests you can apply to your objective to make sure it is not affected by outside factors, and that it is neither too ambitious nor too modest for your speaking situation. Armed with the information you now have, let's look at your objective again to be *sure* you can make things happen when you speak.

2

Testing Your Objective

TESTING YOUR objective to be sure it is the right one for your situation and audience is a process of looking beneath the surface. It means examining both your own and your audience's attitudes and knowledge concerning your presentation for any hidden factors that might have influenced your choice of objectives. Even when your objective seems overwhelmingly obvious, submitting it to the following two final questions will help you detect any buried problems:

—Are you sure that your objective has not been influenced by needs you have other than your professional needs?

—From what you know about your audience, does your objective expect too much or too little from them?

Once your objective has passed this final test—or been modified as a result of it—you can be confident that it is the right objective for your presentation and use it to help you select and focus your content.

Business success demands constant and rapid decision-making. Executives and professionals must analyze business situations on an almost daily basis, and the growing use of computers means the tools of analysis are more and more available. When an important decision is involved, the people in charge don't take the first answer that pops out of the computer; they continue to probe and query to be sure the answer is the right one. The same kind of analysis, in which you constantly monitor your situation to figure out what action is required, should go into every speaking occasion. You must continually assess the context and apply what you learn to shaping and achieving your objective. Since this is the first step in problem-solving, it should be nothing new to people in business, who solve problems every day.

Every speaking situation contains flexible elements that require your constant, keen awareness.

SELF-EXAMINATION: KNOW YOUR HIDDEN OBJECTIVES

"But I have already done a lot of thinking and asked a lot of questions that have pointed me toward my objective," you say. "What other objectives could a speaker possibly have when he stands in front of an audience?" There is always an agenda of "hidden objectives" that will affect what you say just as much as your obvious, explicit objective. If you're not aware and in control of these hidden objectives, they can hamper your ability to reach your professional objective.

Suppose you are on a program with five other executives. You have a very cut-and-dried topic to present, but at the same time you would like to stand out and distinguish yourself from the others on the program. Your desire to stand out is an unstated, hidden objective that has no direct relationship to the goal of your presentation. Now, there is nothing wrong with that—unless your hidden objective interferes with the achievement of your professional objective. And this it can do; your eyes must always be open to the possibility of interference from your hidden objective, because it is always there, no matter how disciplined you are or how restricted your subject matter. Always make yourself aware of your hidden objectives and take them into account in your planning.

Whom Are You Trying to Impress?

Hidden objectives usually have something to do with the ego, so they can affect even the most experienced speakers. I was recently scheduled to participate in a workshop where another speech consultant was on the program. We had never been on the same program before, and I knew most of the people in this group had not seen me "in action" in front of an audience. I went into my planning for that workshop determined to be the superstar. A month beforehand, I found myself trying to come up with gimmicks and different approaches that would, in a subtle way, cut down my competitor's approach. Then I had a flash of realization that made me stop to think about what was going on. My unstated objective of outshining my competition was making me do things I wouldn't have done otherwise. I knew that if I let my unstated objective take over, I would never be able to meet my professional objective of making a clear, useful presentation. That flash of insight allowed me to get my planning back on track; I focused on my objective for that audience and planned my content as if I were going to be on the program alone.

Stiff competition is a part of today's business world. There's a premium on better ideas, better methods, better products; and the person who's first with the most is on the ladder to success. That has made it a world of winners and losers, in which there's a lot at stake in each meeting or presentation. The pressure to succeed gives every speaker priorities that go beyond just presenting a program with a direct, stated objective. One unstated objective is often to "prove" something to somebody, to demonstrate superiority: "I want to show the other account executives that I'm better than they are," or "I'll show the managers that I really know what I'm talking about." The hidden objective is to win, win, win. And because the other person feels that he or she has to win, too, you come up against a lot of resistance. Business people encounter that win-lose atmosphere in practically every job that's worth having. At a subconscious level, you want to go into a presentation and show others how much more you know than they do.

How do most people go about showing others how smart they are? By telling them everything they know in their twenty minutes on the program. The unstated objective of most presentations is to tell the audience as much as possible in the time available. Why else do executives get up at cocktail parties and ignore the circumstances while they give long-winded speeches? Why do people plan presentations that give no clue to the identity of the audience? Because their need to show how much they know becomes more important than the needs of the audience and more important than their professional objective.

Companies Can Impose Hidden Objectives, Too

Your own hidden objectives are not the only ones you may have to deal with in a speaking situation. Companies often feel business pressures that cause them to have hidden objectives, too. These pressures are invariably passed along to employees, who feel them most in speaking situations.

A woman in one of my style seminars worked for a company that supplied research information to banks. Diane had no choice about the information in her presentations; she had to give her banker audiences detailed information designed to help them make profitable long-range investments. Explaining data-filled charts and reams of statistics would inevitably require much of her time. But instead of putting her information in a form her audiences could use, she concentrated on describing the research methodology and proving the accuracy of her statistics.

Diane had another burden beyond supplying copious statistics: Two of the top people in her company had recently left for other jobs. Both men had excellent reputations in the research field, and the company feared their absence would hurt business. So Diane's unstated objective was to let her audiences know that despite the fact that two top people had left, the company was as good as it had ever been. More than that, it was to show that she was as good as the two men who had left.

Diane could have met both hidden objectives if she had achieved her professional objective of giving her audiences information that would let them make better investment decisions. But she never gained control of her hidden objectives or her company's. She always pressed too hard in her presentations, supplying too many details about where the information came from and not sorting out what the clients really needed for their specific investment pro-grams. She never was able to make the distinction between a piece of information that was accurate and one that was valuable to the clients. Diane ultimately left the research firm.

Hidden agendas, no matter whether they come from within or without, are capable of placing heavy pressure on us as speakers. Just recognizing our hidden objectives is not enough; we must also learn to deal with them, since they occur in virtually every com-munication situation we encounter every business day and since they always have the potential to sidetrack us from our real objec-tive.

MANAGING YOUR HIDDEN OBJECTIVES

We can never simply eliminate our hidden objectives. They stem from feelings and emotions that are part of us as human beings. We all want to "shine" in our work, to feel that we are successful in pressure situations. You can, however, manage them so that they don't interfere with your professional objective. Managing your hidden objectives means getting them out on the table —making yourself aware of them and taking them into account in your presentation planning. You can recognize your unstated objectives in the planning process with some simple self-analysis.

Try to be open-minded as you look at yourself. Perhaps your tension level is inordinately high as you are working on an important project. Ask yourself, "Why am I getting so uptight? Why is this so difficult?" If you pull back and do some unbiased thinking about the way you feel about yourself and the audience and what you want to happen, you may find that you are thinking things like "Boy, my boss is going to say I'm terrific when this presentation is over," or "Wait till I'm finished. This will sure show Joe how much more I know than he thinks I do."

We all have these thoughts; they are a part of wanting to be liked and admired and thought well of. Make note of them, even write them down on paper, as you plan your presentation, and then you'll be in a position to deal with them. Your dialogue with yourself may go something like this: "Well, yes, it would be nice if I get a standing ovation while they laugh poor old Joe out the door. But that really has nothing to do with my presentation. My task, my real objective, is to make a professional and informative presentation that helps people make decisions. My objective is not to make the boss think I'm dynamite or to upstage Joe. My objective is to make the marketing people understand that they have to make some different choices about their advertising. And if I do that well, what I want so badly from my boss will happen." There's nothing wrong with wanting approval and recognition. We all want those things and will always think about them when we think about speaking to an audience. But you must recognize that desire, admit it to yourself, and get it out in the open where you can deal with it without letting it get in your way.

Now you have tested your professional objective against the concerns imposed by your hidden objectives. If the objective you originally formulated stood up to the test of unstated objectives, then the test confirmed your original choice. If unstated objectives influenced your thinking about what you wanted to happen in your presentation, then the test made you aware of the influence of hidden concerns on your real objective and perhaps caused you to reformulate it.

AUDIENCE RESEARCH: STUDYING THE MARKET

Now, take a closer look at your audience. You have already asked what your audience needed from your presentation. You still must learn how much they know about your topic and what factors exist among the audience that may affect your ability to reach your objective.

Many business speakers think their job is simply to inform their audience, to provide them with unvarnished facts that the audience may take or leave. But it is never quite that simple. There are said to be two kinds of talks in business—those that inform and those that persuade—but almost all informative presentations have a touch of persuasion. You don't just dole out information the way you might ladle out soup in a cafeteria line; you want your audience to buy that information as persuasive and reliable. If it has been a bad quarter, you want your listeners to know why it's been a bad quarter; if you are giving them results of a research project, you want them to believe the results and act on them.

Your initial audience analysis was a sort of "fact-finding" tour to locate common ground. Now your consideration of the audience is more pragmatic. You have decided what you want to happen as the result of your presentation. But will your audience's knowledge or attitudes keep you from reaching your objective?

Anybody who wants to sell something has to know about potential buyers. Manufacturers don't just throw products on the shelf without testing the market; advertising agencies don't run ad campaigns without knowing their pilot audiences. They perform market analyses to determine the levels of awareness, as well as the kinds of attitudes, their markets have toward a specific product and ways that product might be promoted and advertised. They want to know if potential buyers know about the product and, if so, whether they understand it. If buyers know about the product and understand its purpose, a market study's next task is to determine if they believe in it and if they are ready to be moved to action. Are they ready to buy? Considering the huge investments of time, money, and manpower required to manufacture and sell a new product today, to put a product on the market without a thorough grasp of buyer attitudes would be foolish at best.

If consumers have no knowledge of the product, the manufacturer or marketer must try to create both awareness and interest. Liquid soap is an example of a product that had been used commercially for some time but was not marketed for home use until recently. Home consumers first had to be made aware that liquid soap was a product they could use; next they had to be moved through other stages to the point where they were ready to buy liquid soap to use at home. When automatic tellers first came to the banking industry, billboards and newspaper ads created an initial twinge of curiosity—a need for more information—that was satisfied when the machines were installed and introduced to consumers. Widespread publicity about toxic shock syndrome left many women unsure and confused about a product they had used for years. To counter the negative feelings, ad campaigns went back to square one and, rather than advertising one brand of tampon as better than another, tried to clear up misconceptions about the product. That is a necessary step in dealing with an audience whose viewpoint, right or wrong, is the opposite of what is desired.

Your ideas are no different from a product that is going to be put out on the shelf; a speaker has to do the same kind of "market study." The key questions are similar to those in any market survey:

1. Is the market, or audience, unaware of your subject—that is, totally ignorant of what you're about to tell them? Perhaps worse, are they misinformed?
2. On the other hand, are they at some stage of awareness of what you're going to tell them? Do they, for example, already have some idea of this new accounting procedure that you're going to

install in their department? Do they know about the changes that have been going on inside the company?

3. If they're aware, do they understand?
4. If they understand, do they believe?
5. And if they understand and believe, are they ready to move to action—are they ready to buy your point of view?

These are important questions, because they indicate how far you have to move your audience before you've met your objective. The more stages you want to move your audience through, and the faster you want to move them, the more difficult your task and the greater the challenge you're setting up for yourself as you plan your content. You have to think about moving your audience through the stages from unawareness to awareness to action, and set your goals realistically.

The Marketing Model

To assure that your goal is a realistic one, it is useful to employ a marketing model like the one below. Locate your audience on the scale in terms of what they know about your subject before you speak, and also indicate where you want them to be after your presentation. The distance you are attempting to move them should give you a good idea if your goal can be achieved.

Before you speak, where is your audience in relation to your message?		After you speak, where do you hope they will be?
_____	Stage 1. Unaware or Misinformed	_____
_____	Stage 2. Aware of the Issue	_____
_____	Stage 3. Informed on the Key Points	_____
_____	Stage 4. Believing, Convinced of Your View	_____
_____	Stage 5. Ready to Act on Their Belief	_____

Now reconsider your objective in light of the marketing model: Does your objective take sufficient account of where your audience is on the "Unaware-to-Action" scale?

It is awfully frustrating to walk away from a presentation asking yourself, "Gee, what's wrong? I had all my information there.

Why didn't it work?'' That happened to me a year or so ago in a one-day workshop on better speaking that I was giving for mid-level hospital administrators. These people listened politely all day long, but they asked very few questions and I really had to work hard to keep things going. As I thought about it later, I realized that I had assumed that just because they were in the room, they were at Stage 4—they wanted to be better speakers and understood how it would help their careers. I thought they were ready to be moved to Stage 5—to work hard at gaining the tools to become better speakers. But they weren't committed to better speaking at all; their management was. The group I was talking to was at Stage 1, the unawareness stage, and reacted to my presentation as if they were saying to themselves, "Speaking? What does better speaking have to do with running a hospital?" At the end of the seminar, many of them were aware and maybe a little bit understanding, but they were frustrated and I was frustrated because we were pushing for different levels of awareness and commitment. Knowing where your audience is on the scale can prevent this frustration by letting you set a reasonable objective, one that doesn't try to take the audience further than you can reasonably expect to move them in one presentation.

A production expert outlining major production-flow problems and proposing solutions in a presentation to upper management, for example, is assuming his audience is at Stage 3—informed on key points—and is trying to move them through Stage 4 to Stage 5. Soon after he begins, however, he may find that one or two members of the management group weren't even aware that problems existed. If he had considered this possibility in his planning, he would have in mind relevant information that would allow him to change his objective. He could go back to Stage 1, the unawareness stage, and cite data and cases to convince his audience that the problems did exist. Once he reached that objective, he could then move to convince them that the problems were serious enough to warrant innovative solutions.

You may not be 100 percent accurate in your first assessment of your audience. But if you spend some extra time at this stage determining where your audience is on the marketing model scale, it will not only help you select your content and focus your objective, but also enable you to change your objective during the actual presentation if you discover your audience knows less or more than you thought they did.

AUDIENCE ATTITUDES AS INFLUENCING FACTORS

Your audience's knowledge of your subject affects how far they can be moved on the marketing model scale. Their attitudes toward both you and your message also influence how far and how fast you can move them. Does your objective take into account any influencing factors such as resistance, hostility, or support on the part of your audience? Influencing factors are any emotional issues or feelings about the subject or you, the speaker, which influence how far you can move them. If you are trying to move them too far in your presentation, you should be prepared to scale down your objective and make it more realistic. If you are not trying to move them far enough, you should enlarge your objective and try to do more.

Suppose you are talking about Darwin's theory of evolution. If your audience has never heard of Darwin and his *The Origin of Species,* you can introduce the notion of natural selection to them and make them aware of it. You can make them understand it. But if they believe strongly in Biblical creation, that is as far as they'll go; a very strong emotional factor—religious conviction—influences your ability to move the audience further.

If you are the production expert whose audience analysis reveals that top management is unaware of production problems, an influencing factor might be your track record with the company. If you have a history of good performance, of making recommendations that work, you may only have to explain at the beginning of the meeting that production problems exist. Your awareness of the influencing factor in this case makes your objective more ambitious, since you know you can move your audience further on the marketing model scale. But if you're "the new kid on the block" in that company, you should understand that that's an influencing factor; you'll have to work harder to convince your audience.

Let's look at some other influencing factors that will determine how quickly you can take your audience through the steps in the marketing model. Say you are in marketing research, and for the past two years have supplied a Caribbean island nation with information that has helped it develop a thriving tourist trade. You've given the island's officials four presentations in the two years, and your recommendations have worked well for them. The good results have given you great credibility with these people, and they will be receptive to more of your ideas and eager to try them. But if you had a bad experience with these officials, or if your suggestions failed to give the desired results, you are not going to be able to take them through the steps as quickly.

If you are trying to push a philosophy different from that held by your audience, the potential for audience resistance should influence your choice of objectives. About two years ago, the chairman of a very conservative company went into a meeting with his board of directors determined that they should approve the purchase of a smaller firm. Lamar took a straightforward approach to his presentation, describing the company and mentioning, among a number of other facts, that it recently had been unprofitable. When he had finished, the board rejected the purchase. Lamar asked me later what I thought had gone wrong. I told Lamar I felt he should have spent some time in preliminary discussions with individual board members with the objective of getting them to believe that buying an unprofitable company sometimes makes sense. He then could have used the board meeting to win their approval for this particular purchase. Lamar had set his objective without taking influencing factors into account, in this case, the resistance of board members who had never bought an unprofitable company before and did not want to depart from their conservative philosophy.

Lamar's initial objective was aimed at making something happen with his presentation. But by failing to consider factors that influenced his audience, he failed to reach his objective.

Anticipating Resistance

Anticipating audience resistance to your message does not mean you have to tell your listeners what they want to hear to get them on your side. The prospect of resistance is an influencing factor that lets you know you must temper your objective; if you cannot expect to move your listeners to agreement, you may still decide to provoke them to think about your point of view.

We're all familiar with some of the old stereotypes that are applied to women, especially homemakers. I ran into these lingering stereotypes when I was asked to speak to a convention of distributors who sold a line of products marketed almost exclusively to women through home visits and neighborhood "parties." The products were quite successful, and the distributors were making good incomes using marketing techniques that had worked well for many years. But I think any business must constantly test its methods against new developments in the marketplace; I felt that these distributors needed to take a hard look at their approach if they wanted to remain successful. I decided to say things the way I saw them to this audience of a thousand people, about half of whom were women, not because I thought I could win them over to my point of view, but because I wanted to make them think a little.

Their meeting was in an older city on the Eastern Seaboard, so I used the city as a basis for comparing old and new, saying that despite the benefits of tradition, it is still important to keep up with changing times. I suggested that the way they marketed their products, and also the way the female distributors looked at themselves as women, could stand a second look. One change meant adopting a strong spoken image.

I also told them I was concerned about the messages they sent out with their constant smiles, which seemed to be in place twenty-four hours a day. They were constantly, determinedly "up," when an occasional let-down or a lapse of enthusiasm is normal in the hectic pace of today's business world; it's hard to convince me that people can smile all the time and be sincere about it. I recommended that they take a more "real" approach. I tried to keep a vein of humor running through my remarks, but my challenge to them was unmistakable.

I wasn't too surprised when a woman stood up during the question-and-answer period and said, in a very aggressive way, that she felt intimidated by what I had said. She told me emphatically that she was indeed enthusiastic twenty-four hours a day, and that she didn't appreciate my remarks at all. About half the group of distributors applauded her as she sat down.

Before long, however, another distributor stood up and took my side, agreeing that real success meant trying to stay ahead of the game and not being satisfied with the status quo. The other half of the group applauded these remarks: I think the audience was split almost down the middle.

I had placed my audience on the marketing model and considered influencing factors. They led me to set the relatively modest objective of getting the audience to listen and consider what I had to say. The different points of view that came out when I concluded my remarks—and that were probably explored further during the rest of the convention—meant that I had accomplished my goal as a professional. I hadn't left everybody happy, and I hadn't tried to persuade everybody that my point of view was the only one worth considering. But in leaving them thinking, I had met my objective. An honest assessment of the attitudes of your audience helps you choose a realistic objective.

A direct approach toward audiences with a built-in hostility or suspicion to your point of view can move them to understanding more quickly than if you tried to beat around the bush. I believe it is important in such cases to state out loud, as best you can, what the listeners are thinking. They probably won't have a chance to state it themselves, and yet it remains an influencing factor. By recognizing their concerns, you reduce an audience's resistance and thus can move them further on the marketing model scale.

In Atlanta, the spring rains sometimes send creeks overflowing into the backyards and basements of nearby homes. Burton, a spokesman for the U.S. Army Corps of Engineers, which deals with flood control, was like Daniel in the lion's den when he talked to a group of angry homeowners after a flood. But he waded right in and faced reality: He said, "I wish I could tell you that when I've finished talking, you'll have an immediate solution to this problem. But I can't." Burton explained that months and years of drainage work, dredging, and channel rerouting lay ahead before some homeowners could be sure their basements would stay dry. They weren't too happy about that, but they knew where they stood. As one disgruntled homeowner remarked, "At least I know not to keep my antiques in the basement." Burton established his credibility by being straight with his audience, and moved them to a point of understanding. By placing them on the marketing model and considering the influencing factor that their basements were wet, Burton knew that their understanding was all he could expect. If he had hedged on the issue he would have left them misinformed—that is, feeling that the Corps of Engineers really didn't understand or care about their problems.

THE TEST OF YOUR OBJECTIVE

We've spent a good deal of time learning that the right objective is not the one you pull out of the air. It is the one that takes a good hard look at you, the speaker, and the audience to whom you'll speak. Each step in the process of developing your objective is a way of testing it against the requirements of your speaking situation. Thorough testing of your objective is the only way of assuring that it is the right one for your presentation. Let's review the steps:

—First, ask yourself what you need to have happen in the presentation if you are to be professionally satisfied.

—Next, consider your audience, looking at their background, needs, and attitudes, and the circumstances of your presentation. What do they need to have happen in order to feel satisfied?

—Then make a statement of your objective that takes account of your need, the audience, and the circumstances. State it with an active verb in terms of your audience: "I want them to buy."

—Now, test that objective in two areas: you and your audience. Are any of your unstated objectives influencing your professional objective? According to the marketing model, is your objective expecting too much (or too little) of this audience in terms of their knowledge or their attitudes?

If your objective meets the test of relevance and realism, you can feel confident that the steps to follow will lead you to effective, memorable presentations each time you face an audience.

Now that you have established your objective—know what you want to happen and feel sure that you can make it happen with your presentation—your next step is to look at the message your presentation will convey and how it helps you select and organize your content.

3

Reaching Your Objective: Your Audience Must Get the Message

YOU HAVE now determined your objective and tested it thoroughly. How will you construct your presentation to reach your objective? Your message or theme is the part of your presentation that aims your content at the objective. Think of your message as the recurring chorus of a song, the part you walk away humming when the song is over, except that in a presentation, it's the statement you want your audience to make in response to the question "What did the speaker say?"

The importance of your presentation's message cannot be overstated. Arriving at your message is not just a speechwriting exercise; your message is an organizational fulcrum between your objective and your content. The right message makes your job easier because it does two things: It targets your objective and it helps you select and organize your content.

THE RELATIONSHIP BETWEEN MESSAGE AND OBJECTIVE

Many people confuse their message with the topic of their presentation. Your topic is simply the subject you are talking about. It is likely to be quite broad, since that's just the way people throw things at you. "We'd like you to:

". . . come and talk about tax laws."

". . . address management about the changing roles of women in business."

". . . speak to a citizens' group about nuclear power plants."

".. . talk to the people in personnel about the new guidelines for minority hiring."

Your objective, of course, is what you want to happen. "I want them to:

".. . invest in tax shelters."

".. . set up a day-care center."

".. . support the nuclear power plant."

".. . understand and follow the new guidelines."

Your message is what you want your audience to say:

—"Tax shelters make sense for people in my income bracket."
—"A day-care center would increase the productivity of female employees."
—"Nuclear-generated electricity is safe and inexpensive."
—"These guidelines are consistent with company policy."

Your objective does not dictate your choice of message, but your message must be targeted toward your objective. In the first chapter we saw the example of Frederick, who told his audience of international marketing people about a major sports event with which his company was identified. He wanted them to promote their products in connection with the event, because the exposure would benefit his company as well as theirs. But Frederick lost sight of his objective, and ended up giving a dramatic monologue of exciting sports history. Frederick had a message—"This is a great event"—but it was not targeted to his real objective and therefore it missed the mark. Walking away at the end of his presentation, Frederick's audience was probably saying, "What a great sports event!" They should have said, "If we get involved, the exposure will really benefit our company. We should use these promotions." The message should always target the objective.

SELECTING YOUR MESSAGE FOR THE SITUATION

Any one of several messages may be employed in helping you reach your objective. If your objective is to sell prefabricated houses and your audience needs to solve a local housing shortage, say at an expanding military base, then your message is that your houses will solve the shortage quickly and inexpensively. Another audience may be interested in more than providing housing; if they own property in several cities and need rentals that will create a quick cash flow, for example, then your message focuses on the speed with which your houses can be erected and occupied. If you are trying to sell your houses in developing nations where the building components would be moved over primitive roadways and assembled with local labor, your message is that your houses are easily transported and assembled. Your objective is the same in each case—to sell prefabricated houses—but your audience analysis, by identifying the needs of different audiences, caused you to shift your message to bring out the characteristics of your houses that best meet each set of needs. With no other information, an observer could learn something about each audience simply by listening to each presentation.

Choosing a message that works is a matter of using what you have learned about your audience and your speaking situation through the same techniques of analysis used in fixing your objective.

Judy was a media consultant. Her objective when she came to me was to convince a company's in-house media buyers that her program of ads and media buys, although more expensive, would pay much higher returns than the one they were using. She told me that her first instinct was to go in and lay down the law as she saw it with a barrage of criticism: "Listen, you people are making a big mistake. Everything you are doing with your advertising is wrong."

I urged Judy to be more restrained and to choose her message more carefully. "Think about it a minute," I said. "How are you going to persuade these people to buy your program if your message to them is how dumb they are? Telling them their advertising is all wrong is a message that not only attacks their intelligence, which means they're going to resist, but doesn't advertise you very well either."

Judy had two choices for her message. Following her first instinct would have meant choosing the negative message, "You're doing it all wrong." A positive theme was also available: "My creative approaches to advertising can make you more money."

I recommended that Judy use the positive message. Emphasizing "creative alternatives" was the best way for Judy to meet her objective of persuading the firm to use her advertising plan, and it would not create resistance. The positive message in turn dictated positive content—new creative ways to fill their advertising needs. Judy followed that route to win the media group to her point of view.

Don Keough, president of the Coca-Cola Company, used a systematic audience analysis to determine the concerns of marketing employees in a new division of the company before giving a talk to welcome them. The Wine Spectrum had been formed from a number of smaller wine producers that were purchased by Coca-Cola, and like new kids on a strange block, the employees didn't know at first whether to be challenged or intimidated. Keough decided to reassure them, to make them believe that Coke offered them even more of an opportunity than they had had before. With this objective, several messages were available to Keough. For example, he could have talked about Coke's history as a financially strong company, or the career paths available, or the fringe benefits enjoyed by employees. But Keough chose a different approach.

He told them he had been in their shoes by recounting his own background at Coca-Cola: He had been a successful executive with a medium-sized company that was absorbed by Coke, which was to him a huge, unfamiliar corporation. And like the employees he was welcoming, he was not immediately comfortable.

Keough told the new employees that his own first meeting at Coke had reassured him, and that he wanted to reassure them in a similar fashion. He said, "In case you're wondering what's going to happen to you, the choice is yours. All the opportunities and options you had before are here for you now. What you do with them is up to you." When Keough finished his welcome, the warm applause was like a sigh of relief from the Wine Spectrum employees. He had identified their career concerns and chosen a message that went to the heart of those concerns: "Being part of a large company has worked for me; it can work for you, too."

So your message may change according to the situation. For example:

TOPIC: Tax laws.
OBJECTIVE: For the audience to invest in tax shelters.

Possible message 1: Legal loopholes offer some of the best financial opportunities around.

Possible message 2: The laws favor energy development and that's a good cause.

TOPIC: Nuclear power plants.

OBJECTIVE: To gain support for the nuclear power plant.

Possible message 1: Nuclear is the cheapest power source.

Possible message 2: Today's technology means waste disposal and plant safety are solvable problems.

TOPIC: Minority hiring guidelines.

OBJECTIVE: For the personnel department to understand and follow the new guidelines.

Possible message 1: The guidelines require little additional paperwork and can be complied with easily.

Possible message 2: Compliance with the guidelines makes the company eligible for a research and development grant that management wants very badly.

Your message or theme is what you hope the audience will be repeating to themselves when you're finished speaking. When we ask people if they "got the message," we are asking if they got the overriding theme that was a constant thread through our remarks, much as a theme song repeats throughout a musical. You want to leave a message that keeps going through the heads of the people in your audience, just as they whistle a popular product theme song after the commercial is over. The same principle applies—if they say what you want them to say, they are more likely to do what you want them to do.

SELECTING THE CONTENT FOR YOUR MESSAGE

Your message targets your objective, but it also relates to the content you've got—whatever supporting data or details are available. Think of your message as being a refrigerator. When you open your refrigerator, you don't expect to see a pair of sneakers in there, unless you keep a very weird house. What you do expect to find is an array of shelves and compartments—a vegetable bin, a fruit section, a meat section, and a dairy section. So the very package itself—the refrigerator or the message—puts a limit on the content it would be appropriate to find inside. You would throw out the pair of sneakers you found, or at least put them in a more appropriate place, out of the refrigerator. You would probably put them in your closet, where you would also expect to find suits, shirts, and slacks. You would not expect to find your lunch in the closet, and if you did it would be inappropriate to that particular place. Your message helps you select and organize your content; for your message to work, its contents must be consistent.

Different Messages Suggest Different Content

Choosing the right message can drastically improve the results you can expect, as long as the content supports your message in what it is trying to say. Randall, a salesman with a major soft drink company, came to me to prepare for a couple of important presentations aimed at selling his company's low-calorie drink to two restaurant chains. His first presentation was to executives of a new chain which, his audience analysis told him, was trying to build customer traffic. Randall's other presentation was to a long-established restaurant group which had a substantial customer flow and whose primary concern was profits.

For the first audience, Randall chose a message that stressed his brand's ability to bring more customers into their restaurants. He chose his content to support the message that "more customers prefer our brand." His message to the second group was "our brand puts more dollars on your bottom line"; Randall selected different content to support the new message, although his objective in both presentations was the same.

Judy, the media consultant who changed her message to make a positive impression on the clients she was trying to sell, found that her content changed along with her message. Her content for her original, negative message would have been an analysis of the defects and disadvantages of her audience's advertising program. To conform to her new, positive message, Judy's content became an upbeat presentation of unique approaches to her audience's advertising needs, with examples, costs, and projected results of her ideas.

First Things First: Your Message or Your Content?

When you have finished organizing your presentation, it will have a message that is supported by your content and targeted toward your objective. But how you get to that finished presentation will depend a lot on what kind of presentation you're trying to organize. If you have some choice about the content, you can select your message first and then pick out what data or information will support that message. You can pick the refrigerator as your message and then supply the appropriate food items as your content. Don Keough's speech to the Wine Spectrum is an example of this approach—going from message to content. Another example of this approach to organizing might be a person who comes up with an idea for the greatest ad campaign ever conceived —the message is pure dynamite! Now the task is to come up with some big ideas to support that message, and then identify some evidence to support the big ideas.

But your planning may start from the other direction if you have no choice about the content of your presentation. Suppose you have to include that pair of sneakers in your presentation, as well as the food items. Then you must look for a different container or message. There is always a message, even if all your contents don't fit into the message you choose at first. For example, a message that could include contents as diverse as sneakers and cold food might be a package for the local orphanage or a backpack for a weekend at the lake.

Many business presentations begin with details, number-filled financial data, all of which are necessary to the presentation. One of the biggest problems my students say they face is having to make presentations in which they have little control over their choice of information. It's a good question: How can you make an impact on your audience when you have no choice in the information you present?

Actually, you have more choices than you think. Even when you can't choose your content, you still can choose how it is organized. Organization can have an impact on your audience when your content is a given. First you sort the details into two or three main ideas, then you subordinate the details that don't fit into those big pictures, and finally, from the main ideas you've established, you arrive at your message. You have to find that common thread, because no matter how important it is for you to get all those details into your presentation, the presentation won't work if it's not organized around a message.

Joanne is an example of this second direction for organizing a presentation. She worked in the marketing research department of an advertising agency that conducted a comprehensive national survey on packaging. The survey turned up a lot of information about customer preferences in packaging color and design. Joanne was asked to talk about the survey to an audience of the company's marketing managers. Organizing her presentation from the detailed results of the survey, Joanne arrived at this message: "There are some distinct regional preferences in packaging that our marketing strategy should take into account."

Two Approaches to Content Selection

I've said that whether you go from message to content or from content to message will depend on what kind of presentation you're trying to organize. It will also depend on how you think. Thinking is the process by which we organize information in our minds so it can work for us. Human beings tend to think in rather different ways, and the way each of us does it is the way each individual has discovered it works best for him or her.

We are inclined to stereotype types of thinkers according to the work they do, assuming, for example, that precision characterizes those in mathematical fields but not those in artistic fields. We assume that accountants, for example, because they deal with numbers all the time, think in details similar to the numbers they work with. We attribute to computer programmers the same command of vast amounts of minute data that the machines they work with have.

We tend to believe, on the other hand, that artists think in "broad strokes" of the mental paintbrush—in general rather than in specific terms. Advertising and public relations people are considered to be more interested in the "big picture" of emotional responses than in details. And politicians are generally accused of speaking in generalities, whether they think that way or not. Our stereotypes attribute broad, general thinking to people whose jobs we think of as artistic or creative, and attention to detail to those in mathematics, finance, or science-oriented careers.

Modern research gives us some insight into the way our brains work to reconcile the big, controlling thought with the less exciting, but nonetheless necessary, details which must support it. The right side of the brain, we are told, generates random sparks of creativity, rapid associations, global or holistic images and concepts. The brain's left side is specialized for logic, sequential as opposed to random thinking, and speech. Creativity, the researchers say, is a right-hemisphere task. Yet we know that the sequence of thoughts or acts is just as important in a ballet *pas de deux* as in designing a computer program.

In organizing a presentation, we switch back and forth from one side of the brain to the other. Organizing a presentation is a left-hemisphere task, but we borrow right-hemisphere thinking and use it to enhance the job of organization.

The truth is, there are all kinds of thinkers in all kinds of jobs. Some think in broad strokes, or big ideas, and have to struggle to come up with details, while other people have a command of detail, but need help sorting and arranging the details into bigger ideas that can support a message.

When you are preparing a presentation, it really doesn't matter how your thinking works as long as you can get from one end to the other of your personal spectrum of thought. It doesn't matter which direction you go in, from message to supporting details or from the details to the message. The important point is that when you have finished organizing, your presentation should have a message that is targeted on your message and is supported by your content.

MESSAGE AND MAIN IDEAS: THE MODULAR APPROACH

Your main ideas are the major components of your message— they support the message and organize the subpoints of your presentation. The main ideas correspond to the compartments in your refrigerator, whereas the contents of each compartment compare with your details; the meat compartment compares with a main idea, which is likely to include a steak as one of its details; the dairy shelf is a main idea, the container of yogurt a detail. Just as the main ideas must fit inside the theme, the details must fit inside each compartment and be compatible with it; ice cubes, for example, would not fit well in the vegetable bin. Main ideas emerge from groupings of details that support the same points, just as the contents of each of your refrigerator's compartments support the identification of each compartment's specific purpose.

Thinking big is the key to identifying the main ideas that go into your presentation. The bigger your main ideas, the more easily your audience will identify them as major components of your message. Most people try to put too many main ideas into their presentations, with the result that they leave their audiences confused about the message. Fewer main ideas are better, because they are easier to remember; each main idea is a clue to the message, and most of us simply are better equipped to retain a few sharp, clear clues than many less outstanding ones. The limited human capacity for auditory processing means that using a few large ideas is the best way to make your point.

Go Deeper, Not Wider

Because main ideas are composed of compatible details, not everything you find in the refrigerator has to be part of your lunch. The frozen veal patties and the ice cubes in the freezer compartment aren't necessary if they don't fit among the big ideas that contribute to your message. If it doesn't fit, eliminate it; you don't have to use all the details, or the big ideas either, just because they are there. Most speeches and presentations suffer for this very reason. They try to do too much, and often bury the audience under a barrage of facts.

It is reasonable to ask, as many of my students do, how a speaker can throw anything out that is even slightly relevant when there is time to fill. How can a three-minute speech have as many big ideas as a twenty-minute speech? Conversely, how can a twenty-minute speech possibly not have more big ideas than a three-minute one? To make the most of your time, you should go into more depth with fewer ideas, not spread more ideas around in a shallow fashion.

If you're giving a three-minute talk on boating, you may have decided on a theme that many owners would agree with: "The expense of owning a boat only begins with the purchase price." In three minutes you have time to do little more than state three main ideas:

1. You have to think of the cost of storage both in the summer when you're using the boat and in the winter when you're not.
2. You have to consider repair costs and the condition the boat is in when you buy it.
3. You must consider trailering the boat, or some other means of transporting it if necessary.

With those three points, you have a three-minute speech containing three main ideas—storage, repair, and transportation.

If you all of a sudden have to talk on the same subject for twenty minutes, there's no need to add more main points. There is more than enough to be said just by expanding the ones you already have identified:

1. STORAGE: Here are some problems and costs involved with keeping your boat in a marina slip during the summer boating season; dry storage in the winter can affect your boat's hull and motor, and here are some precautionary steps.
2. REPAIRS: Problems are usually found in three specific areas— mechanical, electrical, and the hull, including the rudder. Here are danger signs and preventive steps in each area.
3. TRANSPORTATION: Moving your boat can be hard on it and the vehicle towing it; here are some ways to reduce the possibility of serious and costly damage.

By expanding on each point, you can easily talk for twenty minutes. If you have to give a two-day workshop, the same three main ideas would apply. People have written entire books on boat repairs, so you won't run out of things to say in two days; a discussion of transporting boats could range from a guide to the Intracoastal Waterway to a list of trailering laws in all fifty states. And I don't think that in two days you would run out of things to say about boat storage, either.

It's easy for speakers who have to make thirty-minute or forty-five-minute presentations to fall into the idea that they have to cover seven or eight main ideas. With this kind of "shotgun" approach that tries to hit everything in sight, the audience leaves remembering little or nothing. If you go into more depth, however, expanding on two, three, or four big pictures to impress them on the audience, your listeners leave remembering your message and what you had to say, which is the route to your objective.

With few exceptions, the material for any presentation can always be arranged to fall under three or four major subject headings that the audience can retain more easily than raw facts.

Time Modules

When you think of your main ideas as modules or compartments in the refrigerator, you are using modular thinking. When you organize your presentation in a modular fashion, you are actually creating space, or time, to be filled as you go on. Each module, or main idea, can be filled as you come up with subpoints and details that support it. You can also subtract details if a main idea doesn't need much elaboration for a particular audience. You may also decide to do without some of the details if you are having trouble remaining within your time limit. It is not unusual to find yourself with too much material if you have organized thoroughly, but paring away details is a task that is a lot more fun (and easier) than scrambling to fill time; now you are able to make choices that will make time work for you.

Suppose you are a CPA making a presentation to a banker on behalf of a client. The client needs a loan to start a new business, and you want to cover three aspects with the banker:

— Description of the new business.
— The market and need for the business.
— Projected profitability of the new business.

These are your three main ideas, and in your planning, each represents a module, a compartment in the refrigerator.

Perhaps the banker has scheduled a thirty-minute meeting and you want to cover all three main ideas in your presentation. You also need to allow some time for any questions the banker might have. Obviously the third main idea is the most important one for the banker, because it relates to how well and how soon the new business can repay the loan. So you allot ten minutes to this main idea. The second main idea is also important, because it sets up your discussion of projected profitability, so you give that five minutes. The least important idea, in terms of the loan repayment, is the description of the business—you give that three minutes. With two minutes for your opening and closing, your presentation totals twenty minutes, leaving you ten minutes for questions from the banker during or after your presentation.

You can still "juggle" the time you assign to each main idea, so it's not important for you to make any final decisions right now. What is more important is that in your plan for this presentation, you are holding spaces open that will be available when you get ready to fill them in. As your planning progresses, you will return to the module on profitability and choose the most important things you can say in the ten minutes you've given yourself to talk about it. You've allotted five minutes to discuss the market for the business, and three for a description of the business, and you can decide later what you want to say about each subject in the time you've got. You can decide to add or subtract from the time you're devoting to each of your main points, if you choose, but you keep each point within its module.

As we move toward a discussion of sequencing your main ideas, keep in mind the advantages of staying flexible. You have been making choices about your objective and your message, and sorting out your detailed data into main ideas and subpoints. Soon you will choose the order in which you will present your points. But making these choices does not lock you into any of them. One choice leads logically to another, each directing and pointing you to the next one, but at any point your choices may force you to look back and return to your earlier choices to adjust them. This is what you've been doing all along, allowing the latest information available to be applied to your planning: Your audience analysis affected your choice of message; your new message may dictate a different choice of content; the details of your content may not turn out to support your message. As you move into sequencing your main ideas, your sequencing method may cause you to re-shape some of your main ideas or even to reformulate your message.

One choice should lead to another, but it should not force another. There should be a built-in element of openness at each stage of your preparation that will allow you to go back as well as forward, not to tear down the entire structure but to strengthen its foundation. The best business judgments are made based on the greatest amount of available, up-to-date information. This is also true in preparing a speech or presentation, and staying flexible allows you to put the greatest amount of information to work in its development.

Keeping Your Thoughts in Order

You have a reasonably good sense by now of how your topic, message, main ideas, and details fit together into a cohesive presentation. All along, you have to keep the elements in order. Many of my students find the following outline form a useful aid. It looks something like the pairings sheet for a basketball or tennis tournament.

In this outline, the random thoughts at the left of the page are refined into subpoints and then into main ideas. These are then distilled into the message, which is aimed at the objective.

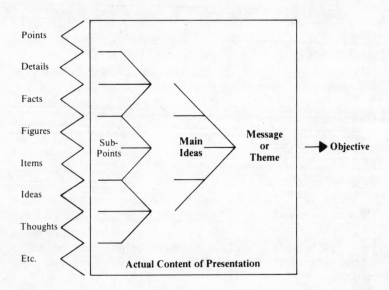

Just as useful, according to my students, is a four-column outline form. As in the thought process you follow to plan your presentation, it makes no difference which of the columns you fill up first. Along with the information you jot down in each column, be sure to include the amount of time you allot to each part of your presentation.

By keeping your main ideas in separate modules along with their supporting information, you maintain the option of shuffling them to suit your presentation. In your presentation on the new business, you may have started by filling in the compartment on "Profitability." You don't have to put it first in your talk, however, and by shifting the module around you can easily mention it where it has the most impact. This may be at the end, where it is most easily retained, and after "Potential Market," because the market will obviously affect profitability. However you go about this process, you are putting your ideas in a workable sequence.

There are a number of methods you can choose for revealing your main ideas to the audience. Some are quite obvious, others are subtle, but all of the sequencing techniques available for business presentations are ways to keep your presentation on course toward your objective. They are discussed in the next chapter.

SPEAKEASY PRESENTATION PLANNER

MAIN IDEAS	Amount or % of time	Supporting Points	Details

4

Sequencing Your Presentation for Greatest Impact

YOU NOW have the heart of your presentation—your main ideas —well in hand. You have identified them and thought them out for the support they give to your message, which in turn is targeted to your objective. This is where many speakers stop dealing with their main ideas and move on to the introduction of their speech or presentation. But there is another step in dealing with the body of your presentation; that is, the arranging of your main ideas to make them contribute as much as they possibly can to the support of your all-important message. The way a presentation reveals its message—that is, the sequence of its main ideas—affects its impact and memorability. The sequencing method you use to present your main ideas exerts a powerful influence on your ability to reach your objective.

The sequencing of your main ideas makes a bigger difference in some presentations than in others; again, the information you have learned about your audience plays an important role. In the presentation on the expenses of boat ownership discussed in the last chapter, for example, it probably doesn't matter whether you talk first about storage or repairs or transportation if the people you're talking to have an equal concern with all three potential problem areas. But if you know your audience consists entirely of big-boat owners, who keep their boats in the water most of the time and don't trailer them back and forth to the lake or ocean, you have extra information to draw upon. As a result, you are likely to spend less time talking about transportation and to give it less importance in your order of presentation.

Among the available sequencing options, some are clearly more appropriate than others for certain situations. Most of them can work wherever they're applied, however, as long as they present your information in a way that is clear and easily remembered and that gets your message across.

TEN SEQUENCING OPTIONS
The List

The most commonly used method of sequencing is the list. More often than not, the speaker arranges his main points arbitrarily, in no particular order according to no particular value. For example, here are three things you need to do to achieve true happiness:

1. Work hard.
2. Play hard.
3. Save for a rainy day.

Here are four reasons why you should buy our product:

1. Price.
2. Service.
3. Quality.
4. Availability.

You assume in listing your main ideas in arbitrary order that each has nearly equal importance, and that changing the order in which you present each point will neither enhance nor detract from the presentation.

But because it is so easily used, the list is easily abused; many speakers use the list when with some thought they could come up with far more creative ways of organizing their presentations. In the presentation on the costs of boat ownership, for example, it is easy to assume that the order of the list makes no difference in a presentation to boat owners who, after all, are faced with all three problems—storage, repair, and transportation. But might it be more effective to begin with transportation, since the small-boat owner has to get his boat to the water before he can use it? Storage can logically come next, since boats must be stored somewhere, either in or out of the water. And the owner can face repairs at any time, whether his boat is in storage or in use, so it may make sense to talk about repairs last. A speaker who uses the list should be prepared to ask questions to avoid being arbitrary: Does the order of the list matter? What are the most important ideas, and where should they go? Without a proper ordering, can listing always be effective?

The list works best as a sequencing method when it contains only a few items of equal importance. The more items on the list, the more difficult it is for people to remember any of them and the less effective your presentation becomes. There's no hard-and-fast rule, but my personal guideline is to use no more than five. Lists get too long, in my opinion, because speakers use listing as an excuse to avoid the harder job of organizing content into main ideas.

A lot of audiences are probably put to sleep by speakers who reel off item after item in a list without any attempt at creative organization. Listing can be appropriate, but there are a lot of other, more effective ways to organize a presentation. You're likely to find some of the following options more attractive and challenging.

Chronological Order: The Way It Happened

Chronological order is the order in which events occur. Thus an advantage of a presentation arranged in chronological order is that it is easily remembered. To use chronological order in your presentation on the costs of boat ownership, for example, you could follow the seasons of boating:

SPRING: This is when you will move your boat to the water, so transportation is the first thing you have to be concerned with.

SUMMER: You will use your boat most heavily during the summer months, so repairs are most likely during this time.

FALL/WINTER: At the end of the season, you must think about the best method of storing your boat until the next boating season.

We have all heard reports that begin with the words "Let me bring you up to date." Chronological order is a natural method for the report that updates its audience on the state of affairs within its particular sphere of business:

PAST (1982): Market share before new packaging.
PRESENT (1983): Market share immediately after introduction of new packaging.
FUTURE (1984): Projected market share for coming year with new packaging.

Broad ideas and concepts in the passage of time, like past, present, and future, are easier to grasp than specific dates, which are hard to remember and are likely to be obscure. World War I, World War II, and the Vietnam War; elementary school, high school, and college; planning, production, and marketing; before, during, and after deregulation—these are all big ideas. They speak of the passage of time but do not confine the listener to specific dates.

Chronological order is not by itself particularly persuasive, but it is an ideal form for many types of business presentations because it presents an unmistakably clear picture of evolving business conditions.

Acronyms: C.U.T.E.

I don't recommend the regular use of acronyms as a way of ordering your presentation, although I hasten to add that I have used them myself on occasion, one being my first book. An acronym is a series of initials combined into a word, which then comes to stand for the idea expressed by the words from which the acronym is formed. In *Speak Easy,* I used E.A.S.Y. as the acronym deriving from the phrases Energy, Audience Awareness, Strength or Self-esteem, and You, the speaker. The acronym described both the way speaking should be—easy—and at the same time incorporated in a memorable way the major elements of an effective speaking style. Some acronyms so effectively express what they stand for that they become words in their own right, as, for example, "snafu," a word derived from the first initials of "situation normal, all fouled up."

It's all too easy to go off on tangents when you struggle to come up with the right "message" word from the initials of the main points you have to work with. If you're not careful, you might find yourself Taking Off-the-wall Options or Creating Unworkable, Tenuous Examples, and that would be T.O.O. C.U.T.E.

Analogy: Learning to Speak Is Like . . .

Learning to give a speech is like learning to play tennis: You must first have a command of the basics but at some point it becomes a matter of practice, practice, practice. Many business people, men especially, use sports analogies frequently. Recent presidents have talked about their "game plans" for getting bills through Congress, implying that passing legislation is like moving a football through interference into the end zone.

Used well, an apt analogy serves to dramatize your presentation. An analogy can paint a vivid word picture: "The Battle of Gettysburg was similar to a political and economic battle being fought right now." The use of such comparative pictures can help the audience remember the message that carries a presentation. An accountant speaking to local businessmen used an effective analogy to describe the effects of inflation. Clayton told the story of a carpenter who built a ten-foot shed to store his tools, using a standard one-foot ruler to determine its measurements. Some time later, however, a friend complimented the man on his twenty-foot tool shed. "But it's only ten feet," said the carpenter, and got out his ruler to prove it. Lo and behold, although the ruler looked the same, it was only half as big, so that when the carpenter measured his shed, it now measured twenty feet. Clayton's point was that the dollar, the "measuring stick" for monetary value, continues to shrink during periods of inflation while the items it buys seem to become more valuable. Clayton applied this analogy to depreciable equipment and buildings, to explain that depreciation is easily understated and profits overstated in business accounting.

Analogies are like acronyms in that they must make their points clearly and simply, without having to be explained; if you try to stretch an analogy too far it will lose contact with the point you were trying to make. Analogies are often most effective as anecdotes illustrating points within a presentation. An analogy that organizes an entire presentation must be strong enough to make a clear connection with each of the main points.

Problem-Cause-Solution

This approach to organizing a presentation lends itself well to business situations, which so often have to do with problem solving:

> PROBLEM: Our product sales are inconsistent from region to region.
> CAUSE: Our packaging overlooks clear regional preferences in package color and design.
> SOLUTION: Adopt regionally oriented packaging consistent with regional preferences.

> PROBLEM: Inadequate cash flow to meet current obligations.
> CAUSE: Large backlog of accounts receivable.
> SOLUTION: Vigorous collection efforts aimed at improving cash flow.

Problem-cause-solution flows naturally from one point to the next and is therefore quite easy to follow, which makes it particularly desirable in a persuasive situation.

Chain Thinking

More stimulating than simply listing your main ideas is a list of related ideas. I call this "chain thinking." For example:

— "These are the political, economic, and social effects of the proposed value-added tax."
— "Read *Inner Tennis*. It can affect you physically, mentally, emotionally, and spiritually."
— "Entering the video-game market will affect the company's cash flow, credit, and production capacity. But a successful entry into the market will improve the company's prestige, employee morale, and investor confidence."

In chain thinking, the related concepts are the big ideas you want to convey to your audience. By expanding your main ideas into concepts, you enlarge them and make them easier for your audience to remember.

Comparison/Contrast or Argument/Counterargument

This sequencing method is effective when you want to present the pros and cons of a proposal or when you want to reply rhetorically to objections raised or criticisms made about an idea or course of action. It is also an excellent way of correcting impressions you feel your listeners have as the result of unfavorable publicity or some other damaging factor.

Don Baeder, then the president of the Hooker Chemical Company, used argument/counterargument in a speech to the Commonwealth Club of San Francisco as a way of changing the popular perceptions of the chemical industry in general and Hooker in particular. He spelled out the erroneous perceptions, or "myths," and countered them with "facts"—information the public had not been given or had not taken into account.

In outline form, Baeder's speech would look something like this:

> ARGUMENT (or myth): The chemical industry has a waste disposal problem.
> COUNTERARGUMENT (or fact): Yes, but the problem is cleaning up old wastes; those generated today are being disposed of safely.
> ARGUMENT: The chemical industry is irresponsible.
> COUNTERARGUMENT: The industry is being blamed for problems no one had the knowledge to anticipate. Now that we have the knowledge, responsible regulations are something we want, too.
> ARGUMENT: The chemical industry is insensitive.
> COUNTERARGUMENT: I'm a human being with children and grandchildren, and I don't want them exposed to hazardous wastes.

Baeder used a similar argument/counterargument approach as he talked about the specific misconceptions arising from the Love Canal publicity:

> ARGUMENT: Hooker recklessly dumped chemicals into the Love Canal site.

COUNTERARGUMENT: A task force of the American Institute of
  Chemical Engineers concluded that the design of the site was
  well within current federal standards for chemical waste disposal sites.
ARGUMENT: Residents near Love Canal suffered widespread,
  serious health problems.
COUNTERARGUMENT: There is no reliable evidence to support
  allegations of widespread health problems.
ARGUMENT: Hooker knew of the problem for years and con-
  cealed what it knew.
COUNTERARGUMENT: Hooker had always advised against dis-
  turbing the disposal site but those warnings were ignored.

A salesman pitching a client on radio advertising would find
comparison/contrast an effective way to present the advantages of
his medium versus newspapers and television.

ARGUMENT: Radio is too expensive.
COUNTERARGUMENT: Radio is less expensive than television or
  newspapers.
ARGUMENT: It's hard to target a specific audience on radio.
COUNTERARGUMENT: Rating services show who's listening and
  when, which lets advertisers target the audience they want.
ARGUMENT: People don't remember what they hear on the
  radio.
COUNTERARGUMENT: Radio's low cost permits advertisers
  "saturation coverage" which listeners will remember.

The employee presenting to her boss on transportation alternatives for product distribution could also use this method effectively if her research has determined that popular accepted
methods won't work as well as innovative alternatives.

Using comparison and contrast is a good way to lay points of
disagreement between you and your audience out on the table,
where they are always easier to deal with. A speaker's first temp-
tation, when he knows his listeners hold opinions different from
his own, is to ram his side of the story down their throats. But
forcing a viewpoint on an audience without considering their concerns diminishes the importance of their feelings and makes them
more likely to resist. By giving voice to the concerns of the audi-

ence and addressing those concerns, the speaker reduces resistance by showing the audience he considers them important. He is reaching out to them and saying, "I see you."

Inductive Reasoning: Facts Leading to a Conclusion

"Induce" means to move by persuasion or influence, or to infer a conclusion from particulars. Inductive reasoning is sometimes known as the scientific method. It presents evidence leading to an apparently logical conclusion, and thus is suited for a persuasive speech.

If you are arguing that no-fault automobile insurance should be instituted in your state, for example, you can cite the evidence amassed in other states that already use this system of insurance. If no-fault has succeeded in these other states, you would use their experience to demonstrate the system's effectiveness. The evidence of success elsewhere tends to lead to the conclusion that the no-fault system is needed in your state.

Inductive reasoning is often used in marketing presentations. If you have just done a marketing study and are convinced by this study that a certain product your company offers will preempt the market and bring your competition to its knees, you should probably use the inductive approach in a presentation to your managers: "We've studied this. We took this survey. We examined this background. And on the basis of all this evidence, we have concluded that this product will make a lot of money for us."

FACT: Studies show that coin-operated video games are popular with many adults as well as teenagers.

FACT: Technology permits video games to be made smaller than the coin-operated commercial versions.

FACT: The technology for video games can be integrated with home television sets.

FACT: Video games can be made at a price that most families can afford.

CONCLUSION: The market is ripe for the introduction of home video games.

The most important thing to remember about inductive reasoning is that it is more of a way to build evidence to support your conclusion than it is a way of arranging or presenting your main ideas. Thus inductive reasoning may employ other sequencing methods in amassing the body of evidence that leads to the conclusion.

THE LIST: "There are four reasons why . . ."

COMPARISON/CONTRAST: "No-fault insurance has resulted in these benefits in other states: . . . But in our state, without no-fault, this is the situation."

PROBLEM-CAUSE-SOLUTION: "Your problem is low profits from fountain sales. The cause is that you are paying too much for syrup. The solution is to use our syrup, which will help you make the profits you should be making from fountain sales."

Deductive Reasoning: If, Therefore . . .

"Deduce" means to infer a conclusion from a general principle. Deductive reasoning begins with a generalization which is your major premise, adds a known fact, and draws a specific conclusion from the combination of the two. An early example of deductive reasoning, arising as it did from medieval thought, is:

MAJOR PREMISE: All men are sinners.

MINOR PREMISE: You are a man.

CONCLUSION: Therefore, you are a sinner.

Deductive reasoning is effective for an appeal to the emotions. Its major flaw is that it depends upon the validity of your major premise, which is the presupposition or "given" that leads your audience to an apparently logical conclusion when the local facts are added. Your argument hinges upon your major premise, and a weak major premise will weaken if not destroy your entire argument. We use deductive reasoning, despite its shortcomings, practically every day. How often have you said, "She's a redhead. Boy, I bet she's got a temper." That's a conclusion drawn from the major premise that all redheads have hot tempers. Of course, since I'm a redhead, I know that redheads are no more likely to have quick tempers than blondes or brunettes, which points out the fallacies of deductive reasoning.

In the marketing presentation using inductive reasoning, we saw a body of evidence leading to the conclusion that home-use video games would make more money for the company. Applying deductive reasoning to the same situation, we find a major premise that was not stated in the inductive process and our thinking proceeds as follows:

> MAJOR PREMISE: The company wants to make more money.
> MINOR PREMISE: Home-use video games will make the company more money.
> CONCLUSION: Therefore, we should make home-use video games.

Reasoning from a major premise that seems to exist for every entrepreneurial enterprise—that its purpose is to make money—is easy enough to accept.

But a word of caution: Since deductive reasoning lends itself to emotional situations, it is great for encouraging audiences which already agree with you. I have heard speakers use deductive reasoning in talking both for and against gun control, school busing, the ERA, and abortion, all examples of emotional issues. An audience which has some reason to resist or suspect you, however, may not accept your major premise quite so easily. The less agreeable and more inquisitive your audience, the more they are going to question a weak major premise. If you plan to use deductive reasoning in a presentation, you should be sure your major premise will hold up under the scrutiny of an informed audience.

Inductive-Deductive Interaction

Inductive and deductive reasoning are natural partners in putting together a persuasive presentation. The aim of most marketing presentations is to persuade the audience to unconsciously make the message or theme of the presentation the minor premise in a deductive reasoning process, leading to a conclusion that fits the objective. The presentation itself amasses a body of evidence in inductive fashion, leading to a conclusion that fits the message. The conclusion/message of this inductive or evidentiary process then fits into your audience's deductive reasoning process this way:

MAJOR PREMISE (generalized supposition): I want to make
money (make a profit; be more efficient; improve sales).

MINOR PREMISE (the message of the presentation): Video games
will make money (that syrup will increase my profits; a new
accounting system would be more efficient; regionally oriented packaging will improve sales).

CONCLUSION (the objective): Therefore, I should get into video
games (buy that syrup; adopt the new accounting system; use
regionally oriented packaging).

The conclusion the listeners draw from their own process of
deductive reasoning is the objective of the presentation. This interaction of sequencing methods can be extraordinarily persuasive.

Inductive-deductive interaction also illustrates the relation of
message to objective, making it clear how the message should
target a presentation's content toward its objective. If a listener
"gets the message"—that is, makes your message the minor
premise in his deductive process of reasoning—he will come to
the desired conclusion, if not automatically, at least with high
probability. When the speaker uses inductive reasoning to provide
the evidence leading to his message, the listener's deductive conclusion will always be the same as the speaker's objective.

COMBINING SEQUENCING METHODS

I'm frequently asked if a speech or presentation can employ
more than one sequencing method. It can. You may find, for example, that your presentation is best done in chronological order
but that within one of the time modules you want to make a point
by inductive reasoning, applying problem-cause-solution or illustrating with an analogy. Any combination of methods is acceptable
and can be effective, as long as your presentation remains clear
and your message memorable. Trying to be too fancy can turn
your presentation into a jumble which may confuse your audience.
Worse yet, you may confuse yourself.

Internal sequencing, or the combining of sequencing methods,
often becomes an unforced and necessary part of your business
presentation. One method may rely naturally on another or con-

tain elements of another, as in the use of other sequencing methods to build the body of evidence in an inductive presentation.

TESTING YOUR SEQUENCING METHOD

Students in my Speakeasy content workshops have tried all of the sequencing methods. Each has its place, and can undoubtedly be used in organizing a variety of business presentations. While there is no prohibition against using any one of them or a combination in a given situation, my students clearly find some methods more effective than others. Some sequencing methods simply lend themselves better to the general requirements of most business presentations. These are the ones that rely less on verbal sleight-of-hand and fancy techniques than on straight presentation and logical progression of the facts as a means of persuasion. Some choices will work better for you than others, and you should always be prepared to test the effectiveness of one method against another.

Paul, who pitched clients for a management consulting firm, is an example of someone who reexamined his sequencing method after an unsuccessful presentation. He had attended a day-long meeting at which he presented his firm's recommendations for labor-intensive-plant development to an investment group. This group had the sole authority to approve a plan and to select a consulting firm from among several competing for the contract. Paul, in his initial presentation, chose the listing method; he simply listed his firm's choices for plant development and tried to show why they would work. He said he "had a little trouble with the main points." When he thought about it later, he decided he would have been more persuasive by using the problem-cause-solution method of sequencing.

Paul said, "The problem was unemployment, and that was why they had sought these proposals in the first place, to do something about the lack of jobs. If I had chosen problem-cause-solution, I would have dramatized my firm's understanding of the problem by stating it at the beginning of my talk. Their unemployment problem was caused by a lack of manufacturing plants that employed large numbers of people yet were also safe and efficient.

Getting those two needs out on the table would have made it easier for me to connect the solution I was proposing—a safe, efficient plant that put people to work—with the needs. It would have led more easily to the conclusion on their part that we were the ones who could show them how to do it best and most effectively.''

Barbara was preparing a presentation that was to be given by the president of her company to a group of foreign investors. The objective was to convince them to buy the company's stock. By reputation and tradition these investors were rock-ribbed conservatives who were not under any circumstances going to put their money into a stock that wasn't a sure thing. According to Barbara's audience analysis, they felt that any company whose stock they bought had to have a reputation as firm as their own. There was no language problem, but cultural differences meant they had a different sense of humor, so it was no spot for joke-making or the hard sell.

Barbara's message was: "This is a strong company with a solid past and a promising future, and therefore you should want to participate." She used inductive reasoning to convince the audience that the company was solid and well managed by having her boss present a history of sales and earnings growth. That was the first main point. Next, she went into the performance and growth potential of the company's subsidiaries. Finally, although she had to be careful about portraying the company's stock in a "bargain basement" light (she felt this would diminish its worth in the eyes of the audience), she presented evidence showing a high return on equity compared to comparable companies. The whole presentation was geared to show the stock was a good value and would continue to be.

"I looked through all the other options," Barbara said. "The ones that could be startling, or dramatic, all seemed to be a little undignified for this group. They are pretty conservative people. This was really the only way to bring them along."

There may be no single right sequencing method for any given business presentation. But some ways of sequencing will be clearly better for your purpose than others. Your audience analysis, especially in small audience or one-on-one situations where you've learned to recognize the audience's preferences for receiving information, will steer you toward one sequencing method or another. But the really important thing is for your sequencing method to keep your presentation or speech moving along toward its objective. The order in which you arrange your main ideas must keep your message on target without deflecting it or confusing the issue. Once you've arranged your main ideas to do this, you are ready to think about ways to open and conclude your presentation with the same effectiveness you've built into it so far.

Openings and Endings

AT THIS point your presentation is already a substantial piece of work. You have determined the right objective by a process of investigation and self-study. You have weighed what you have to say and drawn from your content a message that your audience will remember. You have sequenced the body of your presentation in a way that supports your message. Now it's time to start thinking about what you can do at both ends of your speech to make sure people listen and act. How do you grab their attention at the beginning and hold their attention even after you've finished? First, how do you intrigue them, pull them in so their attention won't wander off the path to your objective?

That is the job of your opening. Your personality and speaking style help dictate the type of opening you use. Since you are likely to be most uncomfortable at the start of your presentation, before you've had a chance to interact with the audience, your opening should be one that puts both you and your audience at ease. First impressions resist change; like any first impression, the one left by your opening is hard to alter once you've made it. So you want to make sure it's a good one. You can see more easily now the advantage of organizing the body of your presentation before you work on the opening; a firm grasp of the subject and where you're going with it will help you figure out an opening that will fit your presentation's sequencing as well as draw the audience in and keep their attention tuned to you and your subject. If you lose your audience in the first couple of minutes, chances are good that you will have lost them for the entire speech. If you establish rapport at the outset, it is likely that your audience will stay with you. This is true in all your speaking situations. Presentations to colleagues, staff members, or your boss need openings just as much as full-blown speeches, because you always need to prepare your audience for what's to come.

The ending of your speech or presentation is as important as its opening. Openings should get the audience's attention and prepare them for what is to follow; endings should stamp your message indelibly in the mind of your audience. The ending is your last chance to place your information in perspective and give the audience a reason to act. The ending should distill what you've said; it should wrap up the package and make it compelling. Presentations should never "just" end. To paraphrase the poet T. S. Eliot, a speech should end with a bang, not a whimper! It is just as important to rivet your audience's attention when you conclude as it is when you begin your presentation.

PREPARING THE AUDIENCE TO RECEIVE YOUR MESSAGE

A woman in one of my seminars described herself as a "hip-shooter," meaning that in her business presentations as well as in her personal remarks, she spoke up quickly without assessing the impact her remarks might have or preparing her audience to receive them. "Quick-draw Peggy" was surprised that her presentations weren't always well received, because she was so sure that her aim was right. Her colleagues agreed that most of the time her information was right on target, but they also said they were put off by the fact that she always launched right into her remarks without taking time to establish rapport with her audience. No matter how perceptive her presentations were, Peggy frequently failed to reach her objective because she had not prepared her audience to receive her message. I told Peggy that paying more attention to her openings would probably solve her problem with audience resistance; audiences would be more likely to receive her messages if her openings laid a groundwork for receptivity.

Your opening leads into the body of your presentation; it must flow naturally into your message. The opening of your presentation is the time to begin using the information you have learned about your audience. You should begin immediately establishing common ground, to make that contact with your audience that lets them know that you share with them concerns, problems, information. Your task at this point is to let your audience know, without actually saying so, that there is mutual benefit in your speaking and in their listening. But remember how you reacted to what your parents said when you were a child demanding to know why you had to take your medicine or eat your spinach: "Do it because it's good for you." The more they told you to do something because it was good for you, the less you wanted to do it.

Every listener is asking the question "Why should I listen?" The question may be only subconscious, but it still is there, and you can't tell an audience to listen because it is good for them, at least not in so many words. No matter how much your audience needs your information—even if getting a job, a promotion, or a raise depends on their absorbing and acting on what you have to say—it is still your responsibility to hook them at the outset by signaling that what's to come will be stimulating and thought-provoking as well as informative. Coming on as pompous and pedantic, with a holier-than-thou attitude about what you have in store for them, will turn them off and create stiff resistance.

You needn't be wildly imaginative or even especially creative to think of a way to pull your audience in with your opening remarks. You don't have to put on a clown suit or bang away on a pair of cymbals to get the audience's attention. But the task does take a little thought, the same kind of thought you put into analyzing your audience and your general speaking situation in the first place. As you have found that you favor some sequencing methods over others, you may also find that some openings are more comfortable for you. Don't typecast yourself with your opening; the ways to open a presentation are too many and too versatile to restrict yourself to one or two. Restricting your options also takes away your opportunity to put some alternating rhythm in your presentation as you continue to balance your needs with those of the audience.

Openings and endings, just as much as the body of your speech, can have a beginning, a middle, and an end. Some openings are one-liners, of course. But other forms can have the same kind of structure as the speech itself, even though the opening will obviously be shorter. Let's look at some of the options.

FOURTEEN OPENINGS

A Dramatic Statement: Startling for Starters

An unexpected, dramatic statement can jolt your audience to attention. Startling the audience is especially effective when they think there's nothing new under the sun they can possibly hear from you. Alexandra, a well-known local activist for women's rights, was urging an audience of women to support laws that would outlaw discrimination based on sex. Alexandra's audience knew she supported anti-discrimination laws. They weren't expecting any surprises, until they heard her first words: "A woman's place is in the home."

The unexpected cliché that embodied the philosophy of their opponents made Alexandra's audience suddenly sit up and listen. It promised something new and different in a too-familiar landscape. It also made them bristle. Beginning this way was risky, even for Alexandra, because she could have alienated her audience, at least temporarily. The way in which she followed her dramatic opening became all the more important.

A dramatic, startling statement at the opening requires strength and authority. The statement must be delivered with energy and allowed to stand on its own. If you follow it with an immediate disclaimer, as if to say you really didn't mean it, you lose the entire impact of your opening. A beginning such as "A woman's place is in the home. . . . Of course, we all know this is ridiculous" deflates the audience no sooner than you've given them a reason, even a risky one, to listen to you. It's important to be able to use pause effectively after beginning a speech with a strong statement; a pause gives your audience time to wonder what in the world you're up to by saying something so outrageous.

Alexandra paused after her opening statement amid a silence that virtually reverberated through the room. Then she said, "That's what the speaker of the state house told voters in his district during his reelection campaign, and that's an indication of how hard we'll have to work if we expect to change discriminatory laws." She had captured audience attention, and then put her message in dramatic perspective with a conversational statement. Alexandra had chosen a good way to follow a dramatic opening statement; she didn't deflate the audience's expectations, but at the same time she injected a personal touch that kept her from overdoing the high drama.

Dramatic opening statements can be very powerful, compelling the audience to sit up and listen, but if you're not careful they also can make you come across as a melodramatic actor. The conversational, human, but still stimulating touch that should follow a dramatic opening will keep you from appearing "speechy," as if you're giving a dramatic reading rather than a serious presentation in which you want the audience to be involved. As in Alexandra's case, the dramatic opening is probably best suited for situations in which the audience expects to hear nothing new or stimulating. The element of surprise provided by the opening gives the presentation enough zest to keep the audience focused on an already familiar subject.

Business presentations can benefit from the element of surprise as easily as other presentations. You would certainly get your audience's attention if you announced at the beginning of a presentation, "Production efficiencies saved the company over nine million dollars last year." The clients you're pitching would be surprised—and interested—to hear you say, "I'm not here to tell you we're the best firm in the country. (Pause) But we are the best firm for you."

Asking for Audience Response

To involve the audience at the outset, you can simply ask for a unison reaction to a direct or a rhetorical question. Questions that would be likely to evoke a response include:

— "Would you like to know how much improved health benefits will cost the company this year?"
— "Raise your hand if you want better public schools in Westchester County."
— "How many of you would like to go to a sunny tropical island for a free two-week vacation?"

The question must always be simple, for the obvious reason that you don't want the audience to spend time mulling over a response before they react.

Like the dramatic opening statement, the effectiveness of soliciting a unison reaction depends on the pause and involves risk. What happens, for example, if the audience does not respond as you expect? Someone may shout out a negative answer, or a different answer than the one you need in order to follow through with your message. If you choose this kind of opening, I suggest being prepared with a rejoinder. You may never have to use it, but it's better to be prepared.

Sam was the travel agent who asked his audiences how they would like two free weeks on a sunny tropical island. He wanted people to sign up for a drawing he was having to promote travel to the Bahamas, and he wanted others to decide to go on their own. At one meeting, though, someone in the crowd shouted back, "I'd rather go skiing." Sam calmly answered, "Water skiing is very popular in the Bahamas, and the free trip includes a choice of skiing or sailing in the afternoons." His response silenced his challenger without ridiculing him, which would have created resistance among his other listeners. And it allowed Sam to move quickly into the other attractions of a Bahamas vacation. Seeking a unison reaction is an opening best used when you want to establish at once that you and the audience have similar, popular objectives. It brings immediate recognition to your common ground.

Using the Headlines

It can be effective to begin a speech with a reference to a recent or a well-known event. If you are talking about the need for stricter enforcement of highway construction regulations, for example, you might start your speech by quoting a recent newspaper headline: "Elevated Highway Collapses, Killing 54 People." If your subject is corruption in city government, you might choose a headline referring to a scandal in the police department to open your speech. You could open a presentation on the need to improve manufacturing productivity by quoting the numerous headlines praising Japanese production management methods. A recitation of headlines referring to attempted assassinations of public figures would be appropriate to begin a speech about gun control.

Guard against using a headline or an event that is too obscure for most of your audience to recognize. You fail to establish common ground if you leave your audience scratching their heads wondering what in the world you're talking about. Ask yourself if you weren't the only person reading that section of the paper that morning, or if you may have been the only person impressed by an obscure event. You should choose an event that most members of the audience will remember vividly. Using a well-chosen, memorable event to open a presentation draws the audience into immediate involvement because each listener has his own images or impressions of it.

Personal Anecdote

An amusing or relevant personal experience, if it is well told, can establish personal rapport with listeners by making them smile or simply establishing in a human way the speaker's connection to the subject. Linda Mathews, a *Los Angeles Times* editor who headed bureaus in Peking and Hong Kong, used a personal anecdote to open a speech questioning the United States' uncritical embrace of China:

"While we were living in Peking, our six-year-old son, Joe, brought home a top-secret art project he'd been working on at school for weeks. It turned out to be a six-foot-long drawing of the Great Wall of China. . . . Atop the wall, repulsing [Russian] invaders with crossbows and cannons, were the Chinese troops. 'They're the good guys,' Joe declared.

"I hope you'll indulge me this story about my son," she continued. "There is a point to it. It seems to me that many Americans, like six-year-old Joe, have made up their minds very fast that the Chinese are the good guys."

Telling the story well is the key to this kind of opening. Humor is hard for many people to handle well, for example; if you're not comfortable with it or are unsure of yourself, you should probably stick to relating a personal experience that is sincere and reveals something about you. Relevance is the other key; your story must have a definite purpose that relates to what you're talking about. If it doesn't connect or if it seems patronizing, your audience will tune out. You can come across as less than professional or as a placator who's trying to score Brownie points with the audience.

It's not a hard-and-fast rule, as Ms. Mathews makes clear in the example above, but I have found that stories involving children or pets can easily become precious or overly sweet. Look at children and pet stories with an especially critical eye as you evaluate the effectiveness of your opening.

In general, the more position authority you have—the higher your position in relation to those you're speaking to—the more successful you may be at using the human touch implicit in an anecdotal opening. The boss can establish common ground by making employees forget her title while reminding them that she's a person, too. Unless it illustrates problems shared in common, you'd be less likely to use a personal anecdote in speaking to others at a similar management level, because in this case you have no need to bring yourself "down to earth."

A Slice of Life

Writers are always trying to find the one example that encapsules all the statistics and puts them into human form, the single telling incident that illustrates the larger picture of what life is all about. The same technique of using a real person or event to illustrate your message is an effective way to open a presentation. If you're arguing that Social Security benefits ought to be increased, for example, a case history of a sixty-eight-year-old widow with no other income will get your point across more effectively than a recitation of statistics about inflation and the rising cost of living.

The chairman and chief executive officer of Norton Simon, Inc., David Mahoney, used an illustrative slice of life at the beginning of a speech on the growing divisiveness among different segments of American society:

"On a shuttle flight between Washington and New York, a non-smoker demanded that the nonsmoking section be expanded to accommodate him, as the rules call for. The smokers sitting next to him refused. They started hollering at each other. The pilot, after his warnings to calm down were ignored, landed the plane not in Washington, not in New York, but in Baltimore. I think this is symbolic of what is going on in our society."

As in the recounting of a personal anecdote, the slice of life must be pertinent or you will leave your listeners scratching their heads wondering how it connects.

Famous Quotations

Many speakers like to open with a quote. A quotation inevitably lacks spontaneity, so if you use one, it must be spoken with a lot of energy in order to be effective. An opening quotation should be brief, to the point, and, like other openings, relevant or applicable to the topic. A mortgage banker addressing the industry's serious problems during the 1981–82 recession began a speech to a convention of bank officers by quoting Franklin D. Roosevelt: "The only thing we have to fear is fear itself." He then went on to suggest that the banking industry could weather the recession by refusing to be timid and by taking positive steps to deal with its problems. The quotation worked because it was brief, it made the point, it applied to the situation, and it was familiar to the audience.

You must choose your quote carefully if you decide to use one. And unless you're an actor speaking to a roomful of theatergoers, you will probably lose your audience if you begin by reciting a dozen lines from Shakespeare.

Quotes are easy to overdo. They can be an interesting part of any speech, not just in the opening but all the way through, because they can set off that special spark of recognition. But remember that your business presentation is not a dramatic reading; you are speaking because you have something to say on a specific topic. A hidden objective may emerge when you make a presentation filled with dozens of famous quotations. Perhaps you are trying to show people how well read you are—or that you consider the words of others more important than what you have to say.

Dictionary Definitions

Dictionary definitions tend to be dry and bookish, and I don't recommend using a definition to open a speech unless it is dramatic and tells the audience something new. Sometimes a word has a surprising definition that, because it is unexpected, brings your message clearly into focus as it leads into the subject of the speech.

In a speech on spoken power for women, I have used a dictionary definition of power, which is "possession of control, authority, or influence over others." The dictionary does not suggest that power is a masculine or feminine word, and it includes none of the negative ideas that some people have developed about power. For the message that I want to deliver, defining power is an effective way of making the point that power or authority in speaking is something men and women alike should try to develop.

"A Moment Ago, the Speaker Before Me Said . . ."

Many speakers seem to feel that a reference to the previous speaker or the person who introduced them is a good way to establish contact with the audience. My advice is that you should refer to the previous speaker only if the reference is spontaneous and an ideal lead-in to your speech. The previous speaker may have stolen your thunder by saying what you had intended to say, for example; you may then want to explain why your remarks will be briefer than expected. Even as an explanation for being caught short, however, a reference to the previous speaker has limited potential for effectiveness. I've been at meetings where almost everybody on the program began by mentioning the previous speaker, usually as a way of recognizing that person's authority. Such openings not only get very boring to the audience, they tend to detract from the authority of what you are saying.

Visual Aid or Prop

In most cases a visual aid is a weak way to begin a presentation. Because the focus is on the aid rather than the speaker, you tend to lose rapport with the audience at the point when it is needed most. However, if you're talking about hunger in India, a slide that dramatically illustrates the physical condition of a starving child will make your audience sit up and listen by drawing graphic attention to the point of your talk. Business speakers can begin presentations with the same dramatic effect. A slide or transparency highlighting a substantial rise (or fall) in profits, for example, could be flashed on the screen simultaneously with the speaker's opening words to dramatize the company's gains (or losses).

When discussion is desired, it is frequently effective to use a "trigger" film or slide show to open a presentation. Public health lecturers say they find teenagers more relaxed and willing to talk about the problems of their developing sexuality after they have seen audiovisual presentations that exhibit an understanding of those problems. An appropriate audiovisual can trigger questions and discussion from the audience and lead into the remarks the speaker intends to make. The integration of visual aids with oral presentations is covered in Chapter 6.

Stating the Main Idea

An introduction should not tell your audience so much about what you are going to say that it leaves nothing to the imagination, but it should give the audience clues that provoke interest. A strong statement of the main idea is one way of doing this, as Herchell Britton of Burns International Security Services did in a speech to the Executives Club of Chicago on white-collar crime:

"Ladies and gentlemen: The security of corporations is seriously threatened by the growing incidence of white-collar crime. It's a major national problem. Right now, at this moment, while you're listening to me, some sixty to sixty-five percent of the companies you represent are being ripped off. And I'm being generous, not sensational."

Another way of stating the main point is to raise the questions that your presentation will answer. An example is provided by the dean of the University of Richmond's Westhampton College, Stephanie M. Bennett, in introducing a panel discussion on women reentering the job market:

"You are here today at a conference that focuses upon the subject of the reentry woman. Just who is this woman we have come to consider, to plan for? How is this woman perceived by her society and its institutions? by her peers? by herself? What do we know about the reentry woman biologically, psychologically, emotionally? And, finally, whose responsibility is it to help the reentry woman? and in what ways?"

Establishing Common Ground

The opening of any speech should be an attempt to establish common ground. Some openings are quite frank about trying to establish common ground, as the one used by former Central Intelligence Agency director Stansfield Turner in a speech to the San Francisco Press Club:

"It is always a treat to have a chance to exchange ideas with the press. I believe that our two professions, journalism and intelligence, have a great deal in common. We have in common the task of finding the facts about what is going on in the world; you, primarily for the American public; we, primarily for the American government."

In a business situation, a marketing executive speaking to a group of educators might say: "Your institutions and companies like mine really do have a lot in common. We in the ABC Company are primarily marketers, but we play a major role in the lives of thousands of our employees as educators. On the other hand, you are primarily educators, but you play a unique role as marketers of your products."

Laying Your Cards on the Table

Remember that common ground is not necessarily positive; it may consist of those things speaker and audience disagree on. Stating negative common ground is what I call laying your cards on the table. When the audience's expectations are different from the speaker's intentions, it is perfectly acceptable to say, "I know you're expecting me to talk about X, but I think it's important to talk about Y." The personnel department representative speaking about the impact of the company's new computer system on personnel operations may be forced to say, "I know the new computer system is great for production and inventory, but it is causing overtime and a work backlog in my department."

Mary Cunningham addressed the Commonwealth Club of San Francisco after the former Bendix Corporation executive had been the subject of widespread gossip in the nation's business press. The combination of her good looks and quick advancement at Bendix fueled rumors about her relationship with the company's president. Referring to the barrage of unwelcome publicity, she told her audience that she was "puzzled if not a bit intimidated by reports of a sellout crowd and an overloaded press table." She didn't speculate about the audience's expectations, but let it be known right away what she would *not* talk about: "I'm not here to do a postmortem on the circumstances surrounding my departure from a large industrial company" or to indict the media "for one of the most sensational fictions of the year" or to "regale you with the latest woes of women in top management." She went on to talk about ways in which business managers could help improve national productivity.

Laying it on the line to correct misguided expectations can be a risk, but it will work when it is done with humor, warmth, and authority. To recognize that your audience's expectations may be different from your intentions requires authority and self-assurance both as a person and as a speaker. Laying your cards on the table means you've thought very carefully about what you want to say and what they expect to hear, and decided that by following your instincts you will be able to connect with them despite their expectations.

Analogy

Analogy is as effective a method for opening a speech as it is for sequencing, as long as the comparison is valid and not labored. An apt analogy is easier to use in the opening where the comparison is compressed, easily remembered, and hard-hitting.

Robert J. Buckley, chairman and president of Allegheny Ludlum Industries, used an effective analogy to open a speech he made to the Economic Club of Detroit in 1981. Speaking on the nation's industrial economy, Buckley recalled "a most interesting medical paper . . . about voodoo medicine. [The author] wanted to know how a witch doctor could simply point to a person and say, 'You will die exactly forty-five days from now, two hours after the new moon comes up.' And, forty-five days later, that person would be claimed by death! And it happened time and time again.

"[The author] . . . discovered that it was not the voodoo doctor who had killed the individual; it was the individual himself. That is to say, the will to die had replaced the will to live at precisely the point that the individual accepted as reality the prediction of death.

"The moral of the story is obvious. People can be programmed to die. But the corollary is equally true: If people can be programmed to die they can also be programmed to live.

"The same is true of society and the economy."

Buckley went on to talk about ways the industrial economy in the United States could be "programmed to live." His opening analogy flowed into the body of his speech without being stretched or strained, which is the ultimate test of an effective analogy.

Jokes

Use humor only if it is not stale, if you handle it well, and if it is relevant to your subject. You must also be sure that the humor is something your audience will recognize and appreciate, not something obscure or esoteric that only a few people would find amusing. Be prepared to look with a cold and critical eye on jokes you are tempted to use in opening a speech; presentations have a way of falling flat when you find that you're the only person laughing at your joke. John, who spoke regularly to civic clubs on behalf of his state's welfare and public health system, found the right formula when he opened his remarks with the following story:

"My next-door neighbor's daughter went off to college last fall, and for a while her letters were upbeat and optimistic. Then they got a letter that really shook them up. It said, 'Dear Mom and Dad: Things have really been exciting lately here at good old State U. The dormitory burned down. It caught fire during a pot party. I'm fine, though. I'm living with Bill, and he's promised to marry me as soon as the baby comes. Then we'll be living with his parents, who run a service station in Alaska. Write soon. Love, Suzy. P.S. The dormitory didn't burn down, I'm not living with anybody, I'm not pregnant, and I'm not moving to Alaska. But I did get a D in chemistry, and I wanted to be sure you kept things in perspective.' "

Of course, John wanted his audience to keep the unpopular welfare and health system in perspective as a government service. His story never failed to get a laugh from the civic club members he was speaking to, because many of them were the fathers of children in college. They could identify with John's story; it relaxed them and gave a signal of what was to come. More important, it made them see John as a human being instead of just another bureaucrat. Humor can work well, but it is very much overused as a method of beginning a speech. If you always start with a joke, why not surprise your audience and try another method?

Combining Opening Methods

Openings, like sequencing methods, are not mutually exclusive. Creative organization frequently points the way to an appropriate combination of techniques, as when a student of mine spontaneously joined humor with analogy at the end of a seminar. Mark began his "graduation speech" this way: "When I first enrolled at Speakeasy, I thought of this course as being like jeweler's polish." He paused for effect. "But now I see that it's really like a plumber's helper." He paused again. "It unclogs the pipes." The rest of the class broke into uproarious laughter, and I had to admit it was an apt analogy for what Speakeasy tries to do for its students.

Humorous analogies or quotes are often incorporated into opening remarks for their unique ability to make a point as they simultaneously establish the speaker as a warm, approachable human being. William F. May, chairman and CEO of American Can Company, combined a straightforward statement of his topic with a lighter touch when he opened a speech to the Conference Board meeting in 1980:

"Good morning. It's both a pleasure and an honor to be here today with such a distinguished group of business leaders to chair this opening meeting on the topic 'Political Activism and the Corporate Dilemma.'

"If these were simpler times I could cover the subject of political activism very briefly by merely quoting one of the many wise sayings of Will Rogers. You may recall that Will Rogers said: 'Thank God we don't get all the government we pay for.' "

DO YOU ALWAYS NEED AN OPENING?

As I talk about openings at Speakeasy, students often want to know if they need an opening in every situation. They ask, "What if I'm just speaking at a staff meeting? Do I really need to spend time working on opening remarks in a case like that?"

Even for a presentation at a staff meeting, speakers should have an opening. But you have to use your own judgment about what kind to use, and stop short of oratorical overkill. A dramatic statement would overdo your opening at most routine meetings, for example, although startling news about sales or other developments could provide an exception. In most cases, however, you may simply need to bring your listeners up to date with a simple introductory statement: "At our last meeting we discussed development of a sales campaign and agreed that today we would talk about the market survey. Since the last meeting, I've been thinking about ways to implement the survey that would give us quicker results."

It is worth your time to think about and work on your opening, no matter how simple it will be or how routine the occasion. Certain questions should always be asked, just as they are in other aspects of your presentation planning. A question like "How am I going to start this thing, anyway?" is just as valid as "Where is the audience in regard to my subject?" and "What do I and the audience want and need from this presentation?"

Your opening is your first opportunity to establish common ground, just as social small talk is a way of breaking the ice and establishing a basis for communication. In a conversation with three or four people, we certainly think in a slightly different way than we do about standing up and giving a speech to a larger audience. But the principle is the same, and those who don't break the ice effectively are not as successful in creating relationships that have the potential to reward both parties as speakers who do.

Al, a sales manager who attended one of my Speakeasy workshops on content, expressed it very well when he said that neglecting to establish personal rapport at the outset always left him unsure whether he had been effective in a business meeting. "You're not sure about the impression you've left," he said. "But in the meetings where you do spend the time at the opening, you get a sense as to whether the feelings were shared or not. What happens in the end is more influenced by the way you start at the beginning. Even if the middle—the objective things—are all handled, there's a subjective element that somehow needs attention in the beginning."

USING OPENINGS AS ENDINGS

Your speeches and presentations should end with a bang. Since the various methods of openings we've seen are designed to be attention-getters, most of the same methods can also be used to end presentations. Some, of course, will be more appropriate than others, but all of them should firm up the common ground you've been expanding from the beginning of your presentation.

A *dramatic statement* can work as well at the end of a speech as at the beginning. Often the dramatic statement comes in the form of a question that challenges the listeners and leaves them pondering a course of action. Charles W. Bray III was deputy director of the U. S. International Communication Agency when he spoke in Seattle about the growing interdependency of the United States with the rest of the world. He closed with a question and a challenge:

"As Walter Lippmann once reminded us: 'You took the good things for granted. Now you must earn them again. . . . There is nothing for nothing any longer.'

"There is truly nothing for nothing any longer. Can we cope with that fact? Will we?"

Quotations like the one used by Mr. Bray can form the basis for a rhetorical closing question. Public relations executive Joseph J. Duome, in a speech to AT&T executives, simply used an effective quote to close his remarks on the value of communicating through press conferences:

"The press conference is a truly valuable medium in today's complex and highly competitive world, and as John Milton once said:

" 'Good . . . the more communicated . . . the more abundant grows.' "

A *personal anecdote* can reemphasize the points made in a talk, as in banker Edward E. Crutchfield's story closing his address at the ninth annual Payment Systems Symposium:

"I played a little football once for Davidson—a small men's college. . . . One particularly memorable game for me was one in which I was blindsided on an off-tackle trap. Even though that was seventeen years ago, I can still recall the sound of crackling bones ringing in my ears. Well, seventeen years and three operations later my back is fine. But I learned something important about competition that day. Don't always assume that your competition is straight in front of you. It's easy enough to be blindsided by a competitor who comes at you from a very different direction.''

A *slice of life* was used to illustrate the ending of a speech made by Harvey C. Jacobs, editor of the *Indianapolis News,* on America's unique concept of freedom. His story was about a Russian grade school class after the launching of the first Sputnik:

"The teacher asked the class if they were thrilled with the prospect of a Russian satellite probing space and perhaps someday landing a Russian on the moon.

"The class smiled with pride and agreed that it would be a great achievement to go to the moon. But one thoughtful student broke the silence and spoke a different kind of response.

" 'Yes, it would be wonderful to go to the moon,' he said. 'But I would like to know—when may we go to Vienna?' ''

Analogy is another way of illustrating and bringing together the main points of a presentation. Reginald H. Jones, then chairman of the President's Export Council, found an analogy was an effective way of concluding his talk to the U.S. Council of the International Chamber of Commerce on excessive export regulation:

"Our economy, like Gulliver in Jonathan Swift's masterpiece, is a giant potential source of strength when freed to serve the nation. But thousands of Lilliputian disincentives and regulations —no one perhaps in itself disabling—are weakening the ability of the business community to serve.

"Let's untie Gulliver. The world community will be better served by a United States that has domestic and international vitality than by a weakened giant.''

Restating the central idea of the speech can be a good way of wrapping up, and so can *reestablishing common ground* with the audience. Of course, each type of ending is a way of recalling the central idea so that it is memorable to the audience and points to a course of action.

SIX MORE ENDINGS
Repeating the Introduction

Repeating the introduction can be an effective way to conclude a speech if the opening was effective. If you've challenged the audience with a rhetorical question in the beginning, for example, repeating the challenge becomes an appropriate conclusion. Jan, a commodity analyst, was speaking to commodity analyst trainees on the fear of failure and how it interferes with the potential for success. He began with the question "How much are you willing to risk?" After his talk he paused, looked at the audience, and repeated with different emphasis, "How much are *you* willing to risk?" His message emphasized the risks inherent in his profession, and the rewards possible for those who take well-calculated and thoughtful risks. His ending repeated and highlighted his message just as his opening had introduced it.

Summarizing the Main Points

A brief summary helps the audience remember the main points of the speech. If you use this method, which is popular with many speakers, you must avoid being turgid or academic, too much like a lecturer in the classroom. Make the summary brief, bright, staccato. The points, when repeated, must hit home quickly. If they are drawn out the audience will begin to wonder why you're repeating yourself.

Monsanto Company chairman John W. Hanley spoke to the Instrument Society of America on the responsibilities shouldered by American business in a climate of deregulation, and categorized those responsibilities in his speech as "self-restraint, self-denial, and self-reliance." Closing his speech, Hanley said, "New and heightened responsibilities rest on all Americans . . .

". . . if we fail to exercise *self-restraint* and instead place our special interests above the common good . . .

". . . if we shun the *self-denial* and cooperation and compromise required of all Americans . . .

". . . if we recoil from the *self-reliance* required to solve our national problems and to make this country again an economic miracle. . . .

"If we fail to carry out these responsibilities honorably, we won't be asked to bear them the next time. . . . Let's seize the opportunity that is ours and make the most of it."

Hanley's summary fit the requirements of brevity and brightness, and was an effective way of recalling the main points of his speech.

Call to Action

Calling on the audience to take some immediate action is risky, but somewhat less risky at the end of a speech than at the beginning, since your efforts to establish rapport will have had a chance to take hold.

A call to action is especially effective when your speech has been convincingly persuasive. Karen, a fundraising volunteer, began an appeal for donations to the local chapter of the American Cancer Society with a dictionary definition of cancer. During her talk, she mentioned that one in four people would eventually be stricken with cancer. There were twenty-eight people in her audience, and she ended her presentation by saying, "Won't you give so the seven people in this room who will be victims of cancer will have a chance?" The effect of her conclusion was stunning and dramatic. It involved her audience directly; it pulled them in and gave them no chance to persuade themselves that the problem she had discussed was somebody else's problem. Karen's pledge cards and donations testified to its effectiveness.

The call-to-action ending literally asks the audience to do something specific, such as donate, sign a petition, or commit to working on a project of some kind. It has the advantage of peer pressure that attaches a certain level of stigma to holding back, almost like the stigma of not putting anything into the collection plate at church. In a speech about public schools, for example, the speaker who urges members of the audience to sign up to work with the principal and teachers for needed changes is likely to produce results in the form of a list of volunteers.

Sam, the travel agent who opened by asking his audience how they would like a free two-week island vacation, closed with a specific call for action: "Please sign the registration form I'm handing around. It is your entry in the drawing for the free trip I mentioned earlier, and it will put you on my mailing list for further information." Sam was building a list of names for future contact, and for that purpose, his ending was as effective as Karen's was for her objective.

Prophecy

Prophecy—predicting what will happen in the future—can be positive or negative depending on your topic. In a persuasive speech about the need to conserve gasoline, a prophetic conclusion would be: "If we continue to use gasoline at our present rate, we will have depleted all the world's known reserves by the year 2000." If the talk is informative, dealing for example with the growing use of computers since World War II, the speaker might conclude by predicting: "By the year 2000 computers will be as familiar to every American as the telephone is today."

Pledge or Promise

Depending on your objective, a pledge or promise can give you an effective conclusion and leave the desired impression with the audience. Your pledge may be a commitment to quality, good service, or quick delivery, or, as in Don Baeder's Commonwealth Club speech, a broader promise:

"I give you my pledge that our company [Hooker Chemical] will continue to make products that are as free from hazards as we can possibly make them; that we will continue to work to eliminate risks from our places of business; and that we will seek constantly to maintain and improve our careful stewardship of the environment that we all share."

Appeal to the Emotions

An appeal to the emotions of your audience requires that you be on common emotional ground to start with, since your appeal relies upon the assumption of common beliefs and feelings. The chairman of a company fighting a takeover bid, for example, may call on company loyalty and history to urge stockholders to reject the tender offer. Appealing to his audience to speak out in defending their beliefs, Washington state's licensing director, R. Y. Woodhouse, closed with a story told by a minister during the Holocaust:

". . . They came first for the Communists, and I didn't speak up because I wasn't a Communist.

"Then they came for the Jews, and I didn't speak up because I wasn't a Jew.

"Then they came for the trade unionists, and I didn't speak up because I wasn't a trade unionist.

"Then they came for the Catholics, and I didn't speak up because I was a Protestant.

"Then they came for me, and by that time no one was left to speak."

ASKING FOR THE ORDER

Remember Frederick, the marketing man in Chapter 1 who lost track of his objective and forgot to ask for the order? As you consider the methods you will use to end your presentations, what you are really considering is how you will ask for the order. Your ending is your last opportunity to "make something happen"— the something that is your objective. The circumstances of your presentation may mean that the best way for you to conclude is literally to ask your clients for the order. But whether or not yours is a sales presentation, you still are seeking a commitment that is the equivalent of asking for the order.

Your objective may not always be to get the audience to sign on the dotted line, but you still must move them in some way, make something happen—cause them to ask for the pledge card, agree with your contention, consider your proposal, keep your suggestion alive for at least another meeting. You may be asking for a commitment from the audience to your point of view, or simply asking them to try to see things your way. You may or may not be asking them to act immediately on the information, beliefs, or opinions you've presented. But you want them on your side or at least tolerant of the view you represent, so that at the end of your presentation speaker and audience share the common ground you've worked from opening to ending to identify, develop, and expand. Making that happen is the essence of effective communication.

6

Using Visual Aids

COMMUNICATION IS not an exclusively oral process. Visual communication has been with us for more than twenty-five thousand years, since the day prehistoric man first scratched into a cave wall an image of what he saw in the world around him. People have been expressing themselves with pictures ever since.

Visual aids can help your presentations make things happen. They might even be necessary to reach your objective. Used correctly, they can make you a better speaker by providing a focal point for your interaction with the audience. They can make your words, at times, unnecessary. They can create excitement and spur emotion.

But communication is the name of the game. A visual aid is not magic; it is just another resource you can employ to help you reach your objective. Don't assume that every time you illustrate a point your illustration must be a visual one. A well-selected story or anecdote can add more vivid color to your presentation than any slides you might select.

Despite the advantages visual aids can bring to a speaking situation, I don't like the way they're used in many business presentations today. Visual aids are too often used as a crutch and a substitute for thorough preparation. When they're added at the last minute, or used just to fill time or give a touch of slickness to the presentation, they merely distract the audience's attention away from you and your message. They can reduce or even eliminate the interaction between speaker and audience, the give and take that communication is really all about. The speaker is there to communicate information and credibility; to reach an objective; to make something happen. To give up the vast power of communication, the unique ability of human beings to exchange ideas, to a chart or piece of film that can't respond to the audience is to

107

avoid the responsibility and miss the opportunity that come with being a speaker.

WHAT VISUALS CAN DO

Visuals should be used to reinforce your message and clarify points that need the help of illustration. You make two mistakes when you throw visuals into your presentations without making sure that they're needed and what they'll do: You don't let the visuals do as much as they can to aid your presentation; and you sell your listeners short by assuming they won't know the difference.

Forrest, a salesman employed by a company that manufactures cold-drink cups, asked me to review a presentation he was planning for executives of a fast-food restaurant chain. His objective was to persuade them to use his brand of cups. He planned to show the restaurant executives how they could save money with his brand and he focused on that point with slides showing cost comparisons with other brands. Then, in the middle of the presentation, he brought up some more slides, this time showing exteriors of the fast-food restaurants and the restaurant chain's logo. I asked him why he was showing the additional slides.

"Oh," Forrest said casually, "I always do that when I'm making a sales presentation. They fill time, and it makes my clients feel good to see their restaurants and their logo on the screen." But instead of reinforcing his point with illustrations, Forrest was diverting his audience by using slides as filler, in a way that didn't contribute to reaching his objective. He simply had not analyzed his illustrations for what they could add to his presentation or for how they could detract from it.

We tend to use visual aids at any cost because we think that pictures are automatically better than words, even when the pictures don't say anything and the words do. People have come to believe that if they use slides in a presentation, for example, the slides instantly make the presentation more effective and professional.

But visual aids are just that—*aids* to communication—and if you approach them that way, you'll find they can have great impact and you'll be able to use them successfully. They should be used only to reinforce your points and make your messages clearer, to aid the job of communication, not to take it over entirely.

Tony O'Reilly, the president and chief executive officer of the H. J. Heinz Company, used slides at the beginning of a talk about Ireland, his native country. "This is Ireland," he said, and the screen flashed with the soft green of the Irish countryside, with its low hills and rich pastures—pictures that showed far better than words why Ireland is called the Emerald Isle. "And this is Ireland," O'Reilly continued, and now the screen showed the ravages of war in Northern Ireland, the street barricades and ghettos shattered by years of religious strife in Belfast. O'Reilly went on to talk about Ireland's history and problems and the island's potential. There was no need for him to describe in words its natural beauty, or the devastation that fighting has brought to the north. Pictures added clarity, and provided a foundation for the talk that followed.

But speakers often use slides that only echo in pictures what the speaker is saying; sometimes the slides are just pictures of words. Don Keough put this tendency in perspective when he said, "Some pictures may be worth a thousand words, but a picture of a thousand words isn't worth much."

What Makes a Good Visual Aid?

If the purpose of a visual is to reinforce your point or to make it clearer, then a good visual should do one or both of these things. A visual can't do a very effective job of reinforcing your point if the visual itself makes more than one point—if it's too busy or contains too much information.

The following examples show the difference between a visual that contains too much information and one that is effective because it makes only one point:

STATUS REPORT

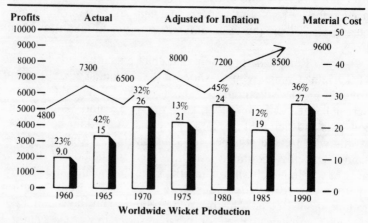

Worldwide Wicket Production

STATUS REPORT

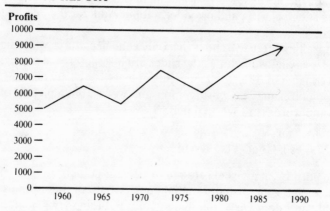

Sometimes, when the purpose of the aid is to make something clearer, you have to include some detailed information. But remember that the best way a visual aid can make something clearer is visually—the more you take advantage of the graphic nature of the aid, the more effective it will be. Try to turn your words and numbers into an easily grasped picture, into lines and shapes. The simplest way of making the point is usually the best.

Wine production statistics of the ABZ Wine Company, for example, can be presented as follows:

Wines	Cases	Percentage
Burgundy	27323	22.5
Chablis	35143	28.9
Champagne	25374	20.9
Chardonnay	10300	8.5
Rhine	8030	6.6
Rosé	15457	12.7

But suppose you want to focus on the Rhine wine segment of the company's production. Then a more effective aid would look like this, which turns the numbers into a picture:

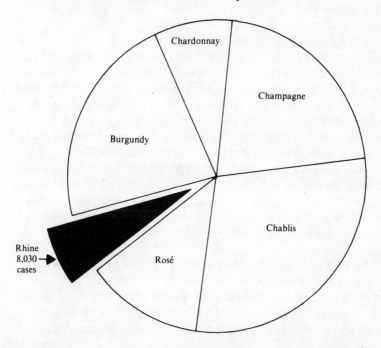

Jim Ruwoldt, who is in charge of meetings for Coca-Cola U.S.A. and whose department handles all the necessary visuals, told me that one of the most successful market research presentations he had ever worked on was a slide presentation done in cartoon style. "It took a lot of arm-twisting to get the presenter to try it," he said. "Most people who work with facts and figures aren't comfortable using cartoon figures with arrows showing 'Up ten percent' or pushing bars on a chart to say 'We're on the move.' But he's been an advocate ever since, because when he was through, people said, 'You know, I learned more from your presentation . . .' The audience retained more than they would have by looking at elaborate charts and data, because only the salient points were made. That's what it all comes down to.''

So a good visual aid is one that reinforces or clarifies only one point and that takes advantage of the visual nature of the aid. It's up to you to decide which important points you need to reinforce or clarify; you needn't be visually oriented to know what needs illustrating and what doesn't. However, you can get help in translating your points from words to pictures.

Except for transparencies made directly from charts and graphs, you're not going to be producing visual aids yourself. Photographers and audiovisual production houses can provide sophisticated illustrations to fit your needs, but remember that these professionals are in the business of selling and producing audiovisual presentations. They will be most helpful if you are looking for a complex presentation that can put their expertise to work on a major scale. That's fine if that's what you are looking for. But if all you need is a few slides to highlight a brief talk or sales presentation, then knowing exactly the points you want illustrated will save the hassle, embarrassment, and potential expense of being supplied with a twenty-minute slide show that breaks your budget and requires a trunkload of equipment to transport and show.

Most large corporations have audiovisual departments that produce visuals in-house or deal directly with outside suppliers. If there's such a department in your company, the best thing you can do is give it time to work for you by informing it of visual possibilities and where illustrations are needed in your presentation.

PLANNING FOR VISUALS IN YOUR CONTENT

If you planned your presentation as described so far, you will be in a good position to decide what and how many visual aids you need. Once you have your objective, your message, your main

Main Ideas	Time	Supporting Points	Visual Aids

ideas, and your supporting points, it should be easy to determine what you want to reinforce and what you need to make clearer. A 50 percent decline in sales, for example, certainly warrants visual reinforcement: "Sales are down drastically—fifty percent," and a slide or an overhead transparency contrasting last year's healthy sales figures with this year's disaster. Again, use this "double-barreled" approach only when you decide the comparison is dramatic enough; you have to be willing to be objective about this, and as the speaker, you have the authority to make such decisions.

Organizing your presentation in modules allows you to incorporate visuals and other resources in its structure just as you incorporate the main points. You can anticipate visuals from the beginning for maximum effectiveness. The outline form, shown here with a column for resources, is an excellent planning guide and can become the notes for your presentation.

When You're Handed Visuals

What happens when, as in many large corporations, the boss comes in and says, "Tom, I know you've got a presentation coming up. Vicki Smith gave a similar presentation last week and it was really effective. Here are the visuals she used." All of a sudden, you're confronted with eighty slides to put into a twenty-minute presentation. Many large companies even mail out packaged presentations with slides or overheads, accompanied by scripts. Good speakers use these packages as a starting point for their planning, not as something set in stone from which they can't deviate. Otherwise, the effect can be the same as presenting too many facts without organizing them into main ideas—your listeners end up with an overload of information that they forget as soon as they leave the room.

When someone throws visuals at you like that, be strong. Look at each visual and decide what concept it illustrates and then decide where it might fit into your outline. Ask yourself, "What is the bottom line with this visual? Does it illustrate a concept that I need, that helps my presentation, or is it extraneous information?" And if it is extraneous or irrelevant, even though it may be a beautiful slide, be prepared to throw it out. You should be able to relate in one sentence the statement that a visual makes or the concept it illustrates. Too many slides are like too many details. You should keep only the ones that really work for you.

Many speakers are drawn along by visuals. Instead of the speaker controlling the visuals, the visuals control the speaker. You must be able to look at them, decide where they fit in, and eliminate them if they don't enhance your presentation.

Planning for visuals means not only deciding where they go in your presentation. It also means being able to use them when the time comes, and being able to do without them in an emergency. Murphy's famous law says that if anything can go wrong, it will. The person responsible for setting up your flip chart may not do it; you might forget your marking pen; the extension cord might be too short to reach the wall socket; any number of mechanical or electrical foul-ups might occur. So don't make your talk absolutely dependent on any visual. If you've used the modular approach, deciding on your content first and then choosing your visual aids to support that content, it will be much easier for you to give the presentation without the aids if and when something does go wrong.

Your planning should always include the mechanical requirements of your situation and your physical surroundings, including the setup in the room where you will speak. Go beyond your normal attention to the electrical, lighting, and sound equipment. The simplest questions are the easiest to overlook: Where are the light switches? How wide are the aisles? Is the screen high enough to be seen by the people in the middle and back rows? You must have as much control as possible over your environment, because your environment can affect your ability to communicate.

WHERE TO PLACE VISUALS
WITHIN A PRESENTATION

How do you know where to place your slides within a presentation, and how many should you use? Do they go only in one place, or can you intersperse them throughout? There's no hard-and-fast rule for the placement of visuals within a presentation, and their numbers are dictated only by your need to communicate. Your objective remains the basic determining factor in deciding whether to use visuals and where they should go. They may appear grouped in one place, or they may be interspersed throughout, depending upon what your modular planning tells you about the need for reinforcement and clarification. If there are parts of your presentation where you can toss a coin over whether or not visuals may be effective, you would do just as well to forget about them and concentrate on making your delivery more effective.

If there's a place in your presentation where five or eight or ten visuals are effective, you should feel comfortable using them there and nowhere else. Once you start with visuals, it's easy to feel that for some reason you have to use them throughout. Remember the children's parable of the boy who called out "Wolf!" and found that it was such a successful way to get attention that he began calling out whether he saw a wolf or not? Pretty soon people stopped paying attention, and when the wolf really came, when the boy really needed someone to notice his cries, everyone thought it was just another false alarm. Using slides where you don't need them diminishes their importance and takes attention away from the places where you really do need them to make your point.

Two of my students were preparing a workshop for supermarket managers on impulse buying in grocery stores. Leslie and Philip planned to use transparencies. The first segment of their workshop was a discussion of impulse buying. They asked questions of the audience like "What percentage of supermarket purchases are made on impulse?" Each question and the correct answer were repeated in transparencies. I pointed out that the transparencies were redundant and really didn't improve on Leslie and Philip's presentation.

Next their presentation moved into a discussion of supermarket traffic flow—the number of shoppers that could be expected to pass through a certain part of the store. The transparencies they used here were simple line diagrams showing the percentage of shoppers that could be expected to move along any given aisle. Here, the transparencies had impact. The diagrams improved Leslie and Philip's ability to communicate their points to the audience in an easily remembered way. As their workshop evolved, Leslie and Philip dropped the question-and-answer transparencies from the first part of their presentation, where they did not improve clarity, and retained the traffic-flow transparencies, which did make their points more clearly.

Leslie and Philip are not alone in their tendency to use visuals throughout a presentation that needs visuals in only one place. A small group of brand managers were planning a briefing to bring a couple of top executives and a new manager up-to-date on advertising and public relations activities on behalf of the brand, including comparisons between their brand's advertising and public relations spending and the competition's. In rehearsals with me beforehand, Logan, the main speaker, used transparencies to illustrate almost every word. But his strong, direct statements really needed no visual backup.

Logan's final transparency, however, illustrated the major components of the brand's overall budget. It was helpful in comparing production with marketing costs, and showed the managers that marketing could justifiably consume a larger share of the brand's budget. In its final form, the brand managers' briefing was a blend of clear, authoritative oral presentation that required no illustration to back up the points that were made, and a visual comparison that allowed Logan to maintain audience contact as he pointed out its highlights. Logan had begun with several slides, but in analyzing what really needed illustrating and what didn't, found he needed only one.

STAYING IN TOUCH WITH THE AUDIENCE

Maintaining speaker-audience interaction while using visuals is extremely important. The tendency to forget about interacting with the audience is strongest when the audiovisuals are slides; flip charts and overhead transparencies encourage interaction, and movies and multimedia presentations are usually self-contained and feature speakers only before and after them. Speakers should never hesitate to take charge and guide the audience, even when it means stepping in front of the screen to direct their attention to a specific point or piece of information. The speaker can act almost like an orchestra leader, directing the attention of the audience between speaker and screen, as if saying, "Put your attention on me, because what I'm going to say now is important. Now, put your attention on the slides, because they make a point visually that I can't make as well verbally.'' To take charge like a symphony director, you must have a command of your content and visuals, and an energetic and committed style. I get a wonderful sense of freedom and excitement from speakers who refuse to be harnessed by a script, who know their presentations well enough to step away from the podium with a microphone clipped on and a pointer in one hand and direct the attention of three hundred people, first talking and then dimming the lights and steering their attention to the screen.

But the need to interact with the audience as well as with the technology of visuals requires extra preparation. Rehearsal is important for any presentation, but it is doubly important for a presentation that includes visuals and that extra possibility for error they present.

A division head of a sportswear manufacturing firm came to me to rehearse a presentation he was to give to more than five hundred employees. Barry was talking about market conditions that had made it a difficult year for his firm's line of women's sportswear. He used slides throughout and stayed virtually hidden in the dim light as he lectured about the company's problems. Barry's visuals only repeated his words through most of the presentation, and I recommended that he drop them except for one point in the middle. There, Barry used slides showing year-to-year sales figures. The visuals painted a graphic picture of the sales trends and let Barry move easily into an oral discussion of the challenges faced by the firm in the year ahead. Highlighting the trends visually dramatized the challenge and was a way to use visuals to support an oral presentation. And using them only in one spot let Barry and his audience see each other during the rest of his presentation. He told me later he wanted to do it that way all along, but it was not until he had rehearsed that he felt comfortable darkening the room in the middle of his presentation to use slides in only one spot.

Let me stress again the cardinal rule governing the use of visuals: Don't use visuals to fill time. Droning along through a tray of unnecessary slides is a sure way to lose contact with both your audience and your objective. A woman enrolled in one of my seminars attended a number of professional conferences, where she was frequently among the major speakers. She told me, "These people usually want me to talk for forty-five minutes, and there's just not that much to say. Can't I get a slide show to carry the ball for fifteen or twenty minutes? Then I can answer their questions in the time that's left." I replied, "Why do you have to fill time? If you're on the program for forty-five minutes and you have only thirty minutes' worth of information, you're not helping your audience by filling that extra time with slides. I think you would do better to say what you have to say and not try to fill the time that remains." The purpose of visual aids is to help you communicate, not to do the job for you.

USEFUL VISUAL AIDS

Visual aids can include almost anything that helps your audience see what you're talking about, any visual tool that moves you further along toward your objective by illustrating your point more effectively than words. Visual aids run the gamut from printed handouts to motion pictures, but no matter which type of aid you use, there are certain guidelines that apply to all of them.

1. Make sure the visual can be seen clearly by the entire audience.
2. Talk to the audience, not to the aid.
3. When you are finished with the aid, remove it or turn it off.

Let's look at the commonly used types of visual aids to see what advantages and problems they give the speaker.

Charts and Graphs

The flip chart, mounted on an easel, is either a large blank tablet on which you write as you speak, or a tablet which you have prepared in advance. The flip chart can be used spontaneously, and that's the main reason I like it. You can keep attention focused on your key concepts and main points by simply writing them on the paper. The disadvantages are that it doesn't work well for detailed information that takes a lot of effort to produce, and it can only be seen by a small audience.

Overhead Transparencies

An overhead transparency permits projection of a large image onto just about any large, vertical viewing surface, whether it's a screen or the wall over the blackboard. The transparency, the same size as a sheet of writing paper, is laid on top of the light source and the image is magnified and bounced toward the wall by a refraction device. Unlike a slide projector, the overhead projector permits transparencies to be changed easily by hand. The transparencies also are inexpensive and easy to make.

One reason I like the transparency is that the speaker can interact with it by marking a number or word or adding some information. It can be used with a good deal of light in the room, so you can maintain eye contact with members of the audience and take advantage of the dynamics of the speaking situation.

The fact that transparencies are so simple to produce makes it easy to overuse them. When you don't give yourself time to think them through as an integral part of your presentation, the audience often ends up playing "read along with me." If the audience reads the overhead (or any other visual) with you as you read it, you lose more than eye contact. Your ability to use your authority as speaker to focus attention where you want it is also lost, and you might just as well type up the information and hand it out.

Slides

Slides offer almost unlimited visual possibilities and at the same time great potential for abuse or ineffective use by speakers. The basic mistake speakers tend to make is thinking that the added sophistication of slides lends more weight to the information you put on them. You now have color and design to work with; you push a button to advance them and project them on the screen. Do these mechanical requirements make your information more valid than if you simply said it? Of course not. The slide's premise is the same as for any visual; a well-thought-out slide should enhance a presentation. Slides are more versatile than overheads. They are a little more expensive to make, but they can attract and hold an audience much better. They can be used not only to direct the attention of the audience to key points; properly produced and presented, they can inspire a wide range of emotions. In more sophisticated applications, they can even be part of movie-like sound and light shows with multiple screens and projectors.

The amount of light in a room is more of a consideration when you're dealing with slides than with overheads. Don't get trapped into being a disembodied voice narrating a slide show in a darkened room. An upturned light at the podium is one way of remaining visible to your audience while talking about the information on your slides. Occasionally you'll run into a slide producer who is a visual purist and feels that the color and visual integrity of his slides are more important than your eye contact with the audience, and that therefore you must speak in a pitch-black room. Don't let that happen. Visual quality is important, but I would always sacrifice some measure of it in order to have interaction with the audience. And there's an added factor: People get too sleepy with the lights off. Of course, there's not much sense in trying to show slides if the room is going to be at full light and nobody's going to be able to see them. Speaker-audience interaction and visual quality ought to be, and can be, compatible. Remember, because most slides are professionally produced, the presentation can appear "canned" if the speaker doesn't really work at audience interaction.

You can gain a bit more control over light by using rear projection, since in this method light comes from behind the screen. But there are limitations even to rear projection when it comes to light control, and you should be careful not to stretch the format beyond its limitations.

Motion Pictures and Videotapes

Film and videotape, like multimedia presentations, are most effective in creating a mood or feeling in an audience. They set a platform from which the speaker can "take off." Motivational or "trigger" films are popular ways of injecting enthusiasm in a sales force or provoking questions and discussion in an audience. One company uses a short, silent film, less than ten minutes long, called *Mountain Climbing*. It depicts the climber's struggle with the elements and the thrill and exhilaration of reaching the top. The film is followed by a speaker who talks about the day-to-day struggle and the tremendous sense of well-being and accomplishment when the task is finished. This motivational film, followed by a twenty-minute oral presentation, forms a thirty-minute package that does a great job of reaching its objective, which is to fire up the sales force. This ability to create excitement is a form of communication that no other medium can accomplish.

Printed Matter and Handouts

Printed materials as visual aids are most often used in workshops and seminars rather than in platform speeches. They can create the same problems as other visuals if they're not thought out. That is, they should be as simple and clean as possible, and attract attention to the points you want to make. To be effective, they should be designed with the overall presentation in mind.

Handouts are often intended as study documents, so it is quite appropriate for them to contain a lot of detail. But if you're going to pass out materials for the audience to study, I advise waiting until the end of your presentation to distribute them. Your listeners' natural tendency is to read what you have handed them, and they can't pay attention to what you are saying if they have their noses buried in the handout; you lose control of the situation by losing audience interaction. Hand out printed material at the end of your presentation for your audience to use as a future reference, rather than playing another version of "read along with me."

Props and Displays

There are other kinds of aids that can help you reinforce the points you're making with your audience. A tabletop model or display can illustrate plans for a new downtown development or office complex, for example. Props can be very effective as long as the speaker maintains control, which means not letting the audience get so involved with the prop that they blank out the speaker. Props are used best with small audiences, of course, but what better way of illustrating the company's new package design than to pass samples around? As in the case of printed materials, this should be done so as not to conflict with the interaction between speaker and audience.

YOU'RE IN CHARGE

Each speaker can affect an audience with more than just his content. Your credibility—who and what you are, your position —also is an important factor. If that weren't the case, you would never have to do anything but hand out fact sheets. No matter what the circumstances, a speaker should never be just a "voice-over." If you allow yourself to be an invisible voice while the action's on the screen, you are not taking advantage of the dynamics of the speaking situation, including the ability to interact with your audience. You could just as well substitute a tape recorder. Never let your visuals do more than aid your ability to communicate, to reinforce or clarify your points as you move toward your objective. That's all visual aids can do, and with the proper planning they can do it very well.

Now you have looked at the planning of your business presentation from start to finish. You've gone from the request that you speak, through the development of your objective, message, and main ideas, through the sequencing of your presentation, the effective use of openings and endings, and ways to use visual aids effectively in your presentation. Throughout the development of your content, you have balanced your needs as a speaker and the needs of your audience. Your presentation is ready to make something happen.

Just as your content considers elements of both the speaker and the audience, the style with which you deliver your presentation must consider the same balance of needs. In the next section, we will look at style for the vital part it plays in the delivery of an effective presentation.

You—your body from head to toe, your gestures, your voice— are a delivery system. Just as your content must be arranged to send a clear message to the audience, your speaking style or "spoken image" must deliver that message effectively. Your spoken image is the combination of your appearance, your stance and movements, and your voice. It is a way of packaging your message for presentation to your audience. Your style should make it easier for the audience to receive your message.

PART II

DEVELOP A STYLE THAT WILL WORK FOR YOU

WHEN PEOPLE COME to me to work on improving their styles, they often tell me they want to be like other speakers they've seen, speakers they know can make things happen with an audience. But you don't have to become other people, or like other people, in order to become a better speaker.

I've learned in teaching and working with many effective speakers that styles can be highly individual while still containing necessary and basic qualities. The people we know as natural speakers, the ones who can make any audience sit up and listen, have unique personalities and styles. Yet they all exhibit authority, energy, and audience awareness—the three basic components of every effective speaking style. The best speakers combine these elements into styles that are confident without being arrogant, energetic without being "hyper," and aware of the audience without being placating or giving up authority. The question is not how to change yourself, but how to work with and improve upon who you are, to put the qualities of effectiveness into your own voice and body. Let's look at the ways these qualities can be reflected in your speaking style.

Authority

An effective speaking style always contains an element of strength. I initially used the word "strength" in my teaching to mean "self-esteem," but the concept has evolved to mean "authority." This simply means looking and sounding as if you mean what you say every time you speak. Having authority in your spoken image does not mean that you are authoritarian or dictatorial, or that you are cold or detached. An authoritative speaker is one whose words proceed from authority; he looks and sounds as if he knows what he's talking about. If your spoken image does not contain authority, if you don't look and sound as if you have the right to say what you're saying, your audience has reason to question your credibility.

When authority is missing in a speaker's style, it's for one of two reasons: Some people don't have it because they've never had

127

it and aren't used to expressing it; others have it and don't use it. Many speakers simply aren't used to showing authority when they speak. Because authority is lacking in their speaking styles, these people have become accustomed to having others dismiss their words and opinions, which reinforces the notion that they have no authority to put into their speaking. Other speakers may have authority, but leave it out of their styles because they think they'll seem too pushy or overbearing. People in positions of authority, especially men who are also physically imposing, are sometimes advised to hold back to avoid intimidating their listeners. But the way to temper your authority is not by suppressing it, but by developing greater awareness of your audience.

Energy

Whereas authority is the impression that you have the right to say what you're saying, energy is the impression that it matters to you. An energetic speaker is involved with what he is saying and sounds as if he cares about it.

It may come as a surprise to you, but effective speaking is hard physical work, and nothing will happen for you if you don't put physical energy into it. When you put physical effort into speaking, you look and sound as if you give a damn. Energy in your spoken image comes from your physical involvement in delivering your message.

When you really work at making your message come alive, you send out the impression that it's worth the investment of your energy. The audience will put only as much energy into listening as your own energy level indicates the subject is worth; you can't hold the attention of your audience for very long if you don't seem interested and involved in what you're saying. An energetic speaker gives to his speaking the amount of energy he wants his audience to give to their listening.

Audience Awareness

No business operates in a vacuum, nor should any speaker. Yet many business speakers exhibit very little audience awareness when they make presentations, a fact I find amazing considering how important the input from an audience can be. You receive a wealth of information by being aware of your audience. A raised eyebrow or furrowed forehead, for example, might signal confusion or disagreement. Signs like these let you know when it's necessary to shift, bend, or adapt your content to become more effective. They let you know when you have to work harder to get your point across. To be effective, you must be willing to see and respond to your audience, yet many speakers ignore the need for audience awareness, especially as they move from small groups to larger ones.

Speakers frequently don't allow themselves to see their audiences because they are afraid of seeing a negative reaction. But speakers who take the risk and learn to see their audiences say the increased awareness of audience reaction makes them feel more confident because they always know how their messages are being received. They're no longer in the dark, which is a very uncomfortable feeling for most of us. Not knowing is more unsettling to most speakers than knowing the audience reaction, even when it's negative.

Audience awareness also means that individual members of the audience feel recognized by the speaker. When you recognize your audience, they feel seen and heard. Because you've involved them, they're more likely to respond to your message.

So audience awareness gives you information from the audience; it can make you feel better; it helps make the audience more responsive to you because you clearly are being responsive to them.

Much in the chapters that follow will focus on specific techniques that you can use to create an image that has these qualities of authority, energy, and audience awareness. But before we look at techniques or even at individual qualities, I want to emphasize the goal or objective of these techniques and qualities: an effective spoken image. A really effective spoken image is more than the sum of its parts, more than an accumulation of techniques and qualities. An effective spoken image makes something happen by reaching out to the audience.

IT ALL ADDS UP TO REACHING OUT

When I evaluate a speaker, I don't immediately pull out a pencil and paper and start critiquing the elements of his style. My first concern is whether he is making things happen for me as a member of the audience. If I don't get pulled in, if I don't seem to want to listen, if I look around and other members of the audience are restless, then I start analyzing the speaker and asking myself what techniques I would recommend to improve his effectiveness. But rote adoption of the techniques is not as important as their all coming together in a whole; if the overall effect is working, it doesn't matter if your style embraces each technique to the letter.

Following each technique rigidly would make you into a robot with no individual characteristics. The techniques in the chapters to follow are simply a base for exploration and experimentation, until you feel you are projecting the qualities of authority, energy, and audience awareness. Even as you strengthen the techniques that make you a better speaker, you can retain the marks of individuality that make you unique.

I continue to be impressed by the fact that the naturals, the speakers who always seem to make things happen with their audiences, combine the basic qualities we've just discussed into styles that reach out and connect with their audiences. The overall effect of reaching out embodies authority, energy, and audience awareness, but somehow transcends them.

An effective style reaches out by sending the speaker's energy forward to his audience. But reaching out is more than a physical quality; it is an expression of the speaker's dedication to delivering his message to the audience. How do you react when you know that someone is paying attention to you and putting effort into making a presentation work for both of you? If you're part of an audience, and the speaker "touches" you by reaching out, you sit up and take notice. If you are the speaker, contact with the audience lets you know that they are listening. If you are convinced about the message you're delivering, reaching out relays your commitment to the audience. When you get more involved, and really work to help your audience receive your message, you reveal more of yourself and the audience can see that it matters to you.

Until you use authority, energy, and audience awareness to dissolve the barrier that exists between you and the audience, you don't ensure that something is going to happen. Reaching out is working to help the audience receive your message, working to connect with them and doing whatever you have to do to make something happen. When you reach out effectively, your audience should feel that the most important thing to you at that moment is meeting them on common ground, giving up nothing of yourself but sharing an understanding. The audience should feel the depth of your commitment in a way that makes them want to match your effort to get something out of the encounter. The audience returns your commitment and involvement with their attention, and the result is an intimate feeling of sharing.

If all this sounds somewhat vague, it is because reaching out is what the French might call a *je ne sais quoi*—an indefinable but essential quality. You know when it's there, but you can't put your finger on it. You know when a speaker has reached out to you when you forget everything else and are pulled into the speaking and listening experience.

SHEDDING OLD HABITS FOR A "NEW YOU"

Much of what you have read so far about an effective speaking style suggests psychological improvement. Words and phrases like "self-esteem," "secure," "having the right," "being willing," and "taking the risk" could suggest that your mental attitude or self-image is the key to developing an effective spoken image. And there's no doubt that one way of improving your spoken image is by working on your self-image.

But I think a poor speaker is usually one who is using ineffective techniques. The qualities of authority, audience awareness, and energy are expressed mainly through the speaker's use of his body and voice. So by working on your body and voice as they are used in speaking, you can make your spoken image more effective, regardless of your psychological state at any given time. Working on techniques that can make you a better speaker is a matter of making choices, and you can observe and evaluate for yourself the effectiveness of each choice.

Learning to speak effectively is really no different from learning to play a sport—tennis, for example. First you learn the basics and then you experiment with individual touches that work for you, as you might choose to try a new grip to see how it affects your tennis game. In just the same way, you can learn to make more effective choices in the way you use your body and your voice in speaking. Why don't we look at speaking the way we look at tennis or other sports—as a skill to be acquired? I think it's because speaking is something we do every day, and tennis is something we have to go out and learn with lessons and practice. We all learned to speak so long ago that the way we speak has become part of what we think of as our identity. We forget that speaking is a learned activity and think of it as an innate part of our personality.

A shy person, for example, projects his shyness in his style. He may think, "I would like to be a better speaker, but I sure can't change my personality. It's me. It's the way I am."

Such a person once asked me if she could develop a special personality that she could turn on like a light bulb in a public speaking situation. I asked Susan why, if she thought she could develop herself as an effective public speaker, she couldn't apply the same lessons to her everyday life. "It's not me," she said. I looked at techniques that might help Susan: She needed to move her feet apart and establish a firm base; she needed to raise her chest, which in turn would raise her head to a level position; she had to learn how to breathe to support her voice; and she had to open her mouth wider when she spoke.

How badly you want to make lasting changes is important. Susan literally watched changes occur in her during videotaping sessions at Speakeasy. Playing a role as a carnival barker, she saw that gestures she had thought were outrageous were actually appropriate and authoritative. She found that people would listen when she projected her voice in a way that signified that what she was saying was worthwhile. She believed that the changes she saw represented a worthwhile change in her life, and she practiced and used them in her daily routine. By working on techniques, Susan quickly changed a spoken image that said "I am shy" to one that said "I am confident, strong and assertive. I have authority." Susan didn't necessarily change on the inside at first, but she changed on the outside.

Susan immediately got better results when she spoke. The sales presentations she made for the interior design firm where she worked became more convincing. By broadcasting her belief in herself, Susan gave an additional message to her listeners—the belief that what she was telling them was backed up by true authority.

What happened then? Susan was amazed at the positive feedback she received when she began using herself with more energy and authority. She soon started to feel more secure, more open, and more assertive than she had when she used herself in a closed-in way that broadcast her lack of confidence. Over a fairly short time, Susan began testing her newfound strength in other situations. She was more lively and willing to state her point of view. She saw that the shyness she thought was part of her personality was really just an accumulation of old habits that could be discarded.

When I saw Susan a year later, I barely recognized her. She was no longer using "techniques" that were "foreign" to her personality. I saw in Susan an everyday style which had incorporated those techniques. She had made them part of her. She said, "You opened a door that showed me I didn't have to be locked into the 'same old me.' " And she said she was taking enormous pride and great pleasure in her "new me."

It isn't only insecure and shy people who can benefit from improved techniques in their speaking styles. David was a successful and confident lawyer in his early forties. He was bright and articulate, but because he felt he had to be taken seriously by judges when he was young and beginning his practice, he had become tight and controlled. He leaned back, away from his audience; he clenched his teeth; his voice droned on in a boring way. Because of the control he was exerting over his body and voice, there was no energy or commitment in his body and no life in his voice. David had plenty of leadership potential for the political career he wanted, but those qualities didn't show through.

I recommended to David that he work on releasing his jaw and opening his mouth as a way of putting energy into his voice, and that he work on reaching out to the audience to demonstrate his commitment to what he was saying. When David saw that image of himself on videotape, he quickly decided he wanted to take ownership of the techniques that had given him that image. A lawyer who was familiar with David's style in court observed later, "David is more interesting than he used to be. He doesn't seem as 'reined-in' and stiff."

Like Susan and David, anyone can choose to change techniques, and the positive effects of those choices can snowball to provide greater, long-lasting benefits. The initial, superficial change can point the way to deep and lasting change.

SPOKEN IMAGE: A TOOL FOR SUCCESS

Speaking skills, despite their basis in techniques that are easily acquired and practiced, are not often ranked among other popular forms of self-improvement, and I'm not sure why. People routinely make adjustments in management style or eating habits; they take up jogging for better health, or learn to play golf to help them relax. And that's acceptable. It's OK to be a better manager, to lose weight, to be healthier or to learn a sport. Improved speaking skills are also beneficial, both personally and professionally, but when someone says he's going to a speaking seminar, he may be greeted with the suggestion that he's going to learn to put on a phony personality that's reserved just for speaking to an audience. It's a common misconception that just as an actor might cover his face with makeup and put on a period costume, speakers must discard their own personalities to become someone or something different from who or what they really are.

As you try out new techniques, they are likely to seem strange and unnatural at first. They feel "not you," and this unnatural quality is what many speakers mistake for phoniness. But as you use and practice new techniques and begin to feel more comfortable with them, the strange "not you" feeling quickly disappears.

Learning to speak well is not learning to assume a different role or character. Standing up straight instead of slouching when you address an audience doesn't make you a different person, for example. It simply makes a better you. Learning an effective speaking style is learning to use your body and your voice the way they were meant to be used.

An effective spoken image is among the many appropriate and legitimate tools to be employed in gaining success. It's like the expertise that has made you a valued financial analyst, made your economic forecasts worth listening to, made your sales and marketing skills important to your company. Your speaking skill is a business tool. It is one of the most powerful self-improvement techniques you can put to work in a business situation.

An effective speaking style is valuable for more than public speaking situations or business presentations. It's something you can use every day, with the same positive results. The habits we adopt for public speaking work in *all* our speaking situations. Conversely, our everyday speaking style, our spoken image, carries over into public speaking; a winning style in one area is a winner in the other. People demonstrate the same weaknesses—and the same strengths—speaking one-to-one as they do when speaking to a group. Speakeasy's students generally see no problem with the way they speak in daily life; they take the course because they want to be better at presentations. They assume that they're effective in the ordinary situations because they're comfortable. They often are amazed to discover that the problems they thought existed only in public speaking situations are actually present in some degree in all their speaking situations. Just being comfortable doesn't make you effective. But when you have developed a spoken image that reflects the best of what you are, that style makes you effective whether you are talking on the telephone, speaking with a friend or a business colleague, presenting to a small group, or delivering a speech to an auditorium full of people. As you think about the role that speaking plays throughout your life, your goal should be to develop a spoken image that makes you not only comfortable but effective.

Everything you read in this section on style will help you develop yourself as an effective communicator. It takes work to become the kind of speaker people call a natural. It takes work to develop any skill, and speaking is just that—a skill. A person born with natural physical prowess does not grow to become a gifted athlete without working to develop finely tuned skills. A child who can draw does not become an artist without practice and refinement. Raw talent never blossoms into skill unless it is nurtured and developed. In speaking, as in athletics and in art, we need to develop natural raw material into skills.

THE CHOICE IS YOURS

Effective speaking is a matter of making choices in the way you appear, and the way you use your voice and body. You can choose to change old habits. You can open a door to the realization that you weren't born shy or afraid to speak out. As you read this section, you will see that people respond to the information you give out about yourself. The vicious circle begins when a shy person, thinking no one can possibly be interested in what he's saying, sends out a message that fulfills his expectation—that what he's saying is not important. So no one is interested; the circle has come around in a self-fulfilling prophecy. You can break that vicious circle. When a person makes a positive change in his spoken image, that is what he does.

To become a better speaker, you must take ownership of new techniques in the same way you would commit to tennis lessons, a personal program of diet and exercise, or a new system of cost management at your office. Taking ownership of new techniques means recognizing and admitting to yourself their benefits, and applying yourself to making them your own. The focus is on you. You are the only one you can change; yours is the only attitude you can control. This section is to give you understanding and tools that will help you feel in control of yourself every time you open your mouth.

I'm told body builders have a saying: "No pain, no gain." The process of learning to be a better speaker isn't always easy, either, because it means taking a hard look at yourself and working hard to practice and develop techniques. Change can be difficult, but it can also be fun and immensely rewarding. I watch students at Speakeasy work to make a breakthrough until they're exhausted. When that breakthrough happens, it's the moment when it all comes together—when the speaker knows he has reached out and connected with his audience, when he knows he has the power to make something happen. My goal for you is that you will experience that breakthrough for yourself and with it the joy that better speaking can bring!

7

Speaking Without Fear

THE POPULARITY of health and exercise clubs testifies to our increased understanding of the value of physical exercise and its relation to good health. Many business people today run, swim, or play a racquet sport. They understand that physical activity helps them relax by releasing tension that builds up during a normal business day.

Most people consider speaking an intellectual exercise, with no physical connection. But the demands of speaking do cause a physical reaction, and you must learn to expect and control it. When you're about to speak, your mind is occupied with the presentation you're about to make, its content, what you've planned to say. So when you feel the symptoms of physical stress starting to affect your body, you're unsure how to handle them. You can't wait until the lunch hour or the end of the day to dispel your nervous energy with exercise. You don't know how to get rid of this kind of tension, and you feel suddenly out of control.

A simple understanding of the body's stress reaction and an "on-the-spot" method for controlling it can help you become a more effective speaker.

My goal in this chapter is to help you understand that in any speaking situation, you can make your body's responses work for you, not against you. Once you understand that you will always have a physical reaction to demanding situations, then you can take steps to make that reaction manageable.

You can make that reaction manageable in two ways: by reconsidering what you need from the speaking situation, and by using specific relaxation techniques. You set yourself up to receive an overload of nervous energy if you see speaking as a battle that you have to win, or if you place impossible demands on yourself to be perfect. Forming more realistic goals from a speaking situation can partially control the nervousness you feel by controlling your expectations. You can also control your reaction by using specific relaxation techniques—not just at the end of the day but when the physical reaction occurs. Training yourself to breathe and relax turns the destructive quality of tension into the constructive quality of energy, which is one of the basic qualities of an effective spoken image.

Reconsidering what you need from the speaking situation is an intellectual process; relaxation techniques are a physical process for dealing with a physical reaction. Both are necessary in helping you gain control in all your speaking situations.

STRESS AND YOUR BODY

Bookstore shelves are practically overflowing with volumes on the subject of stress reduction. If you have done any reading about stress reduction and relaxation, you probably are aware of the "fight or flight syndrome." Our nervous systems are equipped to help us get through tough situations. From prehistoric times, when life was a struggle for survival against wild animals and the elements, our bodies have had a built-in mechanism to respond to physical challenges. When we are physically confronted, the adrenal glands release a hormone called adrenaline into the bloodstream. This hormone increases the heartbeat, raises the blood pressure, and sometimes causes us to perspire. It may also create a sense of anxiety or confrontation. This surge of adrenaline puts us in a state of readiness, giving us a temporary source of extra energy to deal with the challenge. It helps us to either run away faster than we could without this temporary additional source of energy, or stay and fight it out with added strength. Heroic acts— the mother's desperate effort to save her child from a fire; the husband's battle to remove his wife from danger in an automobile wreck—are performed using the extra help the body gives us in these situations.

Most of us don't have that many sudden physical challenges these days. But we are intellectually and emotionally confronted day in and day out. A colleague criticizes our work on a proposal, and our body responds as if to a challenge to fight. The common experience of being caught in traffic and cut off by another driver can cause us to pound the steering wheel in frustration to release our emotional energy. A sales clerk is unpleasant; a waiter informs you haughtily that your favorite soup is no longer on the menu; your spouse complains about the household budget; a neighbor threatens to build a fence because your dog is digging among his roses. Any of these simple, everyday encounters, rational or not, can trigger an adrenaline response.

STRESS AND HOW YOU VIEW THE SITUATION

The stress reaction occurs in any situation or activity that you feel places demands on you to adapt. The demands may be intellectual, emotional, physical, or any combination. You may perceive them as threatening, challenging, or even exciting, but no matter how you view them, these demands will cause a physical response. This response will vary depending on the extent of the perceived demands.

Your body doesn't understand the difference between intellectual, emotional, and physical confrontation. It releases extra adrenaline whenever your brain signals a demand. You might be sitting outside your boss's office or a client's office getting ready for a presentation when all of a sudden, you feel your gut tightening up. You think, "Boy, I didn't think I was nervous." Intellectually, you're not necessarily nervous or scared. But somewhere inside you, you are feeling a response that in varying degrees is universal in a speaking situation—you are getting ready for a battle, either a battle with yourself to be perfect or a battle with another person to win him to your position.

When your body thinks you are getting ready for a battle, it will "juice up" with adrenaline to ready you for action. The way you see each speaking situation will affect the size or extent of the physical response your body gives you. Sometimes we expect too much of ourselves. We each want to be, in our own way, John F. Kennedy inspiring a nation to greatness or Johnny Carson rattling off jokes with perfect timing. We're afraid we'll make fools of ourselves by looking or saying something silly; we don't want to be laughed at. We think that our audiences expect perfection in our presentations, so we end up trying too hard and controlling ourselves too tightly. The first lesson for dealing with the stress reaction is to not expect the impossible of ourselves. Remember, perfection is not what makes a speaker effective.

Another way we increase the size of our stress reaction is by seeing the speaking situation as a battle. The more you feel you have to come out a winner in a "win-lose" situation and the more you view the situation as "me against them," the greater your nervous energy will be.

After my first book was published, I appeared on the *Today* show to talk about it with Jane Pauley. I had hosted a network television show in Canada before moving to the United States, and now was successfully advising business speakers how to be strong and in control before an audience. But when it was my turn to be interviewed on *Today* that morning, I was hyped up and my mouth was dry. I suddenly realized that my stress reaction was bigger than usual because I had made the interview a battle—I was competing with Jane Pauley. I wanted to win, which meant she had to lose. When I realized what was wrong, I was able to relax and continue the rest of the interview without viewing it as a win-lose proposition.

You can reduce the level of physical response depending on how you view the speaking situation. It's unrealistic to think you can eliminate all feeling. The speaking situation will always be demanding and ought always to be stimulating, so there will always be some degree of physical response.

But you will benefit greatly by being able to control this response, because the feeling of being out of control of self probably creates more anxiety than any other feeling in a speaking situation. You must form realistic expectations of yourself, and you must also know how to relax in the face of a situation that causes feelings of stress.

A TECHNIQUE TO HELP YOU RELAX

At the end of a hard day at the office, it feels great to go home, sink into your favorite chair, put your feet up, and let go. You think, "Whew! What a day!" Your "Whew!" is really a deep sigh that releases all the pent-up tension of the day. There are any number of techniques designed to aid relaxation, but one of the most effective is to exhale and concentrate on settling your body comfortably. The goal of this technique is "energetic relaxation," or relaxing while retaining the energy you need for the situation at hand. It's a technique that anyone can use to relax at the end of a day or use on the spur of the moment to relieve the tension of a speaking situation. I've used it for years, and my students tell me they continue to find it effective:

1. Go through some simple movements to relieve tension in your body: Stretch fully; move your arms over your head; bend your spine; roll your head gently in circles.
2. Sit down and gently close your eyes. Consciously choose to let go. Make this an active decision. Talk yourself into it; tell yourself that this is the most important thing you can possibly do for the next few minutes.
3. Now push your seat back into the chair so that you are sitting up straighter than usual. See how comfortable you can become by letting the chair support you totally. Imagine that you are going limp like a rag doll, but keep your head level. Let yourself go and sink as deeply into the chair as you can. I call this "settling in."
4. Exhale deeply. See how deeply and completely you can let your breath out. As the air nears what seems to be the end, try to let out just a little more air. This will lessen your tension tremendously. You are not trying to force or control your breath; you are letting go, releasing. You should be able to feel your ribcage dropping with each exhale. Exhaling in this way should feel like a deep sigh. Do this several times.
5. Scan through your body to pick up points of tension, as if you were "reading" yourself on radar. When you detect tension or discomfort, see if you can think it away. Tell your body to go limp around the point of tension and to release it from your body. Do this until you find no more points of tension.
6. Now that your body is relaxed and your mind focused and both are working for you together, visualize yourself just after successfully delivering a speech. Think of the audience applauding you, of individuals you respect complimenting you, of feeling good about yourself. Let yourself really feel the afterglow of a successful speech.

Practicing this exercise twice a day for a couple of weeks will make it practically routine. You will find that you can do its first four basic steps in a few seconds, and apply it in any moment of stress. Do it in your car on the way to give a speech, and when you're being introduced. When you stand up, take a moment to breathe, center, and settle in before you begin to speak.

This exercise points to the importance of breathing as a key to relaxation. Breathing is as fundamental to relaxation and speaking as it is to life itself.

Breathe to Gain Control

Much of the tension I see affecting the businessmen and businesswomen I work with can be dispelled by the simple act of breathing. Breathing works to reduce the feeling of nervousness that accompanies speaking, because it releases your excess energy and keeps it from being blocked and held inside as tension. Learning to use the exhale technique at the right time is a valuable lesson for any speaker.

Success-oriented people often are so caught up in meeting the unceasing demands of their jobs that they ignore the benefits that pausing to breathe can bring to them. My advice to these harried and harassed business and professional people is to always make the time in their working lives to breathe. We all need to occasionally let ourselves—our minds and bodies—relax, to release the tension that builds up in the course of a working day. If you make time to breathe, you also give yourself time to think. Unless you make a conscious effort to relax, a high-pressure job can keep you in a constant state of adrenaline-charged readiness. If you take the time to pause and breathe, you also will become a better listener; you will see and hear the other human beings with whom you are communicating. Simply taking time to breathe can improve every aspect of your ability to speak and listen—that is, your ability to communicate.

Tony's office was one floor below that of his boss. Every time his boss called him, Tony immediately dashed up the stairs to his office, arriving with a voice that shook with breathlessness from the exertion of the climb. Tony was then embarrassed by his quavering voice, which he felt signified a lack of control, and this made him more nervous, causing his confidence to go from bad to worse.

After we had worked together, Tony began responding differently when his boss summoned him upstairs. He answered the calls by saying, "I'll be up in five minutes." Now, he said, "I take the elevator up to give myself time to breathe. I stop in the hall and take a couple of breaths. And that alone makes me feel different and stronger when I walk in. If I learned one thing," he added, "it was the importance of pausing and breathing."

No matter what you do, focusing on your breath makes you start to focus and listen to yourself. You tune in to the rhythm of your body. That's what relaxation is all about: getting the body centered; letting your weight drop; exhaling to remove the vestiges of tension; having the courage to listen to your body for the information it will give you. These are the basic approaches to relaxation, which every speaker can use as a quick prescription for stage fright: Upon feeling nervous, breathe and exhale deeply to release tension.

MAKING NERVOUS ENERGY WORK FOR YOU

Viewing the speaking situation realistically and then learning to relax and breathe will help you manage your reaction to stress. Then you can harness your nervous energy so that it works for you in the speaking situation, not against you.

The first day of a three-day seminar causes stress in me, keying me up for what's ahead. The people who signed up for it are expecting something significant to happen during the next three days. Their expectations create one set of demands. As a professional, I want not only to meet their demands, but to do it with the high level of performance I expect from myself. My own expectations create a second set of demands. When I walk into the classroom on Monday morning, there are demands on my intellect to get the right messages out to my audience. There are the emotional demands that come when people resist the instruction; for example, maybe their boss required them to attend the seminar, and they start out thinking it's a waste of time. And there are physical demands. It takes a tremendous amount of physical energy to hold the attention of a group over a three-day period.

All those demands, because I care about meeting them, cause

that rush of adrenaline into my system. Even if I don't feel good, or if I'm tired, my energy returns. I may feel tired again after working hours, but not while those demands are pulling a response from me. Since I understand what is happening, I'm not afraid when I feel this physical revving-up or speeding-up beginning to happen. In fact, I've come to welcome this surge of energy as a sign that I'm stimulated enough to do my best.

I am able to harness this surge of energy because I no longer view the seminar as a battle—and, although I place great demands on myself and know that my students expect me to be a real professional, I still don't expect to be perfect. And throughout the three days, especially at particularly tense or tiring moments, I take time to breathe.

You Can Choose to Relax

Tony learned to breathe and relax once he learned what his choices were. Control in a speaking situation comes not in being controlled, but in having many choices. When you try to "clamp down" on your body to control feelings of nervousness, you reduce the number of choices available to relieve your nervousness. So the goal of relaxation is to get the body settled and open, ready to respond when you opt for the choices that will reduce your tension and make you a more effective speaker.

Remember in approaching all your speaking assignments that there are two ways to deal effectively with the physical reaction to the speaking situation. First, reconsider your view of the situation; don't feel that you have to be perfect, and don't make it into a win-lose situation for yourself. Second, use the relaxation technique at moments when you feel the stress reaction beginning to build. Then be prepared to harness your nervous energy to work for you.

Speaking is demanding, but it also can be enjoyable and fulfilling if you choose to let it be. Now that you know you don't have to feel "wrung out" by your nervous reaction to a speaking situation, the chapters to follow will show you how to build upon your new confidence with the look, body image and voice of a confident, effective speaker.

8

Your Visual Image

YOUR VISUAL image is how you look. More than the features
you were born with, your visual image is the composite picture
drawn by the choices you make in putting yourself together: your
personal grooming; the way you wear your hair; the material,
color, style, and fit of your clothing; your glasses, if you wear
them. Facial hair is an added factor in a man's visual image;
makeup is part of a woman's.

What does your visual image have to do with speaking? Although visual image is not the most important part of your spoken
image, it nevertheless is the first impression your audience re-
ceives. First impressions are hard to change. When you walk into
an office or a boardroom, or onto a platform as a speaker, the
audience's first opportunity to size you up is by what they see. If
your visual image interferes with your ability to reach your objective, or is inconsistent with what you are trying to accomplish, it
can damage every other part of your speaking situation. Just as
the opening words of your presentation provide the audience a
reason to keep listening, your appearance sends out powerful signals about you and the quality of presentation you're likely to
deliver. Those signals can work for you or against you.

As you look at the choices available to you in improving your
speaking style, the main reason to look at your visual image is to
see if it's enhancing or interfering with your authority. Your visual
image is more likely to affect your authority than the qualities of
energy or audience awareness, although you can exhibit a lack of
audience awareness if your image strays too far from conventional
standards. Inappropriate colors, poor tailoring, and poor-quality
fabric can detract from any speaker's authority.

BASIC RULES FOR BUSINESS DRESS

In the last few years many books have focused on dressing to be successful in today's business environment. The dark three-piece suit for men and the skirt with matching jacket and soft blouse for women are as much a part of today's business world as the pocket calculator and the briefcase.

Most people in business want to look like business people. The only problem with the recent emphasis on dressing for business success is that too many men and women fear that if they don't wear the right navy-blue suit, their chances for success are diminished. The rules of appropriate business dress are not so strict that they require absolute regimentation. But before you can break the rules, you first must learn them.

The errors men make most often in their search for the right visual image for business can be covered in a single phrase—inattention to detail. Men are now largely aware that colors like navy, gray, and beige are appropriate for businesswear, but they pay too little attention to tailoring and to quality material. A man wearing even a fairly informal outfit, like a navy blazer with gray or khaki slacks, can project an image of considerable authority as long as the clothes are of good material and are well tailored. The man in a navy-blue vested suit will project no authority at all if his suit is of poor-quality material, with an ill-fitting vest and jacket cuffs that dangle to his knuckles.

Don was a seminar student who kept asking how his extra weight affected his image, but he had a bigger problem with his clothing. His suits were dark, all right, but his jackets were too big, his pants were too short, and his cuffs and collars were frayed. Don was one of those people who just paid no attention at all to the details of his appearance. When I mentioned that his clothes were having a negative effect on how his audiences saw him, he said he'd never thought about that part of his visual image; he had always been more concerned with the effect of his weight on his appearance. Whatever the reason, men often overlook details in their clothing and tailoring that can make all the difference in their visual image.

Women have more choices than men in what they can wear in a business situation. The popular "dress for success" look, which means a suit or a jacket and skirt with a blouse, still is right for most women, because it gives them the edge they need in business. For women as for men, tailoring and quality of material count for more than a cheap imitation of "the look."

AUTHORITY GIVES YOU OPTIONS

Investing your visual image with authority doesn't mean locking yourself forever into the monotones of basic business dress. The social revolution of the 1960s and '70s brought more and more women into business roles, which means many women have been in business long enough to be comfortable and relaxed in a business environment. Women who have become comfortable with their authority in a business setting are finding subtle ways to soften the strict "dress for success" image that helped them when they were entering the world of business for the first time.

Five years ago, I almost always wore a jacket or a suit when I spoke. I considered the look crisper, more professional, more finished. Today I no longer feel I have to be in a suit or jacket every time I give a speech, because I am more secure with my authority before an audience than I was five years ago. So I feel comfortable wearing an appropriate dress in a business situation. Your ability to branch out successfully in your choice of business attire depends upon your ability to project authority to your audience.

It is important to learn the rudiments of conventional business attire before seeking individuality. It's important to know, too, that you can't absolutely flout the rules; you can only bend them. We all want to express ourselves as individuals, and we should, because in individuality lies the source of most of our creative work. I'm not one for forcing regimentation on anybody; I don't think all business people have to look as if they were stamped out of a cookie cutter. But I do think it's important to follow a few basic rules, and when a man attends the seminar wearing a pale-green suit, a novelty vest, or a suit with contrasting stitching at the seams, I try to offer some suggestions. When women attend wearing four-inch heels, ankle straps that belong in a discotheque, or clothes that overemphasize their figures, I bring out the rulebook again. These people obviously don't know the basic rules, and I find it helpful to suggest a course or some reading in basic business dress. The basics aren't the only options for an appropriate business wardrobe, but they are a starting point.

Authority is the key to your ability to depart from what people expect in your appearance. If the other elements of authority are there, the overall impression of authority remains intact. Good fit and good quality register authority, and must underlie all your clothing choices in the way that authority underlies all the elements of your spoken image.

Once you've got a grasp of the essentials, it's then possible to add those touches of individuality and color that say, "This is me!" Expressing self-confidence in your visual image is a way of adding authority.

Regional differences naturally have to be taken into account. The checked sport coats and light and brown suits that President Reagan favored when he first took office were not unusual in the mild climate of California, but they looked out of place against the more somber tones of the Washington establishment. Businessmen in Florida find that coats and ties are less of a prerequisite during the heat of summer than at cooler times of the year. And Texans, among others, have taken to wearing cowboy boots and hats in any and all business situations, whether they're in New York or Houston.

Regional differences in business dress are just another way of expressing individuality. If you feel it's necessary to broadcast that you're from Texas by wearing cowboy boots, that's fine as long as it doesn't get in the way of your business objective. But understand that you don't need to wear boots. Acceptable business dress is the same the world over. The well-tailored dark suit, with an appropriate shirt and tie and dark shoes, will serve you as well in Houston as it will in New York, Hong Kong, or San Francisco.

AVOID DISTRACTIONS

Major distractions in your appearance may say to the audience that you don't care about being professional, which undermines your authority, or that you don't care about your audience, which shows a lack of audience awareness. Speakers exhibit audience awareness in content by identifying concerns of the audience, and in style by showing that they see the audience. One way the speaker has of showing the audience that he sees them is to demonstrate with his visual image that he appreciates their standards. You don't have to dress to be exactly like your audience, but you don't want to thumb your nose at them by dressing in a way that shows you're not at all concerned with them. All of us can express ourselves as individuals within the bounds of what's appropriate.

Distractions can include sexy clothes, flashy or jangling jewelry, and sloppiness of any kind. If you are a woman, you distract the audience from your message if you wear excessively form-fitting or revealing clothes or if your hair is too long or too elaborately styled.

Women often are surprised at the effect of elaborate hair styling on their visual image. Sharon was a professional lobbyist who wore her long hair in a bouffant style; the legislators she worked with, mostly men, had always told her they thought her hair looked great. But when she saw herself on videotape for the first time, she exclaimed, "Boy, I thought my long hair was good for my image. But it makes me look like a high school girl. It doesn't look at all like the professional image I thought I projected."

Men often distract their audiences with an abundance of facial hair or flashy accessories. They, too, are often surprised when they see the image they present. Bobby, a publisher's representative, told me after seeing himself on videotape, "I thought I looked like the Marlboro Man, but the fuzzy face I saw on the screen doesn't go along with my serious approach to business." If a man wears bangs, sideburns, a mustache, a beard, and tinted glasses, the total effect is bound to put people off; the average person can't see the message through all the distracting side effects.

Visual image is a matter of balance. Sometimes when I suggest to women that shorter hair would give them a more authoritative image, they give responses like "Why pick on me? You've got long hair yourself." However, taken as a whole—the way I speak and carry my body combined with my visual image—I don't have a problem projecting authority. I'm not suggesting that you have to deny your sexuality or individual qualities to have the right visual image. My point is that you should find an appropriate balance.

In my first book, I made reference to Sally, a pretty, intelligent, and ambitious young businesswoman. On the first day of the seminar, she showed up wearing a silky red dress. When she wore a suit the following day, I commented, "By the way, I think the outfit you are wearing today is much more appropriate." She objected, and smiled when one of the men in the seminar told her how much he had liked the clingy red dress. It wasn't until another of the men said, "Hey, Sally, I really *like* you in that dress," that she got the message. The thinly veiled suggestiveness of his comment convinced Sally that her red dress didn't project the best image for a business situation.

Several months later, at a meeting of business people, a woman approached me during one of the breaks. She was wearing a tailored suit and had a short, attractive haircut. We chatted for several minutes, but when the conversation was over I had no idea who she was. When we met again later in the day, I looked at her nametag. It was Sally. She said, "You didn't recognize me, did you?" She had made such a drastic change in her visual image that, as I was embarrassed to admit, I hadn't recognized her. She told me she had acquired a wardrobe full of tailored clothes and smart shoes. Her hair was shorter. All this came at a time when she was advancing rapidly in her career, and the change in her visual image helped people see her in a much different way.

I saw Sally again even more recently. My feeling after not seeing her for some time was that she had developed enough authority to be able to soften up her image. I shared that observation with her, and she expressed surprise that I'd object to an image that I had encouraged her to acquire several years earlier.

But all I was trying to say to her was: "We change, and everything in our spoken image is a matter of balance. You now have enough authority in your person to be softer in your appearance."

Many successful women say the same thing: The tailored-suit image is a necessary stage to go through, but once you reach a certain point in your career and gain a certain level of confidence, you don't need it as much anymore. You have to decide objectively when you have reached that point. Don't kid yourself into thinking you're there if you're not.

YOU CAN STILL BE AN INDIVIDUAL

Visual image is a very personal thing. All of us assume an image of ourselves that we take quite seriously. We are easily hurt or offended when someone suggests to us that we need to change our image.

In my seminars, people are usually open to making drastic changes in their voices and the way they use their bodies in speaking situations. That's not the case with their hair and clothing. Because visual image is the first thing we notice about people, I used to dive right in on the first day of the seminar and tell clients when they needed to improve aspects of their visual image. They reacted more strongly, and with more resistance, than to practically anything else I did or said during our time together. I learned that a comment like "Have you ever considered trimming your hair?" is much more likely to touch a raw nerve than one like "You need more authority in your voice." Now I wait until students have had a chance to become more open to the idea before I suggest ways they might look better and more authoritative.

If you have strong feelings about your visual image, you may overreact to suggestions that your appearance could stand to look more professional. If your gut tightens up anytime someone makes a comment about your visual image, that's a clue that you should probably pull back and do some thinking about why it's so important to you to hold on to that part of your appearance.

Try to be objective when you dress every morning. Once you have a grasp of basic business dress, it won't be hard to add a touch of yourself here and there. You can avoid looking like just one of the office robots and avoid distractions in your visual image at the same time.

Much of what we do with our physical appearance is the result of habit rather than of careful, deliberate choice. Yet people make assumptions about us all the time on the basis of what they see—our dress, hair, and grooming. If we can step back and see ourselves as others see us, we can increase our awareness of the assumptions people are likely to make about us based on our appearance. With this increased awareness, we are in a better position to make choices that will send out the kind of message about us that we want others to receive. We cannot ever entirely control the assumptions people will make about us, but we can make aware, effective choices that are more accurately aimed at getting others to see us the way we want to be seen.

Your visual image, of course, won't stand alone once you begin speaking to your audience. Other images come into play as soon as you start talking. The other elements of your spoken image are your body and your voice. What they convey—their authority, energy, and awareness of the audience—follow your visual image as the main points of your presentation follow your opening.

9

Your Body Image

YOUR BODY can be a friend or enemy in a speaking situation. You already know that you can make choices that affect the way you feel and your ability to relax. The choices you make about how you use your body when you speak are tremendously important; they can affect your sense of control, and also have a profound effect on the way your audience sees you. Your body can express the basic qualities of an effective spoken image—authority, energy, and audience awareness.

The first thing I do regarding body image in the Speakeasy seminar is introduce students to the balanced stance—the best way to stand in a speaking situation. I've found it best for two reasons: It projects an image of authority to your audience, and it allows you to deal with your body's tension, so it can make you feel better when you speak.

STANCE: YOUR HOME BASE

The open, balanced stance is simple and comfortable, yet few people automatically stand this way when they stand up to speak to a group. The elements of a balanced stance are: feet apart, lined up more or less underneath the armpits; weight evenly distributed from side to side and from front to back, with weight on both the heels and balls of the feet; arms comfortably by the sides. Using the open, balanced stance doesn't mean that you have to be frozen into it, nor does it mean that you never move out of it. Sometimes your legs and feet get tired from standing in one place during a long presentation, and you simply need to move, which you'll see later in this chapter can be an expression of energy. But the balanced stance is your home base—it's where you start and where

153

you return. It is a solid position from which strong statements can be made.

The right stance contributes to authority by allowing you to feel the security of "owning" your own space. It is a confident posture that makes you look authoritative to your audience without looking combative or aggressive. It simply confirms for the audience that you know what you're talking about; you look as if you have a right to be there. And by allowing your body weight to settle, it lets you be more relaxed and aware of your audience.

Don't Stand for Instinct or Bad Habits

When people start to feel shaky and out of control, they instinctively go into a protective mode. Male speakers, if they feel threatened by the speaking situation, are likely to take a "fighting stance" with their feet wide apart, knees locked tightly, chest puffed up, and shoulders thrown back in a classic aggressive posture. The results, unfortunately, are anything but what they want: The locked knees add tension to the legs, causing increasing discomfort; the puffed-up chest doesn't permit proper breathing for speaking; tension across the chest and shoulders increases the feeling of nervousness. Making the wrong choices lets the effects of tension accumulate: The more you try to exert control when you feel nervous, the more you'll tighten your knees, chest, and shoulder muscles and the more out of control you'll feel. And the more shaky and tense you become, the less authority you are likely to project to your audience.

Protective reactions like the fighting stance are instinctive. But it's not a physical battle you're girding up for. You don't have to lock your knees until your legs shake, because nobody is going to try to push you backward. You don't have to puff up your chest and pull your shoulders back until you can barely breathe, because you're not trying to frighten an opponent or take a swing at somebody. You can decide not to do these things. If you make the right decisions, you can proceed with your speech or presentation with a more relaxed body that you can control.

Women also are likely to react instinctively to the implied threat in a speaking situation. A female speaker responding to her nervousness may fall back into a posture that worked when she was younger and things weren't going her way: She crosses her legs at the ankle, folds her hands protectively in front of her, tilts her head to one side with her chin up, and smiles like the cute little girl who had her daddy wrapped around her little finger.

Betty was a woman who had the body image of a little girl; when she spoke, she stood with her feet very close together, clasped her hands in front of her, and tilted her head. On the first afternoon of the seminar, I asked Betty to begin using the balanced stance, lining up her feet under her armpits. When she assumed the stance, I asked her how she felt.

She said, "I have to tell you that this feels uncomfortable, awkward, and masculine."

I told her not to look down at her feet and asked her to look at my stance. "Do I look awkward or masculine?" I asked.

"No," she said. "You look fine. But my feet are a lot farther apart than yours." I asked her how she knew that. "I can just tell," she said.

"Betty, look down at your feet," I replied, and she looked down to discover that her feet were not as far apart as mine were. She was so used to standing with her feet close together that her perception was distorted. Being aware of your options can help you decide not to instinctively use a posture that may increase your tension and make you feel and look precariously off-balance.

People sometimes claim that they feel more relaxed standing with their weight on one leg, with the other knee bent and one hand in a pocket—almost the drugstore-cowboy slouch of the James Dean era that signified not giving a damn. Speakers who use this stance are trying to protect themselves by not seeming too involved, as if a deliberately casual posture is a way of fending off the possibility of failure. This posture looks casual to the onlooker, which detracts from authority. At the same time, the person using it actually is increasing his tension, because one leg is tight all the way down to support his weight. The balanced stance actually decreases tension because it distributes the weight evenly on both sides of the body. Two legs are better than one at supporting body weight.

Charles, a hospital administrator, was a good speaker, but he leaned slightly backward when he spoke. Since he was well over six feet tall, his backward lean made him look down on his audience even more than he would have from a normal stance. The backward lean made him look aloof, as if he didn't want to be open and involved with his audience, and it hampered his authority by suggesting that Charles was really a little scared. I told Charles that he was giving up authority by leaning away from the audience, and I recommended that he put more balance into his stance.

A stance that is too narrow gives a look that is insecure and placating, which also detracts from authority. Keeping the feet too close together denies the speaker a firm base to stand on. Without a firm base, the tendency is to try to struggle harder for support or control, again increasing tension. And wearing high heels makes a narrow stance even more precarious.

Every speaker should use an open, balanced stance as a natural, authoritative base for speaking. Adopting the right stance and using it routinely doesn't mean using your body like a robot. You don't have to use your body the same way as another speaker in order to be effective, any more than you have to dress the same as other executives in order to be successful. But a balanced stance is basic to using your body in an open, relaxed way, saving energy, lessening the tension you feel and increasing your authority by giving you a firm home base.

GESTURES: A NATURAL FORM OF EXPRESSION

Natural movement is an expression of energy and commitment. There is nothing more naturally energetic than movement, but when movement is repressed in a speaking situation, it reduces the commitment of the speaker and eliminates an escape valve for built-up tension.

The energy contained in the bodies of children makes it hard for them to sit still. They seem always to be wriggling and squirming; their bodies and voices are freer than those of adults. When they tell a story or ask for something, their faces, their bodies, their whole beings are involved in the delivery of their messages.

As we grow up, though, we impose a lot of control on ourselves. Probably because of the countless reprimands we received, we stop acting with the openness we had as children. Students at Speakeasy always feel silly and embarrassed in the exercise which requires them to use exaggerated gestures as they pretend to be carnival barkers or flower vendors on a street corner. But then they're amazed at how natural those gestures look when they're replayed on videotape and how much more interesting and committed they look and sound.

I'm not suggesting that you have to return to the flamboyance of childhood to put energy into your spoken image. But there is a happy medium between the uninhibited bodies of children and the controlled bodies of adults. Your goal should be an adult body that is open, balanced, and relaxed—one that will work with you rather than against you, one that can express your commitment. It's naturally better to let your energy out in movement, by involving your body in the delivery of your message, rather than to work against yourself by trying to keep your energy bottled up inside.

Dan was a good example of someone who wouldn't let his energy out. When he stood to speak, he kept one hand on the opposite wrist, usually in about the position where a fig leaf would be. He pressed down with the top hand, while the other kept desperately trying to gesture. I suggested that Dan let his "captive" hand go; when he freed his hands from one another and let them fall naturally to his sides, he began to gesture in a way that expressed his energy.

Unnatural gestures can be distracting. Just as the open, balanced stance is home base for your feet, the home base for the arms is relaxed at your sides. Your arms don't naturally bend at the elbows when you are standing in a relaxed way, and your hands don't naturally fall into a fig-leaf position. Almost any gesture will be effective if it is open, natural, and relaxed.

To keep your movements natural when you speak, remember that your hands, your arms, your shoulders, and your torso are all connected; restricting movement in one area restricts it in another. Men who draw back their shoulders and puff up their chests hinder their ability to gesture as well as to breathe. They restrict their ability to move, and limit the body involvement that should go into delivering their message. Perhaps because of the traditional military image, many men try to convey authority with an expanded chest and squared, pulled-back shoulders. In business speaking situations, however, the military image is reminiscent of a rigid tin soldier; the arms can move only in puppetlike arcs from the elbow.

Some speech advisers suggest that the only "power gesture" is a big gesture above the chest. Very little we say in business or anywhere else, for that matter, is so profound that it demands that kind of dramatic gesture. Moreover, people who use gestures this way never really let go of the arms. The so-called power gesture then becomes distracting, because it communicates tension. If we never drop our arms and let go, it conveys the feeling that we aren't settled and relaxed, that we are protecting and shielding ourselves.

The exception to this rule comes when you are speaking behind a lectern. If you keep your arms by your sides, you're likely to hit the lectern every time you begin to gesture. Most speakers find it comfortable and effective to rest their arms on the lectern in a loose way that leaves them relaxed but free to gesture. Don't lean with all your weight on the lectern, however.

You don't have to gesture constantly to be an effective speaker. I do believe, however, that speakers have to let their physical energy out in order to be effective. When people begin to show their energy and commitment in speaking, they often start to gesture a lot. They also often find that gesturing is not the only way to express and let out energy in a speaking situation.

THE WALK

Walking can be an effective tool for releasing tension and expressing energy. When you're standing in front of an audience and feel some excess energy, you can take two or three deliberate steps to one side. It's much better to take a couple of steps than it is to stand there shifting your weight around, which contains your energy and makes you look restless.

A walking pause serves to emphasize a significant point in a presentation or punctuate a major break in its organization. Used in this way, the walk underlines a transitional statement: "That is what our plant will do to provide jobs in your community." Move a few steps. Stop, take a balanced stance. "Next I'd like to talk about the taxes we will add to your city treasury by locating here." Talk for a while and then return to your original position.

As with any technique, overdoing it diminishes its effect. In the case of the walk, which faces you away from the audience as you move from side to side, overdoing it can jeopardize your rapport with the audience. The more you walk, the more casual your presentation will be and the less committed you will appear. The balanced, planted body has more directness and authority.

If you don't use the walk as an accent for a pause, but rather talk as you walk, the power and force of your words tend to be dispersed toward the walls on either side of the room. You should always look at your audience to retain your awareness and to keep the energy flowing between you and them instead of to the walls. Looking at your audience during a walking pause is dramatic. It holds the audience, but it can seem "stagy" and make them feel uncomfortable if it's done too often.

I ask Speakeasy's seminar students to make walking more natural by practicing. Stand in a firm, balanced position, walk a few feet, and then return to the firm stance. I'm not suggesting that you have to walk in order to be a good speaker, and you certainly should not diminish its effectiveness by overdoing it. But it can be a valuable technique, an option that is available to you when you need it. Gestures and walking—all movements, in fact—are not ends in themselves but means to an end: a more energetic, committed style.

Speaking Behind a Lectern and While Seated

How much do standing and gesturing really matter when you're behind a lectern where people can't see your feet or your arms? The fact is, the stance is important wherever you are, whether you're behind a lectern or beside a flip chart or screen. When you don't have a firm stance, even if most of your body is hidden, the off-balance attitude will be reflected to your audience in your upper body and probably also in the energy you send out to them with your gestures. A firm base allows you to feel better and use yourself more effectively behind the lectern. And remember that if you use the walk, you won't be hidden behind the lectern all the time in any case. By the way, if you're using a lectern with a large audience, be sure to request a neck or clip-on microphone so that you won't have to restrict your movement to accommodate a stationary microphone.

Many people say they do a lot of their speaking in meetings

across a desk or around a conference table. Certainly in one-on-one meetings or small meetings in an office you usually sit, but in a slightly larger group you have a choice. Just because other speakers sat doesn't mean you have to sit. It's easier for most people to be more energetic when they're standing, so you should consider whether breaking precedent in this situation will help you reach your objective. And if people have been sitting for a long time, both you and your audience may be especially in need of the extra energy you can put into your presentation when you stand.

But if you choose to sit, all the principles of being centered, balanced, settled, and reaching out that apply when you're on your feet apply when you're in a chair. The most common mistake people make when they're seated in a meeting is to lean back, which makes them appear uninvolved. Leaning back detracts from your speaking and your listening, because it prevents your energy from flowing to the audience. You don't perform as well and your audience thinks you're not giving out to them.

Your body is speaking for you all the time. You may be more conscious of it if you're up in front of a group without any props in front of you. But your body can work for or against you whether you're out there by yourself, beside a flip chart, behind a lectern, or seated at a conference table. The basics still apply.

You've seen how your body can express authority and energy when you speak and make you feel better at the same time. With eye contact, you can add the important quality of audience awareness.

EYE CONTACT: HOW TO GET IT, HOW TO USE IT

Eye contact is another of the choices you can make with your body that can give you one of the essential qualities of an effective speaking style and also make you feel better in a speaking situation. Eye contact provides audience awareness; it is a continual source of information about your audience and their reaction to your message. It allows you to see and benefit from the support that exists in the audience for your message. And when you don't see support, it allows you to make intelligent adjustments to reach your objective.

It's How You Look at Someone, Not How Long

In every speaking situation, the audience gives out subtle signs to the speaker. Looks of curiosity or confusion let you know your message isn't getting through, and that you may need to adjust your content if you want to be effective. Eye contact is a source of feedback from the audience, and your means of silently "asking" them, "Is what I've just said clear?" The information that comes from eye contact also will affect your style as well as your content, causing you to increase your energy if you see signs of boredom, or to reach out more at signs of resistance or hostility.

Real eye contact doesn't mean scanning your audience, looking at some arbitrary point over their heads, or, if it's just one person, fixing your eyes in the distance over his left shoulder. It means looking at and seeing individuals in the audience as if each one were the only person in the room, the one person whose reaction is important to the success or failure of your presentation. It means talking to individual human beings, not some amorphous mass called an audience, the marketing group, the Downtown Civic Club, or the executive committee of your company.

Good eye contact is developed in stages. The first stage is learning to look at members of the audience and not staring off over their heads. Many beginning speakers find this the hardest part, because they've never really looked at the people they're speaking to before. The second stage is learning to see the people in the audience, so that you know how they're sitting, what color their hair is, and whether they're wearing glasses, for example. The third and final stage, which is what eye contact is all about, is "listening" to the audience with your eyes, using this source of input to sense important developments in their mood and responses. The speaker who is listening with his eyes is aware of frowns, puzzlement, approval—the whole range, in fact, of reactions that any speaker can expect to encounter.

One of my staff members once listened to a lecture by the actor John Houseman. She said that as he went around the room taking questions, he caught her eye and held it. He had seen something in her expression that made him think she had a question. She did not, but he held her gaze long enough to make sure, and then went on. This illustrates a good speaker's sensitivity to his audience.

Eye contact doesn't mean a staring contest, however. Never distract yourself by trying to count the number of seconds of eye contact you have with individuals in the audience. Timing your eye contact is truly form over substance; it may allow you to look at everyone for the same amount of time, but it prevents you from really seeing anyone. Eye contact means genuinely looking at a person, taking in what you see and responding to it as you go on. You should look directly at the person you're talking to, as if you were speaking one-to-one.

It is also important to try to look at everybody within reasonable viewing range. There is a tendency among speakers to avoid seeing people who seem bored, skeptical, or hostile, and instead aim their entire message at the people in the audience who look sympathetic or merely attentive. Those listeners are then saddled with the responsibility of providing feedback to the speaker for the duration of the speech or presentation. Focusing narrowly on one or two members or even half of the audience permits the energy in the rest of the room to fade away and distractions to occur.

Once I was standing at the back of a room waiting my turn to speak at a communications workshop for midlevel managers, and I saw the speaker before me concentrate all his eye contact on the people to his right. They were responding by leaning forward attentively and listening with considerable energy. But the people on the other side of the room were having quiet conversations, looking around, and doodling. The speaker had lost one side of the room, while just across the aisle was an attentive audience.

It's important to include as many people as possible in your eye contact. Look around the audience at random and pick people out; don't try to go row by row or take one side and then the other.

Be aware of room arrangements that can interfere with eye contact between speakers and listeners. A U-shaped seating pattern in a conference room, for example, makes it easy for the speaker to ignore the people at the ends, so don't move too far into the U and leave part of your audience behind you. People on the speaker's side of a conference table can also get left out if the speaker isn't careful, because a genuine effort is required to lean forward and look up and down the row. Sometimes the speakers' platform, if there is one, is too low for convenient eye contact with people toward the back of the room. A speaker who sees members of the audience leaning and craning around the people in front can help them out by occasionally moving away from the lectern.

Learning to See Each Other

Of the many reasons we tend to avoid eye contact, one may be that we are afraid of being seen by others. We translate the nervous energy that speakers feel into the fear that the audience will be bored, skeptical, or disapproving of what we say. Cameron, who found it almost impossible to look at people when he spoke, put it like this in the seminar: "I learned how hard it is for me to see you. It's hard because I'm afraid of being seen. If I see you, there's a part of me that says you'll see me. And you won't like what you see."

I've helped many students work on developing eye contact, but it wasn't until Cameron got up and talked about his fear of eye contact that I really understood how difficult it is for some people to develop this part of their speaking style. But when you begin to see the audience for the first time, you're likely to find a lot more support there than you expect. One of my students was a lawyer who was to argue an important case before his state's supreme court. Since Mitchell was an associate in line to become a partner, the case was also important to his career with his law firm. Mitchell told me he was nervous when he went before the nine justices. But he said that as he began his argument, the justice who had been toughest on a lawyer in the previous case nodded and gave him a look of encouragement. He said that small gesture of reassurance made him relaxed and confident from then on. If he had not made eye contact long enough to see that slight sign of receptivity, he—and his case—might have suffered.

Adam was an engineer who was an adequate speaker, but his delivery lacked the extra measure of life that would have made him really good. He explained his problem as a lack of eye contact: "I began to realize that during the seminar this week, I've been looking at you, but I'm not sure I was really seeing any of you. The thing I need to do is to talk to you as individuals, because you're the ones that make up this whole audience that I'm talking to. As I do just that, it's amazing to me the kind of real communication I have with each of you. It really makes me feel good, and the thing I realize is that I see each of you as individuals, and this helps me to relax.'' Helping students experience real eye contact is always a major goal for me, because once you've experienced it and seen how it can make speaking easier and not more difficult, you'll always want to do it.

Moira was articulate and capable; she said she was nervous when she spoke, but the feedback she got showed that her audience felt she was aloof and uninvolved, and didn't care about them. After a presentation in which I told her to make eye contact with each member of her audience, she sat down and said, ''That's the first time I've ever seen anyone!'' As she began to make eye contact when she spoke, her aloofness fell away and she became much more level, direct, and involved with the people she was speaking to. I saw Moira a month later, speaking to a group of about four hundred people. The audience no longer saw her as cool and distant, but reacted positively to her new impression of involvement.

Like Adam and Moira, students tell me that once they begin to look at and really see people in the audience, they feel they can be more open and honest with the audience and with themselves. Allowing yourself to show your commitment and share it with the audience has an impact on the way the audience sees you. The impression you give is that you're concerned about what you're saying, and the audience finds it easy to become involved along with you.

AUTHORITY, ENERGY, AND AUDIENCE AWARENESS IN BODY IMAGE

So you can stand and move and see in ways that will enhance your spoken image. But because doing these things is a natural use of your body, they also make you feel better and more in control in a speaking situation. The open, balanced stance gives you maximum support and allows you to relax. Gestures and walking allow you to release pent-up tension. Eye contact helps you to be comfortable with the speaking situation, because it allows you to see the audience's interest and support.

Choosing these techniques contributes significantly to an image that has authority, energy, and audience awareness, and also helps you feel more at ease and in control of yourself in a speaking situation.

The elusive quality of reaching out can also be expressed in a speaker's body image. Leaning forward slightly from the torso has the effect of sending your energy out to the audience. Forward-directed energy from your body, face, eyes, and voice spells commitment to your audience.

Reaching out is what you would do if you were asking the location of a restroom in a country whose language you did not speak. You would not stand there with your arms folded in front of you and quietly ask for the restroom, barely opening your mouth to speak. You would reach out with all of the means of communication you had available—your facial expressions, your eyes, your mouth and voice, your body, hands, and arms. You would make a sincere, perhaps a desperate, effort to get people to understand what you wanted.

If you look from the side at an effective speaker, you will see him not just staying inside an upright, rectangular "box" formed by the space around him. An effective speaker leans forward, breaking the vertical plane of his own "space," sending his energy in the direction of the audience and of common ground.

But as I noted earlier, the quality of reaching out transcends the techniques that make an effective body image. Neil, a speaker in one of my seminars, had a firm base and good eye contact and expressed his message with energy. He was a big man who spoke with his hands folded comfortably in front of him. In his final talk, he reached out beautifully—he looked at people, his energy flowed forward, and he pulled in every member of his audience. When he looked at the videotape, however, Neil was disappointed in himself.

"I guess I'm your worst student, Sandy," he said. "I'm still holding my hands in front of me."

"It doesn't matter," I told him, "because in spite of that, you reached out and made something happen." Your ability to connect with the audience is the bottom line in being an effective speaker.

An effective body image does all these things, and forms the second component of an effective spoken image. Your body controls your voice, which is the third component in your spoken image. Your voice, too, can project an image of authority, energy, and awareness to your audience.

10

Your Vocal Image

MOST PEOPLE don't realize that they can make choices in the way they use their voices. They feel that voice is something that they were born with and that if they should try to make changes in their voices, it would involve years of voice study. But you don't need to put in the amount of time an actor or a singer does in order to make your voice more effective. What you do need to do is first of all to listen to your voice objectively. Use a tape recorder and hear the impression your voice conveys to others.

The next step is to understand the way the voice works—and the five elements of voice that really can make a difference in the way you sound.

The last step is to practice, using voice exercises. They will help you to develop an awareness of your voice and to hear the changes that are possible.

Most of the problems in making your voice more effective can be solved by this process of inquiry, understanding, and practice.

HOW VOICE WORKS

Just what can be done with the body's normal equipment for voice production? The physiology of voices goes back to breathing. When the lungs need air, the intercostal muscles between the ribs contract and the ribs swing up and out. The diaphragm—the umbrella-shaped muscle just below the lungs which separates the chest from the abdomen—contracts, then descends and flattens, causing a slight displacement of the abdominal organs and an expansion of the upper part of the abdomen. The size of the chest cavity is increased and air rushes in to fill the vacuum. During exhalation the muscles relax and return to a resting position, and air is forced out of the lungs.

The importance of this is twofold. First, when we inhale, the diaphragm and other muscles are in a state of contraction; when we exhale, they relax and return to a resting position. So inhalation is tensing, tightening; exhalation is relaxation, letting go. Second, the diaphragm controls the rate of exhalation, but the actual push comes from the upper abdominal muscles, sometimes called the "belt muscles." So air is pushed not from the throat, chest, or lungs, but from the abdomen.

This process has everything to do with voice production, because voice is produced on exhalation. As we exhale, the push from the abdomen forces air out of the lungs through the voice box, or larynx, located in the throat. The vocal cords, or folds, inside the larynx vibrate as the air passes through, producing sound in much the same way that air vibrating a stringed instrument produces sound.

So voice is produced by a push from the gut, not from the throat. And since voice is produced on exhalation and exhalation means a physical relaxation, or letting go of the muscles involved, speaking, in a very real physical sense, means letting go.

The basis of good voice production is relaxation—letting it happen the way it was intended to happen. Tension interferes with this natural process. Because voice is a function of the body, tension anywhere in the body can interfere with voice; but the most common tension points involve the muscles surrounding the speech center in the jaw, throat, and neck, as well as muscles in the shoulders, chest, and stomach.

From the above you can see that voice is produced in four steps:

1. Inhale. The inhaled breath provides energy for your voice. Tension in your speech center will limit the amount of breath you can take in and thus limit your energy.
2. Begin to speak. Breath pressure from the exhaled air does all that is necessary to make the vocal cords vibrate to produce sound. Straining or trying to push from your throat will interfere rather than help voice production.
3. Send your voice forward toward the audience to give the voice fullness and carrying power.

4. Open your mouth and let the sound out. Tight jaws and clenched teeth distort and muffle the voice.

The four steps of voice production are interrelated, and each begins with and depends upon relaxation. Tension in your chest and stomach prevents you from breathing effectively and giving your voice a source of energy; tension in your throat strangles the sound at its source and affects the pitch of your voice; tension in the mouth and jaw is felt in the throat and also affects your ability to articulate.

RELAXED BREATHING PROVIDES ENERGY

Relaxation in the chest and throat and proper breathing for a source of energy are necessary to achieve an effective, energetic speaking voice. Breathing is so common to us that we hardly give it a second thought when it comes to speaking. Yet I believe that nothing is so important as the correct use of the breath. Untrained speakers tend to stop breathing effectively for speech whenever they get nervous or tense. If you don't pause and are too tense in the chest to inhale correctly, you will be able to take in only short, quick breaths. If you feel you have to keep talking no matter what, you will speak with far less air than you need.

Tension, the common, unconscious reaction of many speakers to the challenge of a speaking situation, is the natural enemy of a speaker's ability to breathe correctly. Rigidity, especially around the chest and abdomen, makes it nearly impossible to get a good deep breath that allows you to put energy into your speaking voice. Relaxation and pausing to inhale are the keys to breathing effectively for speaking. Fortunately, proper breathing, as seen in the relaxation exercise in Chapter 7, "Speaking Without Fear," is a key to relaxation.

We breathe normally through the nose, inhaling and exhaling at a rate of about four seconds each. Breathing for speech, however, requires more air than we normally use, because we talk for longer than four seconds at a time. And it would make for an awkward presentation if we paused for four seconds every time we inhaled to replenish our breath supply. But since we exhale naturally in the act of speaking, we have to stop talking for some period of time in order to inhale. Frequent brief pauses—less than four seconds—are essential for a good pattern of breathing that will support the voice.

Trying to take in more air more quickly through the nose is noisy and looks haughty. For speech, you should breathe through the mouth. This is perfectly natural, since you must open your mouth to speak.

Many speakers, especially if they are required to use a microphone, worry that the audience can hear them breathing each time they inhale, even though they take in their breath through the mouth. It's one thing if when you inhale you sound as if you are slurping soup. But the sound of natural breathing is nothing to be concerned about. No listener expects you not to breathe and deny yourself the energy you need to speak.

Inhaling effectively for speech should not be confused with exhaling for relaxation. When you're feeling the nervous energy that builds up before a speaking situation, that's the time to use the exhale, the letting go of the breath, to relax and settle down. But before the first word comes out of your mouth, you must fill up with breath to support your voice and give it its energy. As you continue to speak, your concern should remain with the inhale, to make sure that your voice has the support it needs.

ARTICULATION FOR ENERGY AND AUTHORITY

Articulation, the act of shaping sounds into words, gives your voice the qualities of energy and authority. It may seem obvious, but good articulation is first a matter of opening your mouth. Proper breathing is the first step in developing an effective voice, but learning to relax your jaw and open your mouth is a close second.

Well-articulated speech adds authority by sounding and looking more definite. When you articulate, you sound as if you're more involved with the words, which in fact you are—your mouth is taking an active part in the shaping of your message. Articulation also adds energy and commitment. Think of angry speakers you've seen. They inject vigorous meaning into their words, and say them as if they mean them, with an extra measure of expression. Anger usually improves a mumbler's articulation, but you don't have to be angry to articulate.

There are two main reasons why people don't have good articulation. Some speakers have never thought about using the mouth energetically. Their words just kind of slip out in a mumble with a listless, lackluster kind of sound. When you use your mouth with more energy, it makes you feel more involved and in control. That active feeling sometimes gives a feeling of self-consciousness to people who aren't used to it. Other speakers, many of them top executives, subconsciously clench their teeth and jaws as an expression of control. Even though they are committed to their messages and aren't afraid to project authority, the sound doesn't come out because they don't open their mouths.

As you try consciously to open your mouth to articulate, don't be concerned that it feels foolish, flamboyant, or out of control; as with the use of gestures that at first seem exaggerated, what seems overdone and unnatural when you're not used to doing it is seen as sincere and committed by your audience. You don't have to stretch your mouth open. The simple act of opening your mouth requires relaxation; the muscles that hinge your jaw must be relaxed to let the mouth drop naturally open.

Many men seem to think precise articulation is prissy or affected. Roger was a student who had a lazy mouth—he barely opened his mouth or moved his lips as he described the advantages of advertising in the magazine he represented. Potential advertisers thought that if Roger wasn't willing to make himself understood, he must be uncommitted to the value of what he was trying to sell. In other words, they interpreted his lazy mouth as a lack of authority and commitment.

I urged Roger to stop thinking he would be seen as affected if he took the trouble to form his words properly, and to realize that energetic articulation would give his voice more authority and commitment. I told him to begin shaping his words as if he were speaking to people who could only lip-read. He said it felt exaggerated and strange at first, but his fears vanished when he saw a videotape in which he looked authoritative and energetic as he spoke about the value of his magazine as an advertising medium. The more convinced Roger looked, the easier it was for him to convince his audience; the attitude of potential advertisers was captured in a comment by one of Roger's fellow students: "If he's sold, I'm willing to be sold, too."

One of the nicest things about making a change in one aspect of your voice is that other changes will sometimes result. This is because the components of voice production are interrelated. Once I was leading a group of women, all in real estate, through a series of exaggerated articulation exercises. I encouraged them to open their mouths wide and really form their words. They were stunned to hear their voices drop almost an octave. The jaw tension that kept their mouths closed had also caused throat tension, which gave their voices a shrill pitch. When they opened their mouths, their jaws and throats relaxed, which let their voices drop to natural, lower-pitched levels. Their relaxed, lower voices gave them all greater authority.

DOWNWARD INFLECTION: THE SOUND OF AUTHORITY

You can add authority to your voice in another way, with downward inflections. Inflection is the way you vary the pitch and tone of your voice according to meaning. There are two basic types of inflection: upward and downward. Downward inflections make your words sound definite, confident, and persuasive. Most phrases and sentences should end with definite downward inflections. In other words, use your voice to put periods at the ends of sentences. Upward inflections—the tilt to a higher pitch at the end of a word or toward the end of a sentence—carry the sound and sense of a question, as if you are unsure of yourself and a little scared. They make you sound polite but tentative and not very firm, like a person asking for approval. Upward inflections compromise your authority and replace it with uncertainty, insecurity, hesitation, doubt, or surprise:

You should diversify your investments; ↗

invest in property ↗

as well as in stocks and bonds. ↗

The use of upward inflections in the example above makes the speaker sound as if he's not sure of the investment advice he's giving the audience. It would sound much more definite with the voice going down at the end of each phrase.

You should diversify your investments; ↘
invest in property ↘
as well as in stocks and bonds. ↘

Hal, a free-lance investment broker, wasn't getting the results he wanted in his client presentations. He was confident with his content, and asked me to listen to his presentation to see if I could spot the problem. The strongest message that came through was the uncertainty in his voice as he spoke. Almost all of Hal's sentences ended with upward inflections, which was undermining the confidence of his clients in the advice he gave them. When I suggested to Hal that he concentrate on using downward inflection, he told me he wanted to avoid seeming pompous. But when he heard on his tape the uncertainty in his voice, Hal immediately understood why he was having trouble selling his services—his upward inflections were robbing his voice of authority.

When Hal began putting confidence into his voice with downward inflections, his words carried the same impression as his thoughts about his investment advice: "I feel definite about this, and it's what I believe. I'm sharing my best opinions simply and directly, and I have no reason to sound uncertain."

THE PAUSE: INSTANT AUTHORITY

Violin virtuoso Isaac Stern was once asked how it was that all professional musicians could play the right notes in the right order, but some made beautiful music while others did not. He replied, "The important thing is not the notes. It's the intervals between the notes." Just as the best musicians add an extra shade of meaning—the difference between good music and great music—by spacing their notes, the best speakers know the value of pausing for effect.

Pause is an incredibly powerful technique to give your spoken image authority, energy, and audience awareness. Pauses are needed in speech to allow you to relax and breathe to give your voice energy; they give you time to see the audience, to think and gain control of your speaking situation by giving you a chance to "get with yourself."

The pause lends importance to the words just spoken, and thus contributes to the impression of authority. It demonstrates that you are comfortable with silence and that you feel in control of the speaking situation. A common tendency among speakers is to fill the spaces that might otherwise be pauses with "ahs," "uhs," and "you knows," or by clearing the throat. This need to fill up all the "blank space" detracts from authority because it communicates a fear of silence.

Pausing also adds energy to speech, first because it is an opportunity to inhale and replenish the energy behind your voice. Pausing as you walk a few steps away from your centered position before the audience (a technique discussed in Chapter 9) lets you take in energy for your voice by inhaling while releasing excess energy from your body.

Pausing adds energy to speaking in still another way. Here is an example of a dramatic pause that adds energy:

"There is one thing we must do to increase our sales next year." (Pause) As the speaker pauses the audience begins to ask, "What? What is the one thing?" An audience that is asking for your information is going to pay attention to what comes next. In fact, people will become noticeably quieter and physically more attentive as they wait for you to continue. A pause before a point you have led your audience to expect can make the air "crackle with electricity." That is a silence more dramatic than words, and is a good way to lead into your most important points.

Pausing also helps your sense of audience awareness, because it gives your audience time to absorb what you have said and prepare for the next point. By pausing after you make a complex point or an involved statement, you are showing consideration of your listeners' needs in the speaking situation as well as giving yourself time to assess their reactions.

Randy, a government employee who conducted public hearings on health and safety regulations, told me that every time he spoke at a hearing he thought, "If I can just get all this out and sit down, I'll be OK. If I stop, I'll go blank." He also wanted his listeners to know he had a grasp of the regulations being proposed.

Randy's audiences, however, were not impressed with his knowledge of the regulations. By rattling them off without stopping, he didn't distinguish important points from routine ones, and he gave listeners the impression that he wanted to push the regulations through without public input. What's more, he wore his audiences out by being "hyper" and hard to follow, leaving them thinking, "Boy, I'm getting exhausted just listening to him. What in the world is he saying, anyway?"

I suggested to Randy that the solution to his problem was pausing consciously every so often to give himself a chance to breathe and think. Once he forced himself to pause, Randy found himself less out of breath and more in command of his material. And he told me he was surprised to find that his pauses also emphasized what he was saying and gave his audiences a chance to digest the information.

As he got more used to pausing, Randy began to understand that the pauses helped the audience calm down, too. Listeners could focus on him and understand and remember what he was saying. They also began to see him as a really confident speaker, and found themselves waiting for his next words or pondering the impact of what he had just said. They could pick out vital points in the regulations, because Randy's pauses signaled places where he wanted to let the information sink in.

PROJECTION AND RESONANCE

Of course, all the authority and energy in the world won't do your voice any good if it doesn't reach the audience. The last step in making your voice its most effective is to reach out with your voice, and that is what happens when you project. Projection is related to resonance. A voice coach might tell you to project and get more resonance in your voice by aiming the voice forward to the "mask" of your face or by thinking of throwing your voice forward to the audience. My advice is that once you've mastered the other qualities of an effective voice, try to put that voice out almost into the laps of your audience. That mental image together with the physical effort of throwing your voice out in order to connect with the audience teaches most people to project without the help of voice exercises.

Projecting your voice doesn't mean shouting, however, because loudness alone won't get your voice out to the audience. You can reduce your volume, but use your mouth energetically and think about putting your voice forward, and you will be easily understood without being loud. What is known in the theater as a stage whisper is done by removing almost all volume from the voice but using the mouth and sending the voice forward to make the words understood.

Business people should remember that a voice that is too loud seems out of control, which diminishes authority and may seem abrasive. A voice that is articulated with energy and reaches forward to the audience, even with little volume, will seem to be much more in control.

Resonance is a quality of voice that is more easily explained in the classroom than in a book, and problems with resonance are more easily corrected with professional help than by practicing on your own. "Resonance" means "resounding." The sound created in the larynx resounds in the chambers of the nose and throat. This is what gives the voice its quality of fullness. A well-resonated voice has more authority and is easier to listen to. Resonance often results naturally when other qualities of the voice are practiced and achieved, as with the women who found their voices becoming lower and more resonant when they practiced articulation.

Many women complain that their voices don't sound serious enough and don't have enough authority. For most of them, pausing, breathing, and opening the mouth more and relaxing the jaw will tend to lower the voice and to make it fuller. But an additional step is sometimes needed. I think it has to do with the way you feel about yourself: You have to be willing to put weight into the sound of your voice. Think about getting the voice forward and speaking forcefully, rather than keeping it back up in the top of your head, which gives the quality that people describe as light-headed. Work on the basic qualities already discussed to put authority into your voice, and use a tape recorder to experiment with expressing anger until you hear the sound you want coming through.

People whose voices are too high and weak often try to force the tone downward, like a tenor trying to imitate a bass singer. Instead of trying to force your voice lower, it's more effective to seek out your fullest, most natural voice, which is probably lower to begin with. Projecting your voice out toward the audience will keep it from being too light and thin, which detracts from authority.

Ellen was a commodities broker who told me she had always heard her high, weak voice as an expression of femininity. But someone who had heard one of her presentations told me that her audiences thought, "Wow, what an airhead." She sounded like a little girl, and the people listening responded accordingly; they thought she didn't really know enough to be taken seriously. Ellen corrected the problem by projecting her voice forward.

Ellen understood that a fuller voice can be pleasing, and that a woman can be feminine by sounding like a woman and not like a little girl. As Ellen's business audiences listened to the difference in her presentations, they thought of her as having more authority and a fuller personality. Responding to her new authority, they were far more ready to receive and respond to the messages she gave them.

Some of the things that irritate people about their voices, like too much nasality, are also matters of resonance. For a better understanding of resonance and projection, turn to the resonance and projection exercise later in this chapter. Business people who want quick results may also want to consider the help of a voice coach or a speech pathologist.

OTHER VOICE-RELATED PROBLEMS

Speakers who breathe, articulate, use downward inflection, pause, and project have the basic elements required for effective speaking. But people frequently encounter other voice-related problems that interfere with their effectiveness. Speakers occasionally ask me, for example, "What should I do if I'm too loud?" If your listeners are complaining that you're too loud, I'd recommend that you have your hearing checked to see if it is a factor. It's more difficult to monitor your own speaking volume than any other aspect of your voice; recruiting a friend or associate to help you can give an initial indication of whether you should seek the advice of a hearing specialist.

A raspy, gravelly voice is what speech pathologists call "glottal fry." Business people feel it as a tightness in the throat and hear it as a shaky quality that makes them sound tired and nervous. Inadequate breath support and tension in the throat are the main causes of this problem, and sometimes the throat tension may be caused by speaking with the chin pressed in and down upon the throat. The way to deal with a raspy voice is to pause more, breathe effectively for speech, think about putting the voice forward, and open your mouth more when you speak. If a raspy voice persists after you take these steps, you should seek the advice of a professional. It could indicate a physical problem.

What About Accents?

Regional accents are a charming reminder that each of us is an individual, with a background that is at least partially revealed in our speech patterns. Yet people ask me all the time if they need to get rid of their accents. I almost always say no. A regional accent is part of your personal identification, and there's no reason to deny your audience that essential identifying factor. It is one way of reaching out to the audience, giving them another means of getting to know you.

What people often identify as their "accent," though, may be in fact a voicing characteristic or habit that has built up over the years. One of these is nasality, which combined with an accent may impress people as uncultivated. In our American culture, a nasal-sounding voice gives this impression no matter what accent it is combined with. Lily Tomlin's telephone-operator character "Ernestine," first used on television's *Laugh-In,* is a good example. On the other hand, a full sound projected through an open mouth will impress listeners as more refined no matter where you're from. People also tend to believe that lazy articulation is a characteristic of their accents, but this is also easily changed to let the real accent come through.

Before we look at some exercises that will help you develop the qualities necessary to an effective spoken image, let's review the basics:

- RELAX. Relaxation is basic to all aspects of voice production.
- INHALE. Your breath is the energy source for your voice.
- ARTICULATE. Energy and authority in your voice come from good articulation.

— USE DOWNWARD INFLECTION. The definite sound at the end
of words and sentences gives your voice authority.
— PAUSE. Effective pauses provide energy, authority, and audience awareness.
— PROJECT. Think about reaching your voice forward and
handing your words to your audience.

MAKE TIME TO PRACTICE

As you begin to make changes in your vocal image, you should
try to set aside frequent times when you can listen to your voice
on a quality tape recorder, one that does a good job of reproducing
sound. It's better to practice for a few minutes at a time, listening
to the playback after each few minutes of speaking, than it is to fill
up one side of a cassette before playing it back.

Practicing in this way, if you stick to it, will make you an expert
analyst of your own voice. Listen for indications of whether
you're breathing enough, relaxing your throat, bringing your voice
forward, opening your mouth, and energizing your articulation.
Listen for pauses and downward inflections. The more you practice, the more ideas you will have about how to improve what you
hear.

Working on your own will let you explore the sound your voice
makes. Don't deny yourself the opportunity to experiment with
your voice as a means of expression. Mark out some times in the
day when you carry your experiments over into normal conversation. You can decide to pause during a telephone conversation, for
example, instead of saying "uh" or "you know." You can choose
a moment at a cocktail party when you involve your body as you
speak in order to put more energy into your voice. If you can,
listen to yourself in these situations. I recommend setting up a
tape recorder on your desk to record parts of your end of phone
conversations. This is a simple, hassle-free way to monitor how
you're actually using your voice when you're thinking primarily
about other things.

I have found that one of the best ways to practice is to read
poetry out loud. Since poetry usually is written for voice, it can
provide some fun and interesting challenges in the way you use

your voice. It pushes you to use more energy and develop a better tone. I recently met a man who had an excellent, warm voice, and was one of the better speakers I have heard among businessmen. I complimented him about his voice, and he replied, "I read poetry aloud. I wonder if it's helped me." He did it because he loved poetry; he wasn't trying to develop his voice, but it had that effect.

Regardless of how you go about practicing them, the exercises that follow are designed to help you breathe and relax, and to improve all aspects of your vocal image by adding energy, authority, and audience awareness. Almost all of them require the investment of considerable energy. Don't try to go only as far as you think you need to go for your particular situation. Throw caution to the winds! Go to the extremes, and you'll find it is then much easier to return to a happy medium that is best for you and your vocal image.

Once you begin a routine of practicing voice exercises, the results of your practice will quickly spill over into your everyday speech. In no time at all, you may develop a "sixth sense" which tells you each time you speak if your voice carries the authority, energy, audience awareness, and reaching out that you intend to convey. Knowing that your voice is effectively carrying your message and working in harmony with the rest of your spoken image provides a constant source of satisfaction and a sense of achievement. It is the confidence that comes from knowing that your vocal image is revealing you at your best that reinforces your commitment to change.

EXERCISES TO HELP YOUR VOICE

Developing Breathing Awareness

1. Sit with your body relaxed but upright, and in good alignment, with your feet flat on the floor. Relax your arms and hands on the arms of your chair or in your lap. Relax your stomach muscles. Close your eyes and breathe passively. Now notice what is happening to your beltline. As you take air in, your beltline expands; as you let air out, it recedes. This rhythmic expanding and receding of the beltline is what happens during good, natural deep breathing. If this doesn't work for you, try panting very

slowly, like a dog. Now you should feel the movement at the beltline.

2. Tension interferes with this natural process of good, deep breathing. For a graphic demonstration, tighten your belt muscles as much as you can. Now take a deep breath. You can feel the difference: You are not getting as much breath as before. Thus you have little control over the outflow of breath, which produces your voice. You may also feel tension developing in your shoulders, your chest, and even your throat. Tension in these areas surrounding your speech center can interfere with the vibration of the vocal folds.

3. Now relax your stomach muscles and take quick, deep breaths through the nose. Do the same thing again, only this time inhale through the mouth. Notice that this method is much quieter. You don't have to open your mouth wide to get a good, deep breath very quickly with little or no sound at all. This is the way you should breathe for speech.

4. You do not always need to take your fullest breath to say what you want to say. But as you develop your breathing awareness, you will find that the more urgent and numerous your ideas, the more likely you will need to pause and take in a full supply of breath before you start talking. When you need time to think and choose your words carefully as you go along, you can pause frequently and take less air.

5. When you take a deep breath, you do not have to use it all up immediately. You can pause, hold your breath by setting your waist muscles for a moment, and then continue speaking. Say "sh" and take a breath. Say "sh" seven times on one breath. Now say three medium-long "sh" sounds. Finally, say "sh" as one long, sustained sound—"ssshhhh." In each case, there is a difference in the muscular action at the waist. As you pause in producing the sound, you also pause in using the stomach muscles to push out the sound. This exercise is designed to give you a sense of how much breath you need to express thoughts of varying length.

6. Your voice runs out of energy if you do not get adequate air, and you look weaker, too. Standing in front of a full-length mirror, expel the breath from your lungs in one quick exhale, then talk. There is enough residual air to produce voice for a short time, but

notice how little power your body has as you strain to speak. Now take a deep breath, with relaxed stomach muscles and an open mouth, and talk. Notice now how much stronger your body looks and feels, and how much easier it is to produce voice without straining.

Breathing and Voice Practice

1. To check the difference that breathing can make in your voice:

— Tape-record yourself as you count from one to ten out loud, using your normal breathing pattern.

— Now take a full breath before each number and count, trying to use up each breath on each number. After each number, blow out any leftover air and take another breath for each new number. Count to ten this way as you tape-record yourself.

— Now take as much air as you need to say series of numbers of different length. Try to take only as much air as you need for each series, as you say "one, two," "one, two, three," "one, two, three, four," and so on, until you count to ten, again recording your voice.

The latter two examples should sound stronger than the first, since you are taking in more air. The second exercise, in which you breathe for each count, is tiring, since you are wasting air. The last exercise should feel just right, since you were able to anticipate the amount of air you needed each time.

2. Each of the following lines is longer than the one before it. Take enough breath to say each line:

I pause to take a breath before I speak.
To get a breath quickly, I breathe through the mouth.
I relax stomach muscles to give myself a deep enough breath.
I stop every time to take a breath before I read each of these lines.
I can use prose or poetry of any variety to practice breathing on my own.

ENERGETIC ARTICULATION

Tape-record yourself counting out loud from one to ten, using your normal articulation. Now mouth the numbers, using no breath or voice, exaggerating your articulation as if someone were lip-reading you from forty feet away. Keep this articulation relaxed as well as exaggerated, without stretching the mouth tensely. Be sure you release and drop your jaw naturally and easily, especially on the numbers "one," "five," "eight," and "nine."

Now repeat this exaggerated articulation with voice and again record the result. You should hear improvements in voice quality and clearness of articulation; both should contain a sound of energy and commitment. Repeat the exercise again, this time watching yourself in the mirror; your face should look natural and committed as you speak.

Repeat this exercise with a poem or a short prose selection. People who already have good resonance are often surprised to find that this energy in articulation gives them an extra measure of authority.

PROJECTION

This exercise teaches you how to project your voice and give it volume without straining your throat. Many speakers have had the experience of a trip to the mountains in which they've stood at an overlook and called out, trying to get an echo in return. Most people project their voices beautifully at such times; they are relaxed, they take a deep breath of mountain air, open their mouths, and stretch out the vowel sounds as they call, "Hello-o-o-o out there!" Perhaps because they expect no response but their own echo, they don't strain their throats.

The calls of street vendors had to be heard in very noisy environments without straining the throat or damaging the voice, because for these street-corner merchants, their voices were their only form of advertising. Losing one's voice meant being out of business, so a vendor usually used relaxed, easy calls.

In the call "Strawberries, apples, tomatoes," there are three different "a" sounds. Notice these sounds and repeat them, releasing and relaxing the jaw as you use the same three words. For this exercise imagine you're a street vendor selling his wares.

1. Do the call on a comfortably high pitch.
2. Repeat the call again at your lowest comfortable pitch, without straining your throat to go lower than is comfortable.
3. Repeat the low-pitched call, but say "tomatoes" in a speech rhythm while maintaining the forward focus you used in calling it out.
4. Now, take all three words to a speech rhythm, again maintaining the forward direction you used in calling the words. Don't stop between the words; keep them rolling. You are using good, easy projection.
5. Take the words of any speech and rehearse them through these steps. Your best projection and volume come without straining your throat.

With energetic articulation and the projection developed in this exercise, you should have sufficient volume for any situation. If listeners press you to speak louder at this point, you should use amplification equipment or suggest that the equipment you're using be checked. Don't try to do the impossible with your voice, because you could do serious damage to the vocal folds.

RESONANCE AND PROJECTION

With your body relaxed and in alignment, take a deep breath. Now say "mmm," concentrating the sound on your lips and teeth. Touch your lips with your fingertips—you should be able to feel the vibrations.

Now deliberately but gently try to force the "mmm" back in your throat. You can hear and feel the difference—the sound may be a bit choked and you will feel the pressure in your throat.

Once again, focus the sound on your lips and teeth. Your throat is again relaxed and open, the way it should always feel. Now match the "mmm" sound, still focused on the lips and teeth, with a series of vowels, each pronounced as long vowels:

— "Mmmā." Just relax your jaw, open your mouth and allow the "a" sound out.
— "Mmmē." Your jaw cannot drop far on this one.
— "Mmmȳ." Here your jaw does drop, way down.
— "Mmmō." Round your lips and drop your jaw.

String all these together and feel the constant buzzing in the front of the face as you say "mmma, mmme, mmmy, mmmo."

Now repeat the string at a faster speed, making sure you still feel the buzzing, and conclude with this short sentence: "We are too." The forward placement of your voice and the vibrations should feel the same as it did for the vowel string.

To carry over this full, easy resonance into daily conversation, you can use the "mmmhm" sound that most of us use to murmur agreement without interrupting a speaker. Using only the "mmmhms" you would normally use in conversation, you can monitor to see that the sound is placed well forward on the final "m." Listen to the next sentence you say; it should sound as if it is in basically the same place.

OPEN YOUR MOUTH AND GET RID OF NASALITY

The following paragraphs have no nasal (m, n, or ing) sounds in them. You should be able to say them with your nostrils blocked with no difference in sound than if your nostrils were open. If you find as you block your nostrils that the sentences are "plugged up" in your nose, you know that you are saying them nasally. If this is the case, work at dropping your jaw to get your mouth open more. The object is to produce a fully oral tone.

Use your voice well. The work will reward you. Why are there speakers all are ready to follow? Others that bore us, or leave us doubts about their credibility? It is how you say what you say that decides how others react.

If you hold your voice back, if you have a tight jaw, you will look closed. You will look stiff. Your voice will be hard to hear. The vowels will have a flat quality. The look will say that you hide the truth. You are afraid to let go, to share what you have to say with others.

> If you relax your jaw, you will have a fuller voice. If you
> really drop your jaw as you speak, you allow yourself to
> share your voice. The vowels will have a rich quality. Your
> voice will carry better as you let your voice out.

DOWNWARD INFLECTIONS

Practice saying the alphabet with upward inflections on each
letter as you record your voice. Then record yourself again as you
say the alphabet with downward inflections. The downward inflections, of course, will sound much more definite. Practice saying
words in a series using downward inflections on every word:

One ↘ Two ↘ Three ↘
Reason ↘ Will ↘ Emotion ↘
Gold ↘ Silver ↘ Lead ↘

Now say a series of phrases with downward inflections:

This city needs improvements in education. ↘
In traffic control. ↘
In financial planning. ↘

Mark a prose passage or a speech for pauses. Record yourself,
using upward inflections at the end of each phrase. Now record
the same selection with downward inflections at the end of each
phrase. Listen to the difference in the sound of authority.

Even questions demanding a yes or no answer sound better with
downward inflections:

Would you like to become a better speaker? ↗

If this sentence is said with an upward inflection, it sounds as if
you need someone's approval or permission to continue your
speech.

Would you like to become a better speaker? ↘

With a downward inflection, the same sentence sounds as
though you know your advice is valuable and you believe that
people would benefit from hearing it.

IF YOUR VOICE SOUNDS MONOTONOUS ADD LIFE

Choose a poem or a short prose selection, and monitor yourself with a tape recorder as you read it:

1. With no movement at all.
2. With large, exaggerated movements. Get your torso as well as your arms and hands involved in the movements. The movement creates vocal energy, as your voice follows the lead of your movements. As a result, your delivery has both excellent vocal energy and variety in vocal expression that is natural and spontaneous. Imposing changes in the pitch, rate, and volume of your voice without involving your body can sound studied and phony, but when the variety originates in movement, it always sounds real because you are putting more of yourself into it.

As you apply this exercise to real speaking situations in your business life, you naturally should use movements appropriate to the situation. Larger-than-life, sweeping movements may be fine for musical comedy or opera; much smaller ones are better for business.

Next, tape-record steps 1 and 2 of the following exercise.

1. Say the word "no" as strongly as you can without movement.
2. Practice a karate chop or any aggressive, slashing motion of the arm and hand. Try to put your back into the movement.
3. Now say the word "no" as you use the motion you just practiced. Your "no" should have become much more energetic and forceful.

To develop an effective voice for speaking, you don't have to put in the hours at voice exercises that a singer or actor, for example, would require. But a little bit of practice with a tape recorder will go a long way toward helping you make things happen with your voice. The exercises are meant to be just that—what I'd call sort of light workouts in the areas of your voice that need improvement. Just reading the chapter and skimming over the exercises won't open the door to changes in your voice; you have to hear the sound of your voice if you want to improve it. If you really want to make your audiences sit up and listen, a few extra minutes of work on this vital part of your spoken image can improve your effectiveness in every speaking situation.

11

Resistance

You NOW know all the techniques necessary to become a comfortable and effective speaker. This entire book has been an effort to convince you that improvements in your presentation planning and delivery are both possible and desirable. Yet most of us resist change, even when it means improvement, and our resistance can be a barrier to adopting new speaking habits. Trying something new demands that we test unfamiliar methods that can feel uncomfortable at first. We are reluctant to adopt a new style because we don't know for sure that it will work. We are anxious about adjusting a style that has brought us success even if the adjustments would make us better. We sometimes resist getting in touch with ourselves, slowing down, and relaxing, because we see ourselves as hard-driving and intense. We all see ourselves in certain ways; change means altering that familiar picture and admitting to ourselves, perhaps, that we are not always all that we could be.

We face resistance from outside ourselves as well. The listeners in a speaking situation also resist and have a right to do so, because the speaker is making demands on them, asking them to change in some way. An audience's resistance to the speaker is the normal resistance to unfamiliar or competing points of view.

Audiences resist in different ways—sometimes with anger and bitterness, but more often with a stubborn reluctance to be moved. This kind of resistance, which we encounter more frequently, is passive resistance. It slows you down and, like quicksand, makes it harder to get where you want to go. Most business people experience some kind of passive resistance in almost every presentation they make, not because business people are disagreeable, but because most business decisions must justify large investments of time, money, and manpower. Because of this, the average business speaker needs to focus on passive resistance rather than on confrontational styles of resistance that a political speaker would be more likely to encounter.

There will always be some degree of resistance in a speaking situation, and you ought to expect it, but it's more important that you deal with an audience's resistance in some situations than in others. The degree to which it matters depends on your objective. A bank official speaking to civic club members about how to borrow money in a tight market may find that a fourth of his listeners disagree with his conclusions. Resistance from this audience, however, doesn't block his objective, which is to inform and present a point of view but not necessarily persuade the audience to accept that point of view. If the same bank official were speaking to the loan committee of his bank defending a loan he had made, he would be more concerned that the audience accept his views. Thus, if a fourth of this audience resisted, their resistance could interfere with his reaching his objective, and he would have to spend more time dealing with the resistance.

I was giving a videotape presentation to an audience of about two hundred potential clients when I was confronted with resistance from one member of the audience. The presentation was designed to show improvements that students had made in their speaking styles during a short time at Speakeasy. Before I could begin, however, I saw a hand waving wildly from the back of the room. A man leaped to his feet and asked in a belligerent voice, "Under what conditions were these tapes made?" The tone of his voice said, "I don't believe what you're about to show me." I ignored the challenge and simply told him the tapes were made in Speakeasy's classrooms under normal conditions. Then I went ahead and showed them.

At the conclusion of the tape presentation, I was talking about the importance of body to spoken image when the same fellow jumped to his feet again. He said, "You don't mean to tell me that this body-image stuff is important, when everyone knows it's only mind control that counts." He was insisting on challenging me in front of two hundred people, and my first reaction was to cut him down. His own body image, after all, was tight and hyper, a good illustration of what I was talking about. But to cut him down, I would have had to make a fool of him in front of his colleagues, and I would have lost my authority by responding in that way. So

I just looked at him and said, "A lot of people feel that mind control is important," and moved on. I didn't agree or disagree with him; I only recognized him with my comment and continued with my remarks.

If I had needed every person in the audience to agree with every word I was saying, I might have taken him on. But most of the people in the room seemed to agree with me, so resistance from one person didn't interfere with my meeting my objective. If the hand waver had been a student in a seminar, or one person in a group of five who really was having trouble understanding the importance of the body to speaking, then his resistance might have interfered with my ability to reach my objective. I would have tried to learn why mind control was so important to him and why he was resisting the idea that body image was important.

Most business presentations are designed to persuade as well as inform. If your most frequent presentations are to clients or to in-house audiences, you will probably always be trying to move them in some way. So knowing how to deal with resistance is necessary if you are to become a better and more effective speaker.

REDUCING RESISTANCE
IN YOUR CONTENT PLANNING

Your first opportunity to deal with resistance occurs during the planning stage, as you look at your content. Here, your most effective tool for reducing audience resistance is a thorough audience analysis. Anticipating your audience's needs and attitudes reduces the potential for resistance from them. As you know from the content section, audience analysis will affect the objective you set, the message you choose, and even the particular opening you use.

You increase audience resistance when your professional objective asks or presumes too much, when you plan to move your audience too far on the marketing model scale. Analyzing your audience in terms of their knowledge and acceptance of your topic helps you decide how far you can reasonably expect to move them. Remember the group of midlevel hospital administrators I couldn't move to my objective in my presentation on more effective speaking? My objective for them hadn't been realistic; I didn't know where they were, so I tried to move them too far. Their resistance to my message, in the form of blank faces and a kind of sullen reluctance to be moved, is an example of how you can create or increase resistance when your professional objective isn't realistic for your audience.

Your hidden objectives—the personal, unstated things you need from the situation beyond getting the sale or persuading the audience of your point of view—can also increase audience resistance. Hidden objectives can confuse, distract, or overwhelm your audience. Since your hidden objectives consider only your own needs, you can easily overload your audience with too much content, or divert them from your professional objective with content that is irrelevant. In either case, a hidden objective that interferes with the ability of the audience to grasp your message is a source of resistance. To decrease audience resistance in your content planning, you must have your hidden objectives under control.

Allen, the assistant director of a professional association, had just been appointed to succeed the retiring director. His predecessor was an excellent communicator, and Allen was attending courses so that he could do as well. He was also working on a master's degree at night and on weekends. To say he had a lot of irons in the fire is an understatement. His achievements and the frantic pace of his activities were all he talked about when he introduced himself to the group in the seminar.

Allen's style lacked energy, so I assigned him an energetic character to role-play. His choices were a carnival barker, a baseball manager disputing an umpire's call, or a panhandler. But when Allen came in on the day of the assignment, he proudly announced to the class, "I decided that instead of just doing one of the assignments, I would do all three."

It was obvious from the fact that he wanted to do all three assignments when asked to do only one that Allen's hidden objective was to focus attention on his abilities. He needed his audience to know how much he could achieve. In doing the three assignments, he was saying in effect, "Look what I can do!"

In Allen's real speaking situations, the equivalent of doing three role plays would have been to overload his audience with content so they would know how smart he was. This hidden objective—to impress the audience with his intelligence and achievements— would create impatience and then resistance in any group.

REDUCING RESISTANCE WITH YOUR STYLE

Your speaking style can also raise or lower the audience's level of resistance. The lessons contained throughout Part II of this book on putting authority, energy, and audience awareness into your spoken image all are ways of reducing the likelihood of audience resistance.

Authority in your spoken image reduces resistance, because it does not challenge or bully. It doesn't provoke your audience to fight back. Authority also means that you don't try to placate or "cozy up" to your audience, which would invite resistance by implying that the audience must like you in order to accept your message.

Your energy makes it hard for an audience to resist getting involved with your presentation, for the simple reason that you are obviously involved in it. The energy that shows the audience that you're committed to what you're saying says it's worth their commitment, too.

Audience awareness decreases the chance or degree of resistance, because by being aware of the audience you communicate that you care about them. It's difficult to resist someone who demonstrates in his style that he cares about you. Physically reaching out, with evident movement toward the people you are speaking to, is another way of showing them you care about them and inviting them to reciprocate. And audience awareness and its extension in active listening, a concept discussed fully later in this chapter, let you monitor resistance and deal with it before it becomes insurmountable.

Your hidden objectives can affect your style as well as your content, and can raise or lower the amount of resistance you can expect from an audience. Allen, whose hidden objective directed a choice of content that increased resistance, also had a style that encouraged resistance. Although he spoke from a balanced body and had a smooth, articulate facade that conveyed authority and

revealed no signs of nervousness, Allen didn't give out to his audience. He was just there. He gave no sign that he wanted to
connect with the people who were listening. I pushed Allen to put
energy into his voice and body. That's what he did in his three
role-plays, following instructions by putting a great deal of energy
into each of the characters. His energetic performances showed
his ability to master an assignment, but no commitment of his own
energy to his audience or to an idea that he believed in and wanted
to share. His energy was self-focused, and his emphasis on himself
continued to say "Look what I can do!" when he should have
been saying "Look what we can share!" Allen's style would create resistance in the audience as soon as they realized that all his
attention was directed to himself.

TECHNIQUES FOR
MEETING AUDIENCE RESISTANCE

It is not reasonable to expect that you will be able to breeze
through all your presentations with no resistance whatsoever. The
audience has the right to resist you as a speaker, because each
party brings different needs to the speaking situation, and this
means there will always be some level of resistance. But what
happens when you've done everything possible in your content
planning and your style to lower audience resistance, and it meets
you head on anyway? Perhaps there's more resistance than you
expected, or it's different from what you expected. Maybe the
resistance you're getting isn't even fair. You still have some
choices in how you respond.

Changing Your Objective

Your first option is to change your objective, making it less
ambitious to account for the greater-than-expected resistance. In
my session with the hospital administrators, for example, I could
have scaled down my objective as I realized that their lack of
awareness was preventing them from committing themselves to
becoming better speakers. That had been my original objective,
but instead I could have made them aware that better speaking

could help them in their careers. At another session, I might have won their commitment.

The executive officer who tried to convince his board to buy an unprofitable company might also have fared better if he had scaled down his objective to account for their resistance. Rather than "going for broke" and trying to win the conservative board's approval in one meeting, he would have been more realistic if he had limited his objective to making them aware of the potential benefits of his proposal. He might then have reached his original objective at a second meeting.

Many business people may feel they have no choice about their objective, and couldn't change it or scale it down even if they wanted to. In that case, there are other options to explore when you face a lot of resistance.

Active Listening

Active listening is one of the most effective things you can do to overcome resistance. It is a concept that is vital to a truly committed speaking style. Active listening means momentarily suspending your needs as a speaker to focus on the concerns of the audience. Carl Rogers, the man who first defined active listening, described it as listening without making judgments. He called it the greatest gift you can give someone. The actual techniques aren't as important as imagining what it would be like to be in the other person's shoes. You begin this by relaxing, pausing and using eye contact to really see the audience, giving them the gift of your time, used to gain a better understanding of them.

I spoke about two years ago to a small group of sales managers. My topic was effective content organization for their business presentations, but when we met, they were distracted: It was between Thanksgiving and Christmas, which was the busiest time of year for these men and women; they were worried about slow Christmas sales, high inventories, and the fact that their company had told them to take time off to attend the workshop where I was one of several speakers. I knew in advance they'd be busy, but thought they were ready to listen to what I had to say.

The sales managers resisted. They kept up a steady stream of questions, and insisted that I deal with specific cases from their business, and then threw up reasons why what I was saying wouldn't work. It was very difficult to maintain a focus on what I wanted to accomplish with them. I couldn't abandon the professional objective that had brought me there in the first place. But active listening told me why these hassled sales managers were distracted, and gave me a choice about what to do next.

I decided to get right to the point. I said, "I want you to know that I realize you are very pressured right now and that business is hard. But I also have to say that I am not here as a business consultant, to discuss your specific business needs. I'm here to tell you ways to organize your presentations that will make them easier and more effective. So let's move on, understanding that our purpose is to explore principles of presentation planning, not to deal with your specific business strategy." Being straight with the sales managers allowed me to stick to my original objective.

Laying Your Cards on the Table

Laying your cards on the table, as I did with the sales managers, is an option that not every speaker is willing to take. But the more confidence you develop in yourself as a speaker, the more you may find it an attractive choice in dealing with resistance. Jake, a young lawyer, was speaking to executives of an electric utility in the weeks before a state legislature was to convene. His job was to give the utility executives tips for effective lobbying, so they would be equipped to work against any anti-utility legislation introduced in the pending session. Jake had had some political experience and was just beginning a promising career in law, and he wanted to be taken seriously. But the utility people made it clear from the beginning that because Jake didn't know a lot about their industry per se, they felt there was little he could tell them about lobbying on its behalf. Jake fought for their acceptance, but the harder he fought, the more they resisted and even baited him, and he found it impossible to get beyond the wall of their resistance.

Jake told me about his encounter with the utility executives several years later, when he was taking the seminar. "If I were doing it today," he said, "I think the audience would be the same —serious and inclined to resist what I was telling them. But I would certainly do some things differently. I wouldn't fight them, and I would level with them more. I believe I'd just tell them, 'I'm not an expert in your industry. I deal with many different industries and interest groups which need advice on lobbying. Here are the basic rules for lobbying effectively. If you want to try them, that's up to you, and if you don't, that's fine with me, too.' "

Jake, having developed confidence as a speaker and a professional, would have laid his cards on the table and stuck with his original objective.

If scaling down or changing your objective isn't possible or doesn't work, and the audience still resists; if active listening fails to provide the answer; if after laying your cards on the table the audience continues to resist, you may decide at that point that you have but one option left.

Terminating the Speaking Situation

If you've thought about what matters to you, and what you need from your audience, you may decide that if the audience doesn't want your content, then it's their problem, not yours. Sometimes, when you can't make contact no matter how hard you try, you have to make the decision that it's time to walk away.

Effective speakers always have to work and bend in order to reach common ground. But you sometimes reach the point where you can bend and reach out no more, and that point is when you begin to feel you are compromising your integrity and giving up who and what you are. You must then make a decision. If you are pursuing a client that you want at all costs, you may feel you have to swallow his resistance. I believe, however, that when only one party tries to compromise, the relationship will never be successful. A business relationship won't work if you lose respect for yourself and the other person loses respect for you.

People deal differently with resistance, of course, because of their backgrounds—some people were raised in families and got into jobs in which they've made a habit of saying yes all the time; they constantly are swallowing their pride and personality in order to get by. If this is what you have to do to make a situation work, you may have to ask yourself if it's worth it. If you have adapted and bent and the other person just won't move, there comes a point beyond which you give up who and what you are. Before you do that, you ought to walk away.

Now you've seen the choices you have for dealing with resistance you encounter in spite of your careful planning and effective style.

— Be prepared to scale down or change your objective.
— Use active listening to detect underlying reasons for resistance.
— Consider laying your cards on the table.
— Be aware of your option to terminate the speaking situation.

Each of these choices is available. But your ability to choose the best response to resistance at the moment it happens depends on having your unstated objectives well under control.

MANAGING RESISTANCE FROM YOUR HIDDEN OBJECTIVES

Most of the reasons for resistance come from inside of us. If we can deal with our hidden objectives, our presentations will probably be as effective and successful as they can be. The final responsibility for effectiveness lies within ourselves, not within the audience.

Most people look for resistance from the audience before they look for it in themselves. They want to know, "What technique do you use when someone in the audience disagrees with you?" Or, like one student who spoke in a tight voice with his shoulders squared and ready for action, they say, "How do you handle those people in every audience who are out to get you?" What these speakers want is a list of techniques that will guarantee success anytime there is any kind of resistance coming from any other person. They see resistance as a battle, to be won or lost.

When a member of the audience resists, you cannot control or manipulate that person to bend him completely to your will. There are no formulas for dealing with various "kinds" of resisters. All you can change is you. The only choices you can control have to do with you. But by controlling yourself in the face of resistance, you can almost always control the situation and come away the winner.

People always seem to think there are rules for avoiding confrontation that will work no matter what. I've worked with a lot of people who know what they should do to keep from getting into confrontations with the audience, and the rules always seem to go out the window when they tighten up and lose control of their hidden objectives. None of the formulas ever worked for me, either, until I was ready to look to myself to see what I was fighting for, what mattered to me, or what I was afraid of losing. Unexpected or excessive resistance always puts pressure on your unstated needs from the situation, and your first response is likely to come from those needs. Unless you have them under control, you're not likely to choose the most effective way of dealing with the audience's resistance.

In my talk to the sales managers who were distracted by the Christmas business rush, for example, active listening let me understand the reasons they were distracted. So even though their comments and questions were aimed at me, I didn't take them as personally threatening or insulting. With my hidden objectives under control, I was able to make the right choice of responses—to encourage their attention by laying my cards on the table.

Jake, on the other hand, made the wrong choice in his encounter with the utility executives he was speaking to about lobbying. Their resistance threatened him and made it hard for him to control his unstated objectives, which at that point in his career were to have his advice accepted and to be respected as a professional. So he fought back, which caused his audience to escalate their resistance. You almost always increase resistance by viewing the speaking situation as a case of win-lose or as a battle, because it's in such cases that you're most likely to lose control of your hidden objectives.

You Don't Have to Fight to Win

I was recently in California for an appointment with the representative of a company that was interested in using me as a consultant. The final step in the approval process was the vice president in charge of marketing, and I reached his office about four-thirty on a Friday afternoon. He was sitting at his desk. He didn't rise to greet me, but instead occupied himself shuffling papers and opening and closing the drawers of his desk. He acted very hassled and distracted, and informed me in a rushed, irritated voice, "We don't have very much time. I have to leave for a basketball game." The message I got from him told me that he considered himself far too important to be wasting his time with me on a Friday afternoon.

I felt my gut tighten, and my immediate reaction was to fight back. But I caught myself and thought, "Hold on. This is a no-win situation. If you try to beat this guy at his own game, you can't be yourself and you'll lose." I exhaled to relax and repeatedly told myself to slow down and stay calm as I kept looking at him. As I looked at him, I talked slowly and rationally at the side of his head while he fished around in his desk drawers and asked questions in his hurried, harried voice. As I continued to talk and look at him, however, he began to slow down and listen. Soon he stopped rummaging among his papers and became attuned to me, and we had a satisfactory conversation.

This was an interesting lesson to me, because by not fighting the battle, I had won the war—I had reached my objective. By remaining slow, steady, direct, and calm, and maintaining my focus, I made it very difficult for him to resist being pulled in. By reaching out, I managed to bring my audience of one into my atmosphere.

When I walked into his office, active listening let me see that he was insecure and had a need to let me know that he was in control and could push me around. I gained insights that helped me know how to react in order to control the situation. My choice of reactions turned out to be the right choice under the circumstances. But if my original choice, to be calm and reasoned and to bring him into my atmosphere, had failed, I could still have made the choice to walk out. When Carl Rogers said that active listening is the greatest gift you can give someone, he might have added that it's also a great gift to give yourself in a speaking situation.

Active listening gives you information that can help you win without fighting. The other person's major need may be to feel in control, even if it's temporary and illusory; if you deny him that by fighting back he'll fight even harder. Soon a simple situation that can be dealt with easily and painlessly escalates into a confrontation, and nobody wins. If you can simply listen, avoiding the critical self-judgment that you're giving up control and letting someone push you around, what you're really doing is controlling yourself. By holding on to who and what you are, you can usually prevail. This means also avoiding the value judgment that the person resisting is a fool or a boor who needs to be put down just to satisfy your ego; if indeed he is, he will almost certainly reveal it without your help.

Listen to Yourself

The episode with the hand waver also showed me the value of pausing to look inward, of trying to understand my reactions to certain situations. In making the choice to avoid a fruitless battle, I gained an important source of information from pausing to listen to myself. The presentation was on the West Coast, two thousand miles and three time zones away from my home. I had arrived late the night before. The airline had lost my luggage, including papers I needed for my presentation. I was physically exhausted and mad at the world when I woke up the next day. Because I realized this, I took a quiet walk and did some breathing. I tried to listen to myself, and what I heard was, "Sandy, you'd better be careful today. You're tired, you're on edge, you're mad at the airline and the world in general. If anybody looks at you wrong today, you're going to want to fight." In other words, my hidden objective was to take out my frustrations on the first person who crossed me. So when I saw that aggressive wave from the back of the room, I was able to remind myself, "Watch it. Take it slow. Think of what you're going to say before you say it."

Taking the time to listen to yourself is just as important as listening to your audience, so that you understand your reactions under stress and remember that on certain days you are more likely to get caught up in battle. When you listen to yourself and react to the information you receive, you are recognizing and controlling your unstated objectives.

Because people don't agree with us 100 percent doesn't mean they oppose us completely. Speaking is not a battle with the audience, to be won or lost. You don't have to take a step toward confrontation when you deal with resistance from the audience. Remember that your objective when you speak is always to expand the common ground between you and your audience. Confrontation supposes that your differences are greater than your common ground. Fighting with the audience enlarges the differences, letting them get bigger and bigger until there's no way you can get beyond them to your objective. Avoiding the conflict and enlarging the common ground keeps you on course toward your objective, and you can only do this when you are in control of your hidden objectives.

You now know a variety of ways in which to deal with resistance —you can ignore it if it doesn't interfere with reaching your objective; you can adjust your objective; you can ask questions of the audience; you can focus on audience needs with active listening; you can lay the cards on the table. Finally, you can decide that you have to walk away.

But just as there are no pat formulas for the right way to speak, there is no formula for dealing with resistance. We each bring our strengths and weaknesses, our own tension levels, our own styles of listening, to the speaking situation. The more you understand yourself and what you need from your audience—your own hidden objectives—the better you are able to handle resistance.

You should understand that there will always be some resistance. It is the audience's right to resist, and you should expect resistance. You can only really control and change yourself. But with the right kind of planning and the right kind of delivery you can greatly reduce the likelihood that your audience's resistance will prevent you from getting the results you want.

12

Special Business Situations

THE BASIC lessons of presentation planning and delivery are the same no matter what the situation. Finding the right objective, establishing your message, and organizing your content to support that message are things you must do to get ready for any presentation, whether it's a quarterly meeting of sales managers, a conference with one client, or a speech to a large group. Authority, energy, and audience awareness in your content and style remain constants in making yourself effective.

But some frequently encountered business situations make additional demands on you, the speaker, not in planning or delivery, but in preparation, rehearsal, and the task of becoming familiar with the mechanics of sophisticated media. So some extra pointers can be helpful. What should you know, for example, about writing, editing, and delivering a manuscript speech, and working with speechwriters? How do you deal with the media encounters that seem to be becoming a daily part of business life? How can you communicate effectively on television and in long-distance teleconferencing? What should you do when you're called on to speak to foreign-language audiences? How can you keep from getting lost in the shuffle at large meetings?

Here are some tips that will help you maintain in these special business situations the effectiveness with your planning and delivery you have already put into your presentations.

SPEAKING FROM NOTES

Speaking from an outline is always more "alive" than reading from a written document. Most business presentations don't require fully written speeches. But many of my students want to know how they're supposed to speak for twenty or thirty minutes and remember everything they have to say without a speech in front of them. There's a middle ground—you shouldn't read a speech word for word most of the time, but neither should you try to speak without notes. Every speaker has the right to have an outline of his talk when he gets up to speak, and to do otherwise shows a lack of preparation. The outline serves as a "road map" for what you want to say in the time you've got.

The number and extent of your notes will depend on your familiarity with the material, but they probably should contain at least your opening and ending and the heading for each module or main idea within the presentation. You may want notes to remind you to use a certain visual aid or resource, and to remind you of the time you've given yourself for each point.

The form in which you keep your notes is up to you; use what works best. Some people prefer legal pads, others small index cards they can keep in an inside pocket until they're ready to speak. Whichever you prefer, I'd recommend that you find a place to put your notes down so that you don't have to carry them or keep putting them in and taking them out of your pockets, which draws attention to them unnecessarily. You don't need, and probably won't have, a lectern for most informal talks and presentations, but it's perfectly acceptable to keep your notes on a clipboard on a table, for example. All you need is a place to put them where they're available for you to check when it's necessary.

THE MANUSCRIPT SPEECH

Speakers can be "locked in" to speaking from a manuscript whenever a strict record of their remarks is important.

If a speech is to be recorded or printed, for example, many more people may hear portions of it on radio or television, or read it in the newspaper, than will hear it delivered. Large companies may have a half-dozen or so top executives simultaneously delivering identical speeches on important areas of company policy to various audiences around the world, and for the sake of consistency each speaker must deliver the same message. Misinterpretations that can arise through the use of slang, figures of speech, or industry jargon when their remarks are being interpreted into a foreign language often require business speakers to follow a script. Other reasons speakers may have to stick to a script include legal issues and the use of audiovisuals. And top-level executives find that they are frequently asked to speak to a variety of audiences on topics on which someone else, a speechwriter or a researcher, will have to do the research and writing.

What can you do to turn an inanimate product—a manuscript— into the dynamic, living process that is speaking? To give life to any speaking situation, you must connect and interact with the audience. The manuscript is a barrier to that interaction, and endangers the basic qualities of an effective spoken image: If you read a speech you lose authority; if your energy goes down to the lectern instead of out to the audience you seem to lack commitment; it is difficult to have audience awareness without eye contact. If you can't do without a manuscript, your goal should be to retain authority, energy, and audience awareness by using a delivery that is as extemporaneous and alive as you can make it.

A manuscript speech must be written and edited for speaking, and thoroughly rehearsed if you want to deliver it well. Let's look first at the beginning of the process.

Preparing the Manuscript

The best planning guide for a manuscript speech is the same three-column outline you used to organize your content for an extemporaneous presentation. The outline form works whether you are writing the speech yourself or someone is writing it for you. Its purpose is to organize your thinking into big ideas to which you can add supporting material and which you can arrange to support your message. Let's suppose for discussion purposes that you're working with a speechwriter, but I think you can read between the lines and apply the same principles to preparing your own manuscript.

Many executives think about their topic first and what they want to say second. Thus, you might say to a speechwriter, "I'm speaking to the Commonwealth Club about interest rates and the national economy. Bring me a speech." The speechwriter scurries off and comes back a few days later with a bundle of pages that you look at and declare, "This isn't very good. This isn't what I wanted to say."

As you have seen before in this book, you don't get the results you want without devoting time and thought to your objective and the message you want to deliver. You can't say what you want to say by giving up your responsibility for your content to another person. If the writer doesn't push hard enough for direction, it is your responsibility to provide it.

Once you've discussed with the writer what you want to say and the main ideas you think should go into the speech, your next step is to ask the writer for an outline, not a finished speech. First, you can make necessary changes before hours are spent preparing a document that will have to be done over from scratch if it's not right. Second, a speech written without your input is likely to have none of the personal flavor you would put into it, in which case you might as well be what television people call a "talking head" or a "reader." These are not complimentary terms, for they indicate a person who doesn't know what he's talking about. Once you do know what you want to talk about and have it outlined to your satisfaction, then the writer can do the time-consuming job of research and fitting the pieces together.

Using the three-column outline as a working guideline or a discussion document identifies the main ideas and their supporting material, as well as any resources you may use for illustration.

I have found that one of the best ways to put "live," spoken language into a manuscript speech is to actually talk it through. When you have your outline and the writer or researcher has provided the supporting details you need, sit down with a tape recorder and, from that outline, talk over each main idea within the time you've allowed yourself for that point. If you've allowed yourself five minutes for the first main idea, talk it through for five minutes. Then play it back to see how it sounds. When it sounds pretty good to you, go on to the next point, and so on through the speech. Then have it transcribed. With a bit of editing, that should be the final version of your speech, and it's done with the dynamic spoken word—your own spoken words, at that—and not written language that is more appropriate for an article that is meant to be read, not heard.

Editing the Manuscript

If you've used the tape-recorder method above, the manuscript probably won't need as much editing as one that was written from the beginning. But when you look at the transcription, be careful not to put the written word back in by eliminating contractions, lengthening sentences, and doing other things that will make the language more formal and stilted.

If you are working with a manuscript that began as a written document, your goal is to make the written words into effective spoken words. Here are some tips for editing:

—Use short, direct sentences, because that's the way most people talk. Only Howard Cosell and William F. Buckley, Jr., can get away with talking the way they do; the rest of us should be less ponderous. If a sentence is more than two lines on a page, it's too long for you to say comfortably and probably too long to have much impact on your listeners.

—Use simple, direct language. Cosell and Buckley are the exceptions here, too. Don't try to impress your audience with your vocabulary; they'll think you're pedantic, which means ostentatiously academic. Language that goes right to the point is best.

—Use contractions. You use them in daily conversation, so why not use them when you speak to an audience? They're among the natural mannerisms that bring you down to earth as a speaker and make you real and human to your audience.

—Mark your script where you will pause. This is a better system than underlining for emphasis. People talk in gushes of words, in phrases that have rhythm and flow. Reading can kill the natural rhythm of conversation. By marking where you pause when you're talking through the document, you'll keep that conversational rhythm in your speech. If the pause is in the right place, the emphasis will be in the right place. You'll also breathe in the right places, so you won't be gasping for air at the end of each sentence. An effective way of editing your manuscript and marking it for pauses is shown in the following example. Note that single slashes are used for pauses and double slashes for the ends of sentences:

~~THANK YOU, MR. BROWN. AND~~ GOOD MORNING, ~~LADIES~~
~~AND GENTLEMEN~~ . . . FELLOW EDUCATORS ^AND^ . . . FELLOW MARKETERS // ~~IT'S~~
~~A DISTINCT PLEASURE TO BE WITH YOU TODAY.~~
'S   THOSE
IT ~~IS~~ NO ACCIDENT THAT I JUST USED ~~TWO~~ TERMS ~~A~~
~~EDUCATORS AND MARKETERS //~~ TO DESCRIBE US // . ~~YOU AND ME.~~
THE REASON THAT I CHOSE ~~TO RELATE~~ THEM / ~~QUITE SIMPLY,~~ IS
YOUR
THAT ~~THE~~ INSTITUTIONS ~~YOU REPRESENT~~ AND COMPANIES LIKE
DO   LOT
MINE / REALLY HAVE A ~~GREAT DEAL~~ IN COMMON //

WE IN THE ABC COMPANY ARE PRIMARILY MARKETERS /
PLAY
BUT ~~HAVE~~ A MAJOR ROLE / AS EDUCATORS IN THE LIVES OF
THOUSANDS OF OUR EMPLOYEES // ON THE OTHER HAND, YOU ' ARE
PLAY
PRIMARILY EDUCATORS / BUT ~~HAVE~~ A UNIQUE ROLE ~~TO PLAY~~ AS
MARKETERS OF YOUR PRODUCTS // ~~NOW, IF WE CAN UNDERSTAND~~
~~EACH OTHER IN THIS CONTEXT, WE CAN REAP CONSIDERABLE~~
~~MUTUAL BENEFIT, NOT ONLY DURING THIS MORNING, OR DURING~~
~~THE YEARS OF THE COMING DECADE, BUT ALSO FOR MANY YEARS~~
~~TO COME.~~ WE HAVE A LOT TO LEARN FROM EACH OTHER /
THAT COULD HELP BOTH OF US / NOT ONLY NOW / BUT FOR
MANY YEARS TO COME //

GOOD MORNING, FELLOW EDUCATORS AND FELLOW
MARKETERS //
IT'S NO ACCIDENT THAT I JUST USED THOSE TERMS TO
DESCRIBE US // THE REASON THAT I CHOSE THEM / IS THAT
YOUR INSTITUTIONS AND COMPANIES LIKE MINE / REALLY DO HAVE
A LOT IN COMMON //
WE IN THE ABC COMPANY ARE PRIMARILY MARKETERS / BUT
PLAY A MAJOR ROLE / AS EDUCATORS IN THE LIVES OF THOUSANDS
OF OUR EMPLOYEES // ON THE OTHER HAND, YOU'RE PRIMARILY
EDUCATORS / BUT PLAY A UNIQUE ROLE AS MARKETERS OF YOUR
PRODUCTS // WE HAVE A LOT TO LEARN FROM EACH OTHER / THAT
COULD HELP BOTH OF US / NOT ONLY NOW / BUT FOR MANY YEARS
TO COME //

The goal of the editing is to make your manuscript sound as natural, as "talky" or conversational, as possible. It should make the inanimate product that is the manuscript come alive with spoken language. It follows that the only way you can edit it effectively is to talk it out loud. If you do it silently, it's not going to work for you as a spoken document. You can even whisper it, but you have to feel and hear the rhythm of the words.

Delivering the Manuscript Speech

Writing and editing the speech, or having it written and edited, gives you an effective document from which to speak. But you have to devote time to practice and rehearsal if you are to do more than just stand up and read to your audience. The audience will know if you have rehearsed or not: If you keep your head buried in the speech, stumble over your words, and make little or no eye contact, you clearly have not devoted enough time to rehearsal. A manuscript speech, like one that's extemporaneous, should sound as if it's coming from your gut at the moment of delivery.

There is no such thing as too much rehearsal. Almost any speaking situation requires some rehearsal until you have an effective grasp of what you want to say and how to say it. It's the same kind of preparation you'd put into any other business situation or learning a sport; rehearsing is something the naturals do without prompting. You may feel reluctant or embarrassed to rehearse in front of your colleagues, but if you don't you'll do your experimenting at the wrong time—in front of your audience.

Rehearsing doesn't mean that you should memorize your speech or rehearse it by rote, because then you're not thinking. The minute you stop thinking about what you're saying, your delivery goes flat, and the audience can tell the difference. Thinking keeps your voice and delivery full of energy, just as thinking about it puts energy into your message. An extemporaneous speaker doesn't have this problem; he must think all the time about what he's saying. Speaking from a manuscript requires the same effort, and one way speakers have of making a manuscript speech come alive is to add impromptu conversational statements as they go along.

Without adequate rehearsal, the main problem speakers have in

delivering manuscript speeches is losing eye contact. Many speakers try to remedy this by simply looking up and down a lot as they
read. Not only does this not provide real eye contact, but half their
content is being delivered down to the lectern. I recommend that
speakers look down and silently read to a pause mark, then look
at the audience and speak the phrase, with full eye contact and
awareness. Then look down at the next phrase and then look up
and give that out. This may sound stilted or artificial, but your
rehearsal should have given you enough familiarity with the material so that a quick glance at the page takes in a lot and you'll find
yourself needing fewer downward glances than you thought.
Maintaining eye contact even when you read gives you a much
more energetic, committed delivery.

Turning pages can be distracting for both you and your audience. Many people prefer to slide pages to one side as they finish
them, which has the added benefit of letting the speaker follow the
words from the bottom of one page to the top of the next. There is
on the market a device called a "speech box"; a speaker can carry
his speech in it and also slide pages into it as he's finished reading
them. If you must use loose pages, make sure they're numbered
in case you drop them and wind up literally "groping for words."

A manuscript is a barrier to the interaction that can make things
happen between speaker and audience. But manuscript speeches
can be done well, and with the same results as an extemporaneous
speech, if you put the right amount of time, thought, and energy
into them.

Speech Prompters

There are two kinds of speech prompters: the plastic "lectern"
which gives the speaker a reflected view of a large-print manuscript as he speaks to a large audience; and the TelePrompTer, a
device that runs the manuscript, again in large type, across the
lens of a camera as the speaker reads for television. The audience
is supposedly unaware of the prompter in each case. While
TelePrompTers were originally used solely in television studios, I
now see them increasingly often at large business meetings where
videocameras and screens make live speakers larger and more
"real" to audiences in huge convention-style auditoriums.

A prompter of either kind can be useful to you as a speaker, but to be used effectively it demands rehearsal time. It can be an effective tool, but don't make the mistake of treating it as a gimmick to take the place of rehearsal or to give the illusion of eye contact.

The plastic lectern type of prompter is used in pairs, ahead and on each side of the speaker. The manuscript, which rolls through from bottom to top as the speaker reads, is invisible to the audience. The prompter thus lets the speaker look up toward the audience, giving the impression of eye contact while still reading his manuscript. But as you know from the style section of this book, the audience can tell when someone is really trying to connect with them. Simply moving your head from side to side as you look from one prompter to the other may give the illusion of eye contact, but none of the benefits of the reality; you'll sound flat and look flat, and the audience won't feel talked to. On the other hand, if you've rehearsed a manuscript well enough to deliver it with a lot of eye contact and genuine reaching out, you'll be much more effective than someone who is unrehearsed but uses a prompter.

Speech prompters and video screens are becoming more a part of business life as meetings get larger and use more complicated audiovisual support and technology. Their increasing use points to the need for more rehearsal time rather than a chance to avoid it. One reason is that the people who are rolling the manuscript through the prompter need time to become familiar with the speaker's pace.

Recently the president of a major corporation was announcing a new advertising campaign to an audience of between three and four thousand people. His close-up image was being projected on a large video screen behind him, and a TelePrompTer in front of the camera lens contained his notes. He had rehearsed and was well prepared, so he was able to reach out and connect with the audience. I felt his reaching out was due more to his rehearsal and preparation than to the mechanical prompter, because the size of his projected image would have revealed any nervousness or discomfort affecting his delivery.

On one occasion I watched an executive use a prompter to deliver a speech he had given several times before. The practice apparently made him overconfident, because this time he left his manuscript backstage. He had placed all his trust in the technology, and halfway through his speech the prompter broke down. He was unable to fake it for more than a few minutes, and someone finally had to run backstage to get his script. It's one thing to have technology support you, but this was a graphic demonstration of the need to recognize its limits and to realize that there is no substitute for thorough preparation, rehearsal, and attention to detail.

LARGE MEETINGS

They don't always include speech prompters or project speakers on video screens, but large meetings are a part of business life today. Annual sales meetings or conventions, important awards ceremonies, educational conferences, and meetings of national interest groups, associations, clubs, or fraternal orders are on practically every business person's calendar. Many companies, when they bring large groups of their people together, put on real extravaganzas. They feature slick motivational films, multi-screen slide-tape shows, and even live orchestras. When something as important as the announcement of a new marketing campaign is scheduled, these meetings can take on the fully scripted and choreographed aspects of a Broadway show. Films, slides, and music may be used to motivate the audience and provide feelings of excitement and *esprit de corps* at many large meetings. Computer technology in graphics and projection methods can produce multimedia presentations that are dazzling kaleidoscopes of light and sound. These carefully orchestrated gatherings, which can last from one to several days, are usually produced by professionals. Some companies have their own meeting production departments, but a number of independent consultants also are in the business of arranging and producing meetings.

As a business speaker, the important thing for you to remember about large meetings is that your role remains vital despite the involvement of professional producers. The glamour of the "production numbers" should never displace your importance as an individual speaker. Although meeting producers are sometimes inclined to pay more attention to the razzmatazz, good speakers can compete successfully.

I watched an executive rehearse his speech, which was on a

prompter, on the eve of a large meeting. He was working with the meeting producer, and he read his speech off the prompter straight through, without errors. The producer walked up to him afterward offering congratulations. "You were terrific, just fine," he said. "That's it."

The speaker turned to me and said, "What do you think?"

And I said, "I think you need more rehearsal."

The meeting producer was concerned with the films and the visuals, and because the speaker managed to get through without stumbling, he was satisfied. But the speaker and I were looking for a lot of reaching out and audience contact, which meant he had to feel comfortable with the technology around him, and the person rolling the manuscript through the prompter had to be comfortable with his pace. Speakers must be willing to insist on taking their proper place in a large meeting and not let visually oriented producers slough off their needs in favor of the technology.

Because of the production needs of large meetings, you may be asked months in advance to provide a script or an outline of a speech or presentation. Your first reaction may be to say, "Why do I have to think about it now? I don't have the slightest idea of what I want to say." But a lot of the components of that meeting can depend on what you are going to say. If you expect the producers to work with you, you have to reciprocate. Being realistic about the advance timing and meshing your schedule with the meeting planning will help assure you a more effective presentation.

Preparation and practice are the ways to hold your own amid the sound and lights of large meetings. The human touch that comes from individuals communicating with other individuals is the most important part of any meeting. Good speakers are remembered.

It is also helpful to remember that a large business meeting or convention, though it is a special business situation in itself, is made up of other meetings that are smaller and more manageable. There are likely to be manuscript speeches, classroom-size seminars and roundtables, and a variety of audiovisual presentations. Each of these is a component of the whole. Looked at individually, they are simply forums in which to apply the basic lessons of effective communication.

TELEVISION: COMMUNICATION BY VIDEO

Like the increasingly sophisticated large meetings that business speakers are likely to encounter, television has become so common in our business and personal lives that every speaker should know how to communicate by way of this powerful medium.

Television long ago emerged from the living room to become a familiar part of the business world. I think most executives approach television defensively—that is, they want to learn its ins and outs primarily to avoid embarrassment in on-camera interviews. But the business person's need to know more about television stems as much from its potential as a positive tool for business communication as from its ability to discomfit and embarrass.

The media encounter is certainly one reason why business people should learn about television, and I'll be discussing media encounters elsewhere in this section. But the uses of television go far beyond the occasional interview, be it friendly or hostile. You may be making a training film or tape for your company. You may be recording a greeting to new employees for a meeting you can't attend in person. Your company may be doing more teleconferencing to save travel money. For its business applications as well as interviews, panel discussions, and the like, there are things you can learn about video that will place you in a position to use this potent tool effectively. If you can communicate well via television, your ability to reach and touch people, to make things happen, is dramatically extended.

What is it about television that puts us off, that seems to increase the feeling of nervousness we get in other speaking situations? The mechanics of the medium are foreign to most of us; like large, heavily produced meetings, television makes us feel less in control than we are in situations not so thoroughly dictated by sophisticated technology. When we're not in control, we feel we can't be as effective.

We also think we somehow have to be different for TV. We are so used to seeing other people's warts exposed on the screen that we think television requires us to be perfect. Perfection is not only an intimidating goal, it's an impossible one.

What scares people the most about video, however, is the same thing that provides the medium with its unique, special magic: the intimacy of the close-up. The title of CBS anchorman Dan Rather's book, *The Camera Never Blinks,* describes the frightening quality of television. The camera zooms in for a close shot, and suddenly we see people in a way that we never see them in real life. When you are looking at a full-face shot of a newscaster, or a business person being interviewed, you see that person as closely as if the two of you were kissing. When you watch yourself in a shot like that, the magnification of the camera is so great that you see things about yourself that you don't normally see, things that raise questions: "That freckle on my nose . . . was it there this morning when I was brushing my teeth?" And those questions can grow naturally into fears: "Is my hair really that thin? Do I look that pale?" Unlike your gaze into the mirror as you brush your teeth and comb your hair, the camera is an unbiased, objective—unblinking—viewer. It doesn't allow us the view of reality that we prefer.

But if the close-up isn't used, television isn't nearly as interesting; the intimacy of a single, animated face is one of the things that makes video such a wonderful medium. It brings us much closer to the person and makes us feel as if we're seeing more of him, and that's what makes us want to watch it.

What does this all mean for you, the businessman or businesswoman who must deal with this wonderful, terrifying medium? Throughout this book, you've learned that effective speaking is a matter of making choices that work for you and project the best of what you are. You have to know what you want to happen and focus on conveying your message and connecting with your audience.

The rules for effectiveness are the same for television as for any other speaking situation. People who apply their own energy, demonstrate an awareness of the audience, and are prepared to say what they have to say with authority can communicate as well on television as any media professional.

Getting Familiar with Television

When you know you're going to be on television, whether you'll be talking to an interviewer or just to a camera as in a taped message to colleagues or employees, you should take some time to familiarize yourself with the mechanics of the medium. Local television stations offer tours that take visitors through and show them the whole process. Many of them will probably do this for you privately, and even let you sit in the back of the studio while the local news is being aired.

No matter how you choose to go about it, you should treat this familiarization with the TV studio as part of your job. It's as basic as locating the hand and foot controls in an automobile and learning traffic signals before you learn to drive. If you approach it as a job-related project, you'll quickly learn that an appearance on television is not a trip into the mysterious unknown.

The action in a television studio takes place in a small circle of light. This is the set, or the area where the interview is being conducted. Activities outside that circle of light, while they may be interesting and will certainly be distracting, should not concern you. People will be dragging cables around, moving cameras from side to side, even talking to each other. Even the set will be distracting; the expensive-looking anchor desk you see on the screen is hammered together out of plywood, and the plush carpet that looks so luxurious on the air is usually unbound, ragged at the edges, and dotted with cigarette burns and wads of chewing gum. It's good for you to notice all this, because it helps keep the medium of television in perspective.

When a camera crew comes to your office for an interview, the mechanics are much the same. There's no question that it's hard to concentrate when even one or two uninterested strangers, the technicians, are standing around listening to you and an interviewer talk to each other. But television has to carry a lot of baggage around with it. While you're being interviewed, light stands seem to teeter in every corner of your office, threatening to fall or be kicked over onto your potted plants. The camera tripod digs into your carpet. There are cables everywhere. Sometimes the power used by the bright TV lights will blow the fuses in your office. The camera operator will shove his way behind your desk to get a reverse, or cutaway, shot of the interviewer; the lighting technician is going to leaf through the books in your bookshelf; the sound man may yawn a lot. No wonder you're distracted.

Once you've seen all this, forget it. All that matters is the way you relate to the interviewer. Everything else that's going on has to do with the technical requirements for getting this brief moment of television on the air. This is somebody else's concern and you don't need to worry about it. Concentrate on delivering your message.

"Where Do I Look?"

When you're being interviewed, the message you're delivering is to the interviewer. When you're alone with the camera, your message is to the people who will view you through its lens. Almost all of your media appearances will involve exchanges with another person or other people, as in a panel discussion. Focus your attention on the people who are there, to whom you are talking. Don't worry about the camera. That's the job of the production crew. Even though you know that from a business standpoint you are there to sell your point of view to the audience at home, you do that best by coming across in a committed, sensitive way to the people in the studio. The only way you can show your commitment and sensitivity is to the live human beings who are there interacting with you and with whom you must establish common ground and rapport. If you get an exciting exchange going with the interviewer, the feeling of excitement is passed on, vicariously, to the viewer.

Nothing can make you look more foolish than a shot that finds you looking at the wrong camera. It looks to the audience at home as if you're ignoring the human beings there with you and talking to the air. Don't try to beat the professionals at their own game. It's just too dangerous for a television amateur—which is what most business people are no matter how much time they spend being interviewed—to try to outguess the camera by following the little red monitor light around.

As a former television interviewer, I can say that what always made an interview interesting was the direct interaction between the people talking. This was just as true in a "friendly" interview as in one in which I was more aggressive. And as an interviewee, I have found that the more I focus on establishing that relationship and conveying my message to that questioner, not to the camera, the more effective I was.

When there is no interviewer or no panel members, as when you are making a promotional tape, delivering remarks welcoming people to a convention or meeting that you can't attend, or doing a training tape of some kind, the only thing that you can do is to talk to the camera.

Some people say that you have to fall in love with the camera. That's not an easy image for business people to relate to, and I'm not so sure it's accurate, anyway. What you can do instead is "replace" the camera in your mind's eye with one person, someone who is likely to be in your audience. Envisioning your viewer as you talk to the camera is a good way of forgetting the notion that you're talking to a machine.

When I was the host of a children's show on network television in Canada, I opened the show by talking directly to the camera. I found it helped to visualize a young niece of mine, and every word that I said was to her. By talking to that child I think I came across in a direct and intimate way to the children who were watching. A local television anchorman once told me that he tried to envision a gray-haired grandmother, rocking and knitting, with a cat in her lap. And the host of a public affairs talk show says that when he talks to the camera, he tries to see a crusty former governor on the other side of the lens.

When I prepare tapes for workshops at Speakeasy that I can't attend, I find a subtle difference in tone when I haven't spent enough time visualizing the audience in my mind. Without being able to "see" whom I'm talking to, I feel a slight lack of the energy and awareness that makes my connection with the audience more real. Without that energy and awareness, my message is less effective. Remember your audience analysis. Since you've learned something about your listeners in planning your content, you should have a picture of them and reflect that awareness in your style.

None of this means that you have to be an actor to be effective when you talk to the camera. You are only placing yourself in a real situation as much as you can by visualizing one person to talk to instead of a machine. Imagining that you are talking to someone rather than something also makes it easier to forget the strangers in the room.

Conveying Authority on Television

By now everybody knows television is not a miracle medium whose best practitioners all are perfect. Knowing that being effective doesn't mean being perfect is the first step toward being in control, which is in turn the first step in projecting authority.

Acknowledging the presence of TV's technological requirements and the occasional problems they create is one effective cure for the feeling that you have to be perfect for television. If you flub a line in real life, in a personal conversation, or in a speech or presentation, you don't have the chance to go back, erase it, and start over. In an interview, you would correct a mistake after the fact, just as you would in any conversation. When you're making a videotape, there's nothing to prohibit letting a minor human error stand alongside your correction.

I saw one chief executive muff a line during a videotaping session for which he'd had little time to rehearse. Instead of halting the proceedings to correct his error, he shrugged, smiled, and said to the camera, "Well, that's what happens when they give you these things to read at the last minute." It was really the moment when his speech came alive. He had said, in effect, "Hey, I'm not perfect." And he had admitted what everybody watching would know anyway—that he was in a situation dictated by technological considerations. But instead of being the victim of the mechanical circumstances, he took control of them and established his authority. He went ahead with his message, as if to say that the mechanics were not important enough to make him interrupt what he was giving to his audience.

It takes a strong, confident speaker to make that kind of admission. But one who does it relates better to his audience because he strips away the mechanical barriers that separate them. You gain control and show authority on television as you do in any speaking situation, but you should also seek a comfortable relationship with its mechanical aspects so you can assure that they won't interfere with communication between you and your audience.

Teleconferencing

Teleconferencing is basically a conference call with video. Advances in communications technology are bringing its costs within reach of more businesses, so teleconferencing is becoming a cost-conscious alternative to business travel. While communicating via a video screen is no substitute for the warmth of a handshake, teleconferencing does permit the display of elaborate graphics and, in some cases, the exchange of hard copies between conference sites. For many business needs, it's the next best thing to being there.

A teleconference with two-way video is much like the live exchanges you see between a television anchor and a reporter in the field. If you've seen ABC-TV's *Nightline*, with Ted Koppel in Washington conducting live interviews with newsmakers in TV studios around the country, you have some idea of the effect. The conversation flows almost as smoothly as if you were face-to-face, but while you still have audience awareness, you can't notice or respond quite as quickly to audience reaction.

To appear natural during a teleconference, just look at the person you're talking to. Of course, this means you'll be looking and talking to a face on the screen, but it will help you relax and make your voice more conversational. Talking directly to the camera can be effective, but at a teleconference, with other people in the room who are all going to be looking at the screen, looking anywhere else when you speak will probably distract you too much from the message you want to deliver.

Avoid the urge to shout; speak in a normal conversational tone even though you may not know the exact location of the microphone or microphones. Use the lessons you learned for projecting an effective spoken image—it will probably be easier for you to be heard at the other end of a teleconference hookup than if you were speaking to a large audience in a ballroom.

Camera operators at a teleconference can be expected to seek the same kind of intimacy in their shots as any television camera person. Wide-angle shots make the interchange less satisfying and make audience reaction less visible to people at the other end. If your audience awareness is blocked in this way, don't hesitate to say so, and if the camera can't move to a close-up, consider asking the people at the other end to be more specific in their reactions than they might be if you were in the room together.

Although a teleconference is usually less expensive than a face-to-face meeting, it's still not cheap. Time on the communications satellite or long-line hookup is costly, and it's billed in increments of minutes or half hours. You should be prepared at any business meeting, but the costs of teleconferencing make solid advance preparation doubly important. Rehearse and structure what you're going to say, and remember that the meter's running.

The teleconference is no different from any other speaking situation in that all you can control in the situation is yourself. So you should try to speak with authority, listen with real involvement, and put yourself physically forward all the time to keep the energy level high and flowing toward your audience, even though they're many miles away.

Two Tips for Television

No discussion of speaking on television would be complete without mentioning the requirements of dressing for the camera, and moving in a way that lets you express energy and be comfortable without being distracting.

If you watch much television, you probably have a pretty good idea of what kinds of clothes work best. Solid colors and muted stripes are better than busy patterns. Avoid shiny fabrics that can reflect the glare of the lights. You're generally better off avoiding black, white, and red and sticking instead to the blues, grays, and beiges of conventional business attire. Keep your hair style simple. Wear a minimum of jewelry, especially the dangly, jangly kind that might make noise, catch the lights, or otherwise draw attention to itself.

A balanced, settled posture is the best base from which to speak for television, as it is for other speaking situations. Any movement should be the result of your trying to convey a message. People seated for a television interview often release their nervousness by swiveling furiously in their chairs. This, or any other motion that doesn't stem directly from the expression of your message, can be extremely distracting on camera. Sit quietly when you are not speaking.

PITCHING A CLIENT

More and more businesses and professions today depend upon pitches or presentations to bring in new business. Many investment specialists, advertising agencies, and accounting, public relations, marketing research, engineering, and architectural firms, to name a few, employ people who do nothing but pitch potential clients. They usually hire a professional to write a basic pitch, which is accompanied by a slide presentation. The danger is that the presentation may become so slick and "canned" that audience interaction, which is so important to establishing a relationship with a client, is lost.

I worked with a firm of certified public accountants on improving their presentations, but they didn't quite buy my message about not using too many slides or trying to be too slick. The accounting firm went on to make a professional presentation to a medical practice group, but didn't get the job. The managing partner of the accounting firm asked one of the medical group's board members why. "Your presentation was professional, and the slides were terrific," he replied, "but we never got to know the people who were going to be handling our money."

A lot of people in sales and marketing are looking for formulas to give their presentations more "oomph." A young man in a recent seminar, for example, had a five-step approach that he used every time he made a sales presentation. But formulas don't usually allow for differences between one audience and another.

If your presentations say the same thing to every client, they can't consider or respond to the needs of the audience. To take in the needs of the audience, you have to be a little less slick and polished and allow for audience interaction. Like the attorney who found out about Speakeasy before he told me about his firm, you should not just tell potential clients about yourself. You should find out what your clients need and respond to their needs in each presentation, following the same thoughtful, creative process that I recommended for your content planning.

QUESTIONS AND ANSWERS

The question-and-answer sessions that follow many presentations can be almost like media encounters, and are a good introduction to them. Question-and-answer sessions can be lively and stimulating. They give the speaker the opportunity to deal directly with the audience. They are often the time when the speaker is most real, because there is no script or outline to follow. And when someone asks you a question, you know he wants your information. I'm always amazed at the dramatic drop in the tension level when speakers move from their planned remarks into the questions and answers. When the first question comes, the speaker suddenly realizes that people are listening and interested in what he has to say.

Active listening is the best approach to a question-and-answer session. Speakers often hear only the first words of a question and then launch immediately into an answer. They don't pause long enough to think about what the question really means. Active listening is a way to take in the whole meaning from the questioner —his words, the sound of his voice, and his body language.

In situations other than media encounters, it sometimes can be difficult to get a question-and-answer period going. I have found that instead of asking "Do you have any questions?" it's better to state the question positively: "What are your questions? What else would you like to know?" Pause is part of successfully beginning a question-and-answer session, because the first question often comes from the person who is most uncomfortable with the silence. Not long ago, in Chicago, I opened a seminar by asking, "What are your expectations for our meeting today?" My audience hadn't expected to be put in the spotlight right away, and they were slow to speak up. But I waited, and someone finally spoke. The authority of the pause can draw out a reluctant questioner.

If the pause becomes awkward as you wait for a question, there are several ways to gently force the issue. You can ask the first question yourself, introducing it with some remark like "A question I'm often asked is . . ." or "An audience like yourselves, with an interest in marketing, would probably want to know how a marketing survey is conducted.''

If you know an individual member of the audience, you can pick him out and ask for a question directly. You should be careful about pushing too hard, however; your listeners usually didn't come expecting to be dragged into the spotlight, and they have a right to resist it.

Just asking for questions usually isn't enough to get the audience to respond; you have to show by your style throughout your presentation that you really do want to get questions. By reaching out, you let your audience know you are interested in what's on their minds and in answering their questions.

What should you do when people interrupt your presentation to ask questions? Your reaction should be determined by your objective. You certainly have the right to ask the audience to hold their questions until the end. If you're planning later in the presentation to cover the point you're being asked about, you can ask the listener to bear with you until the point's explained, and then ask a question if he needs more information. You, the speaker, should dictate the flow of the presentation and the timing of questions and answers.

On the other hand, you should be prepared to be flexible. A really good, pertinent question can sometimes lead you to explore interesting new territory with your audience, and when you can, you should be flexible enough to shift gears to follow an interesting question. Even if you have to throw away part of your presentation, you may find you can reach your objective in another way if audience interest is strong enough. Changing horses in midstream to get to your objective is simply taking your audience as they are, and dealing with reality.

MEDIA ENCOUNTERS

You won't have to struggle to draw out questions during encounters with the media. Just as in any presentation, to make something happen in an interview with a television, radio, or newspaper reporter you have to be certain of your objective. What happens isn't totally up to the reporter, and what you want to happen can determine how you choose to answer certain questions. So your approach to a media encounter should start with organizing your content according to your analysis of the situation and audience.

Nor is a media encounter different from any other speaking situation in that you need to be prepared. Rehearsal, in which you have someone ask you the tough questions, then becomes a must. Don't rehearse with the idea of memorizing the answers to all the questions you anticipate. Rehearse to get comfortable with the really tough questions that may bring out your hidden objectives. No matter how well you think you know the answers, how you feel about the subject, and what your unstated objectives are, until someone really presses you, you won't know what you're comfortable with and what you're not.

I was preparing an executive for a stockholders' meeting which was to be covered by the media and at which a major stockholder was expected to mount a takeover bid. Every time the executive was asked about the takeover bid he gave a weak, wishy-washy answer. At the end of the rehearsal session the executive wanted to know how his style had been. "Your style was fine," I answered. "The question is, what was your answer on the subject of a takeover? You've been waffling, and right now you don't know what it is you want to happen. Before you go into that meeting you have to make a fundamental decision about what you want to happen, and neither I nor your public relations people can do that for you." Rehearsal forces you to come to grips with where you are with the content. Dealing with the hard questions beforehand also can help you arrive at substantive answers. If you don't beat around the bush during an interview, you'll be more likely to avoid escalating an encounter into a confrontation.

The lessons contained in the style section of this book will help you avoid confrontations; authority and energy give your answers the credibility they deserve, and audience awareness keeps you from antagonizing reporters.

Keeping Media Encounters from Becoming Confrontations

Media encounters become confrontations because when somebody pushes, the natural reaction is to push back. The pushing starts when we give wishy-washy answers to a reporter's questions, when we don't exhibit the authority, energy, and audience awareness of an effective spoken image, and when we don't know what it is we want to say. Reporters and interviewers, like most of us, meet resistance with resistance.

Executives are used to being in charge. But when the tables are turned and the control is elsewhere, powerful executives often see themselves in a win-lose situation in which their first reaction is to try to regain control. The results are often just the opposite of what they want.

Speakeasy worked with one industrial company that sought advice on media confrontation. The company wanted to counter a well-publicized series of government charges that it had failed to comply with environmental regulations. In the "aggressive reporter versus stonewalling executive" role-playing that is a feature of many media confrontation courses, I played the reporter firing hard questions at the company president. I would bark a question into the hand-held mike and then shove it under the president's nose, then yank it back again to ask another question before he had a chance to answer. He became enraged. He just couldn't believe he was not going to have control over the microphone. This typical situation is remarkably frustrating for anyone who is used to dominating his surroundings, and that's why media interviews can be so difficult for many top executives.

Executives involved in provocative media encounters should realize that they can control their content, but not the mechanics of the situation.

I have seen some practiced politicians, who know when the camera is probably on a head-and-shoulders shot in a stand-up interview, gently grasp the microphone and hold on to it while they're giving their answer. They usually got away with it because they looked almost like commentators themselves. But instead of fighting for physical control of the microphone, it's better to say, "I'd like to answer your questions if you'd just give me the chance." Such an answer, combined with a low tension level and relaxed voice tone, can avoid heightening the atmosphere of confrontation. It certainly serves to point out the reporter's unfairness in not allowing the person being interviewed to answer.

When you're pushed, pushing back is rarely your best response in a confrontation situation. I was working once with a political candidate who had made the usual number of mistakes and misjudgments that could be magnified in the heat of the campaign. A debate among several candidates was coming up, and the man with whom I was working wanted to rehearse his responses to questions. He was concerned that his answers to reporters not give these things more than the minor status they deserved. I asked him some straight but tough questions. He was direct with his answers and felt satisfied with his performance. But as we kept going, I began asking questions in a harder, pushy way. As my questions got more and more aggressive, his answers too became hostile and aggressive. The more I pushed, the more he came across like the person he wanted to avoid being seen as—someone whose defensiveness made it seem as if he had something to hide.

The same techniques that can work to reduce resistance in other speaking situations apply in media encounters. I was once interviewed by a TV reporter who was hyped-up and totally self-absorbed before the live interview. On the set, she threw me a question and immediately looked down at her script. Then she busied herself with some quick primping before the camera came back to her. My immediate reaction was to rush into what I had to say and get it on the record quickly, but I decided instead to exhale, slow down, and talk to the reporter. I made up my mind that I could set the atmosphere, and as I continued to talk to her she turned toward me and became more attentive. Once she focused on me, the interview went much better. It's preferable to get out less information that works than to spout out everything you want to say in an atmosphere that doesn't allow you to be effective.

If you don't know the answer to a question, don't be afraid to say so. A simple "I don't know" is a better response than a "nonanswer" in which your lack of knowledge becomes clear in any case. Admitting that you don't know can also save you from creating new questions or misunderstandings. A vague, muddy answer that tries to make it look as if you know something you don't promotes misunderstandings. It may be hard to confess that you don't know all the facts or details, but honesty removes the possibility that you'll give misleading or wrong information. And if it's all that important, as when a reporter is working on a deadline story, you can always offer to get back to her with an answer. You can even have associates pursue the information as the interview continues.

Sometimes, of course, you may not want to answer a reporter's question in an interview. Reasons for this could include pending legal action, trade secrets, and any of a host of other factors involving sensitive business operations. Personnel matters, for example, usually aren't talked about publicly in most organizations. Or you may have other good reasons for not wanting to answer a question. Your company may have its own carefully orchestrated timetable for releasing information about new board members or a new product it plans to market, for example. Again, stating your case is usually the best way to handle this—"I can't answer because we're in court on that issue," or "I prefer not to say right now. We have a news conference scheduled on that matter in two days." These may not be the answers the reporter would like to have, but he understands them. They make it clear where you stand, and why you're not giving him the real answer. This is a part of the everyday world of media encounters.

Getting Your Answers Out

As in any speaking situation, you want to make something happen in a media interview. You have a message just as in any presentation, points you want to make and information you want to get across. But sometimes the questions don't allow you to make your points. If the line of questioning doesn't give you an opportunity to give information you think is important, don't hesitate to turn the interview to your agenda. You can usually do this inoffensively by saying something like "That's an area we haven't explored, but we've developed information in another area that I think you would find interesting." This tactic will sometimes help a reporter who is struggling to get a handle on a difficult interview. And, of course, it will certainly work to your advantage, up to a point.

Delivering your own message is a tactic to be used sparingly. If you overuse it, if you never answer the reporter's questions, it becomes quite obvious in a very short time. You exhibit a lack of audience awareness when you continue to say, in effect, "Well, I hear that, but I'm ignoring it, and I'm going to say what I want." People have every right to get irritated in such a case, and you're often better off just saying that you can't or won't answer the question. And don't make the mistake of thinking that you can avoid discussion of a sensitive area if that's what you've agreed to be interviewed about.

When Not to Say Anything

Don't feel compelled to fill silences. This is one of the surest ways of blurting out information that you don't want to relate. Suppose a reporter has asked you a question in an interview, and you've answered it, or at least you've said as much as you want to say. But instead of asking you another question when you've finished, the reporter waits. The silence grows. It's as if he knows you've got more to say, and he's waiting for you to say it. He keeps waiting. Finally, you're desperate to end the silence, and out tumbles the very thing you didn't want to say. This, of course, is the one thing that will make the news, because instead of thinking about what you really want to say, you're thinking about filling that awkward silence.

This happened in a television interview with the head of Atlanta's convention bureau at a time several years ago when the city was suffering image problems—and a potential loss of convention business—because of the widely publicized murder of a conventioneer. The executive felt he'd handled the interview well until he saw the story on network television. The story carried only the very end of his interview, when he had become bothered by the silence and blurted out, "If there is one more murder of a conventioneer in this city, we're flat out of business." It's the reporter's job to fill the silence; let him worry about it. Push back your social instinct to keep the conversation going. Give your answer, and then keep quiet until you answer the next question.

Avoid "Insiders' " Language

I've already mentioned the importance of talking in clear, direct language that people can understand. This is good advice in any speaking situation, but it's especially important in media encounters, when the people you actually are talking to are the general public through the television screen, radio speaker, or newspaper. Remember that while you are familiar with the jargon of your industry, most people aren't. Translate for them. Speak in terms that "break the code" and let the public know in everyday language what your message is. Discard the initials and acronyms that are part of your office talk, and try to think how you would like to have things described if you were an industry outsider. Clarity of language, just as in the manuscript speech that you try to write in short sentences and direct language, is the essence of effective communication in any situation.

SPEAKING TO FOREIGN AUDIENCES

Avoiding the use of jargon helps you relate better to any audience, but you should pay special attention to your language when speaking to foreign audiences. Being sensitive to the needs of a foreign audience doesn't mean you have to imitate them. There are those people who believe that they have to be different, that they have to slow down their speech and mirror the dominant style of that country in their body language and mannerisms. The Japanese, for example, are thought of as reserved and less flamboyant, so some people speaking to Japanese audiences tend to suppress their own energy in order to come across in a low-key way. Another example, again a generalization, is the use of excessive gestures while speaking to an Italian audience.

Not only does this mean you've fallen victim to national stereotypes, which are usually inappropriate, it's not effective in any event. I believe that when you're dealing with a foreign-language audience, much of the feeling that they get from you will come from your body language and the sound of your voice. And I think this is true if they speak your language as a second language, or if they don't speak it at all and it's being interpreted. If your delivery isn't open and spontaneous and reaching out, then they're not going to get a real natural flavor of you.

I worked with employees of a Mexican division of an international company to help them prepare manuscript speeches for delivery at a large meeting of the division. Spanish was their first language and the language in which they would be giving their speeches. Helped by an interpreter, who provided line-by-line Spanish-to-English translations, I worked with the same concepts I use with English-speaking students at Speakeasy—authority, energy, sensitivity to the audience, and reaching out. The results were exactly the same with people who speak a different language as with those who speak English. Those who had authority and energy, those who opened their mouths and articulated, who really worked at seeing their audience, were the more interesting speakers. At the meeting where they gave their speeches, I could tell from the reaction of the audience around me who was the most effective.

Another executive I've worked with speaks frequently to international audiences in a lot of different countries. Charles finds that it's impossible to take on the personality and style of every different country that he's in, and that trying to learn bits and pieces of all the different languages is a losing proposition. All he can do, he feels, is to work with the best interpreters available and be as relaxed and open with his own style as possible. This became an issue for Charles when he was speaking in a country in which a great deal of protocol was expected from all the speakers. They were supposed to greet the honored guests elaborately and at great length, and to name all the politicians in the audience with effusive praise. Charles simply got up and said, "Good morning," then went ahead with his talk. To recite the list of names he'd been given would have ruined the timetable for his talk and the rest of the meeting, too, so by breaking tradition he was really exhibiting audience awareness. When your analysis of the situation leads you to make a choice, it doesn't always have to be business as usual. You must be secure enough with yourself to choose a different way of doing things.

I recently worked with a group of executives for a large international corporation. Prior to the meeting for which I was helping them prepare, they all had been speaking in different countries. There was also a large foreign contingent expected at the meeting. After hearing them rehearse, I felt they lacked energy, mainly because they were speaking at an artificially slow pace. I suggested they speak at a more natural pace, but at first they protested. They said, "Improvements in style are fine. But we're going to be interpreted, and so we will all have to speak very slowly." Their previous appearances before non-English-speaking audiences had begun to make them into stiff robots. Their company used top-notch interpreters who were quite capable of keeping up with the natural pace of speaking. But the speakers, somewhere along the way, had developed the idea that they had to be very slow and stiff in order to be understood. They were amazed, and somewhat relieved, to learn they could act more naturally when speaking.

It is simply impossible to be a different person for every audience. It will work against your style if you try to "change colors" like a chameleon. Your best approach to any audience is the approach and style you know best, and that is your own.

Obviously you have to be sensitive with foreign audiences to the way you use slang or colloquialisms. Some expressions that are perfectly normal to us have negative connotations when they are translated or interpreted into other languages. Use a thorough audience analysis; make sure in assessing your foreign audience that your speech or presentation does not contain expressions that are innocent or humorous to you, but offensive to your audience.

EVERY BUSINESS SITUATION IS SPECIAL

Every "special" business situation we've talked about in this section isn't really special at all. You could encounter any of them on virtually any business day. Sure, you won't be making a major speech to a Spanish, French, or Japanese audience every week. But suppose you're asked to show an overseas tour group through your home office, or attend a reception for your city's consular corps. Media encounters are more and more an everyday occurrence. You may be the person tapped by your company to give a manuscript speech to a local civic club, a club which always asks speakers to include a question-and-answer session. And teleconferencing will become as popular a business tool as today's routine conference call.

There are firms today that specialize in each of these activities. There are companies that put on big, extravaganza-style meetings. There are companies that help you design sales meetings. There are companies that will help you with what they call media confrontation. There are companies that say they have the only way to write a manuscript speech.

It probably won't surprise you, having gone through this book and this section, when I emphasize again that these situations are different only in their particular mechanics. When you become familiar with the mechanics, and when you've learned the basic lessons of objective and message, and of putting authority, energy, and audience awareness into your content and style, you should be able to handle these so-called special business situations effectively.

I believe effective speakers are no different whether they are on television, before an audience, in direct conversation, or in any number of other speaking situations. This section is included in this book not because "special" situations require you to be different, but because they are part of the world in which business people live and work. They are important, but they're not different in that they require different rules. With proper preparation and effective delivery, you the speaker can make choices that will get the results you want in any situation.

PART III

INTERVIEWS WITH THE NATURALS

THE NATURALS I described at the beginning of this book are the speakers who can make any audience sit up and listen and somehow understand what the speaker expects of them. In the following section are interviews with a half-dozen top business and professional leaders whom I consider among the naturals. Although their personalities are unique, they all are able to use a combination of content and style to make something happen, to reach out and connect with their audiences.

The popular view of these naturals is that they are somehow exempt from the steps most of us have to go through to become better speakers, that they're among a special few who can get up and just start talking. So it should be encouraging to see, as they make clear in these interviews, that despite their experience and high positions, these naturals continue to believe that good speaking is worth the effort. Although they emphasize different areas of their speaking—some tended to talk more about content organization, others about style—they all have worked hard to develop approaches to speaking that work for them. Some of them took lessons, or studied speech or debate. All have focused on speaking in some way because of experiences that forced them to speak and to develop themselves as speakers.

The interviews show that good speaking doesn't just happen, not for anyone. You have to work at it. Behind every natural are basics that can help anyone become a better speaker. These interviews bring us back to the point I began with—that naturals are made, not born.

Don Keough

DON KEOUGH is president of the Coca-Cola Company and has served as Coke's senior executive vice-president, president of Coca-Cola U.S.A. and president of the company's Americas Group. A native Iowan, Keough was educated at Creighton University. He is a board member of major American business and educational institutions, including IBM and the University of Notre Dame, and his reputation as a speaker is well known in business and education circles. I interviewed him in his spacious office on the twenty-fifth floor of the Coca-Cola Tower in Atlanta.

S.L. Let's discuss the importance of speaking to a business career and to yours specifically.

D.K. Well, I never think in terms of speaking, because that's sort of a one-sided adventure. But I've always been fascinated by the thought that one human animal is able to communicate with another in a unique and special way. The ability to communicate with the spoken word separates man from all other animals. The ability to formulate and share ideas—that's what gives man his dignity. It is a vital part of being a full, complete, and total human being.

S.L. It's rare for an article to be written about you and not have it mentioned that you're a good speaker. You've been called the Johnny Carson of the corporate world. How do you feel about that?

D.K. I'm always a little concerned about that, because it really talks about an art form. I'm really a lot more interested in the substance. I sort of think of a Shakespearean actor who develops every hand move, and every stance and posture, and worries about his resonance and so on, without thinking about what Shakespeare wrote. The fascinating part was what Shakespeare had to say. So when somebody says, "He's a good speaker," if it means that he has developed all the techniques and skills and maybe has some natural voice qualities, if that's the bottom line, it isn't a heck of a lot.

S.L. You're not saying that an effective style takes away from the substance?

D.K. No, not at all. But first you have to talk about the substance. Then, if you believe what you're communicating is important, the delivery system that communicates that idea also has to be important.

S.L. I'd like to talk a little bit about the way you prepare for speaking situations. You spoke a couple of years ago at a meeting of bottlers that was a challenge for both you and the company.

D.K. It was the first time in a decade that the company had met with all of the bottler community in the United States. Getting ready for it was terribly important. There was no room for niceties. There was only room for truth. I guess there were three or four thousand people there, and each one brought his own perceptions of us. There was a fundamental difference of opinion with many, but even if we disagree, we're family. Some came believing that we would give them the old pep-rally experience with a lot of hoopla and balloons; some came out of curiosity; some came with a certain degree of animosity.

I spent probably two or three months just thinking about the audience, the people who were going to be there and the mental baggage they were bringing with them. I concluded that they weren't going to have a chance to say what was on their minds, so somebody had to say it for them. I decided I would. And so I began to construct in my mind a kind of viewpoint that had an element of the old Greek teaching style of Socrates or Thomas Aquinas, where you get all of the objections out on the table before you make your point. Otherwise I wouldn't develop the credibility for myself or the rest of the meeting, and we couldn't really get down to talking about our future relationship.

S.L. Do you always spend that much time thinking about the audience?

D.K. Always. And anybody who tells you that making a speech is an easy exercise is kidding themselves. When you're preparing for a speech, a tough presentation, or a negotiating session, if you're going to do it well you have to think a lot about it, and the people who are going to be there, and about what you really want to say. You can't do that by sitting down and writing notes on a piece of paper five minutes before you go in.

S.L. Did you work with a speech writer on this speech?

D.K. Once I determined the approach I wanted to take, the issue became "What were [the bottlers'] perceptions?" I brought in a speechwriter with whom I had worked before on speeches I considered significant. I walked through some of the perceptions I had sensed, and he went out to see if they were accurate and valid. In that first interview, I pretty well laid the speech out on the table and then he researched it and polished it. He then brought me back a proposed draft. This was probably three months before the speech.

Now, I carried that document with me everywhere I went for those three months, and what I ended up with probably had changes taking place in it an hour before I went to the podium. I probably read it aloud in airplanes, hotel rooms, my home, maybe fifty times, in order to hear myself and the flow of the speech and whether what I was saying was as precise, as polished, and as accurate as I could possibly make it.

When I stood at the podium, I felt totally comfortable that I had done everything I could do to try to communicate with a terribly important group of people, and that in preparing for that speech I had cared for them.

S.L. Do you always know that you have successfully made that contact with the audience?

D.K. You can never be sure for any single individual whether or not you've been a good communicator, because that is a subjective determination. And if you relied on feedback you'd be mistaken, because how many times have you been discourteous to a speaker? The only important feedback is your own analysis: Did I, in my own judgment, do all that was necessary to communicate as well as I know how, in that situation, with that group?

S.L. I want to suggest that by putting yourself in their shoes and stating their perceptions, what you said to them was, "I see you. I hear you. I accept where you are." And because most people want to be seen and heard, they were then able to go along in the direction you wanted them to go.

D.K. Right. You acknowledged them. You said, "I know that you think that sometimes we're X." It gets it on the table. It sets it aside, at least for the moment, so you can get on with the agenda you are there to present.

S.L. Even though you are an experienced, comfortable speaker, do you experience any "wound-upness," a little tightness, in the moments before a speech?

D.K. Everyone experiences a certain amount of anxiety. The adrenaline is flowing; the anxiety builds an inner tension that is very positive. You hear stories about actors who have to be pushed onto the stage. When you're nervous and tense, and you can feel your blood pressure bouncing and your heart pounding a little . . . a little tightening of the breath, a little dryness of the throat . . . you learn that it can be positive rather than negative.

S.L. It's probably a revelation for those people who say "He's a natural" to know that you, too, get nervous.

D.K. Absolutely. That's why I kind of silently resent it when somebody says, "He can do it in his sleep"—"Wind him up"— all those little asides that we tend to attribute to people who do things well.

S.L. They don't know how hard you work at it.

D.K. They don't know how hard you work at it, and how hard you continue to work at it.

S.L. Do you do anything, use any techniques, to prepare yourself?

D.K. I really don't want many human contacts immediately before I'm going to give a speech, because my mind is sort of getting ready for the act of communication. Just before I'm going to speak, I usually take several deep breaths to get my lungs full and the oxygen in my system. Aside from that, I'm not in a big hurry [when I speak]. I think there is a tendency for people to be afraid of silence, but I think that's a vital part of a speech.

S.L. So you are not afraid to use the pause. How do you use it in a speech?

D.K. I think that pauses can be enormously eloquent. There's a difference between a speech and a spiel. The guy on the corner selling neckties doesn't want to lose anybody and he just rambles on—that's a spiel. A lot of speakers tend to imitate that style, and they're afraid to think while they're speaking. I think it's an enormous tribute to an audience to let them know that you are not only talking to them, you're thinking right in front of them. If your speech is effective, if you're crossing the bridge to the audience, they also have to think. The whole act of communication is the combination of thinking, listening, speaking. When I sense that a speaker is thinking out loud with me, I feel that he's willing to be vulnerable, willing to let the thoughts that are flowing into his head right at that moment be out there for me to evaluate. I think he is being respectful to me.

S.L. Do you feel differently about a small versus a large audience?

D.K. I never think about the size of the audience, because you're always in the very human act of trying to talk to one person. The fact that there are two there means you have to acknowledge their presence. You do that by looking at them, by directing your words to them, your whole body and your whole being to them. If there are five, it just means you have to broaden your perspective. You know, the ability of a single human being to stand up in front of several hundred people doesn't limit his ability to let each one of them know that he's talking to them. And a person does that by simply being aware that they're there. And if you're aware that they're there, your whole body is going to encompass them. Instead of having your head focused directly on one person, you've got to move your head sufficiently to let them know that you see them.

I was talking recently to a large group of people . . . a big convention . . . and there were probably one hundred and fifty people on the podium behind me. I couldn't believe it was that large a group. Well, I couldn't help but turn around in the course of my speech to let them know I was there, and that I knew they were there and part of the audience I was trying to communicate with.

So I don't consider the size of the audience a burden, although some of our habits may go back to the days before amplification was so much of a routine thing—your gestures tend to be a little broader. I believe you reach out a little more. But I've never felt any conscious effort to be different. You're simply talking to a group of individuals, not some large, amorphous mass called an audience.

S.L. You're known as a good speaker. Do you still run into resistance from your audiences?

D.K. When you're in the business of persuasion, the premise is that there is going to be a certain amount of resistance on the other side . . . resistance, apathy, inertia, or whatever. The worst thing in the world is for somebody to be introduced as a great speaker. That automatically sets up a great resistance. I remember Bob Hope saying once that he just dreads it when somebody says, "We're going to hear now from the King of Comedy, one of the funniest men in the world. You're going to fall down laughing when he gets up to speak." He said the audience then thinks, "All right, you'd better be funny!" That's resistance.

One of the best ways to deal with resistance is to be a listener before you're a speaker. It's to get things out on the table, because there is a great advantage to a kind of catharsis. When someone who has a problem or a concern or who feels he isn't being treated properly comes to see me, my first reaction is, "Well, tell me about it." Often when that happens people begin to sense that they are not only a victim of the issue, but they are a part of the issue. Any time you get into a situation where there is resistance and potential confrontation, you have to be prepared to listen, and to give that other party the first opportunity, it seems to me, to state his case. And when you do that, you're now dealing not with some amorphous thing called resistance, but you're dealing with issues and with ideas. You are in the act of communication, and you can't deal with that unless there's dialogue.

S.L. How would you describe the role that your ability to communicate has played in your own career?

D.K. If you mean has it been important in the development of my own career, the answer would be yes. Once you reach certain levels in an executive capacity, you begin to go from the particular to the general. I came up through the marketing route, and some of my skills were in knowing what package to decide on, the quality of advertising, and a number of these kinds of things. As you move up, you tend to leave behind these specific issues and become more of a generalist. When you become a generalist, you're really dealing no longer in the bits and pieces of the business, but in the broader policy issues . . . the direction that the business ought to go, the motivation you try to impart to your associates, the things that are important. You try to articulate the direction of the company.

It seems to me that the ability to communicate perhaps a little better than others is a tremendous asset once a person reaches that level. I find that most senior executives that I know have developed that ability, regardless of what competence brought them to their positions in the first place. When you think, for example, about a great surgeon, there comes a point in his career when he has to begin to convey that knowledge to others. To the extent that he is able to articulate his profession, I think he plays a much larger role than if he just is in the operating room.

S.L. What weight is placed here at Coca-Cola on one's ability to communicate?

D.K. Well, this isn't a company manual, but in my own career, it's been very important simply because as you move up through your career path, you're judged on your ability to articulate a point of view. You know, I've gone through four mergers in my career and in fact have worked for four different sets of owners. And my guess is that it would have been entirely possible for me to have gotten lost along the way if I hadn't had some abilities to speak and listen on significant issues that affected the health of the business.

People say that in big companies, it's so hard to get an idea through. I think that's a valid protective mechanism, because ideas float around a company like Coca-Cola by the thousands. An idea that is going to demand the resources of the company needs a champion, and it needs a champion who has got the ability to convince others. Well, how is he going to do that? He's going to do it by the written and spoken word, and more of the spoken word.

S.L. If a person is an effective speaker and listener, I'd guess he or she can relate to someone several levels higher up, and that executives like you would prefer that to subservience.

D.K. I think you're dead right. The thing that just disturbs me no end is when people are obviously postured, trying to be somebody other than who they are. So many people have so many props that the props overwhelm the person. The idea is a hell of a lot more important than the prop. And the man or the woman is a lot more important than the prop. Sometimes I'd love to burn the props and say, "What do you really want to tell me? What do you really believe?"—instead of spending most of the time trying to place little things on an overhead projector. Because you're assessing not only an idea, but you're assessing the credibility of the person who is presenting it.

A lot of presentations deal with very specific things . . . numbers, pro formas . . . that are helped by being able to see visually. These kinds of presentations are helped by slides, but I sort of draw the line there. Some pictures may be worth a thousand words, but a picture of a thousand words isn't worth much.

S.L. What would you say to younger executives about the role the ability to communicate effectively can play in their careers?

D.K. We're in the business of persuasion. That's really our basic commodity in one sense. That's why we encourage our executives to develop those skills and use the services of places like Speakeasy. It seems to me that what that says to our up-and-coming executives is that we consider this important, because that's using the resources of the company for them to improve their own personal communications skills.

I believe that for a top executive not to realize that he has an enormous obligation to try to communicate as effectively as possible is just not facing up to a major responsibility. It's almost a contradiction in terms to see someone in a senior executive position who isn't able to communicate well.

Faye Wattleton

FAYE WATTLETON is the president of Planned Parenthood of America, the nationwide nonprofit organization whose emphasis is birth control and family planning. Since being named to head Planned Parenthood in 1979, Ms. Wattleton has become a national spokesperson for freedom of choice in birth control and abortion. Audiences don't always agree with her on these controversial, highly emotional issues, but they agree that she is an articulate speaker who projects authority without losing warmth and intimacy. When I interviewed her last year in Planned Parenthood's New York headquarters, I found that she was also articulate on the subject of speaking.

S.L. Your training and education seem to be entirely in health. Now you're not only managing but also the spokesperson for a large national organization. Did you have any particular training, or anything in your background, that helped you to become such an articulate spokesperson?

F.W. I am a professional nurse. I have my master's in nursing and I'm a certified nurse midwife. I received management training as part of my graduate studies, and I was chosen [as president of Planned Parenthood] because there was a feeling that the organization needed strong management at the national office and a new sense of purpose. There was nothing in my professional training that did much to contribute to my spokesperson role—virtually no public speaking, certainly no background in interviewing, or being interviewed by the media. I think they felt in the back of their minds that if I did a reasonably good job of being interviewed and being a public spokesperson, that would be fine, too. So it really came as a pleasant surprise for all of us that my skills in this area really seemed to be very much greater than I, and the organization, had anticipated.

I should add that six months before I was named to the presidency of Planned Parenthood, I was asked to co-host a television show in Dayton. I did it because I thought it was fun—it was a lark —and it had very good ratings. As a matter of fact, after I left, the show was discontinued. That was excellent training in that particular medium, but beyond that I had no on-the-job training or professional training.

S.L. One thing that struck me in watching you on the Phil Donahue show [she had appeared with U. S. Rep. Henry Hyde of Illinois in a show that focused on abortion] is that you have a voice that is extremely well articulated, beautifully modulated, and comes across with authority, but also with warmth. So I wondered whether you had been in plays in high school, for example, or whether the role models you had growing up were conscious of the way they used their voices.

F.W. I was in only one high school play during my high school career, which really didn't last too long because I graduated a year early. I think that if I had any training or role models at all, it came about through my upbringing, which was very much in the church. My mother was a minister. We spent a great deal of time in church and I have been the recipient of many, many sermons. I suppose that my style is not altogether unlike some of the role models that I listened to as I was growing up in that environment.

My mother was a very strong role model. I think more than anything, she contributed to a great comfort in speaking to large audiences without being intimidated. She would say that she was equal to the highest calling in the church—the ministry. I didn't recognize it at the time, but it took a great deal of courage to stand up and become a respected minister within that particular denomination, which was very fundamentalist, both theologically and from the standpoint of delivery.

S.L. Some people say that good speakers are born, but I don't believe that. I believe that at some point in their lives, whether it's courses in speaking or experience, something happens to make them more comfortable with speaking.

F.W. My mother offered me that in terms of not being intimidated. I think that's perhaps the first rule, or the first obstacle to overcome. She was very courageous in what she said, and she certainly always said it with authority.

I think she offered another lesson, too, and that was to always be prepared. She said that you never go before anyone unless you are very well prepared, unless you know your material and can articulate it from many different perspectives. That has really been the foundation for me, I think sometimes to the consternation of my staff. I'm often very demanding and very precise in what is prepared for me, and in what I will, and will not, agree to say.

S.L. Let's talk a bit about that. Having someone to help you prepare material for speeches is something that heads of organizations or corporations have to deal with a lot. What procedure do you go through if you know that you have a major speech coming up a month from now? Does someone always do the writing?

F.W. Someone always does the writing. It depends on the event, how much time is being requested, and, obviously, who the audience is. I do have a person available to me. My speechwriting at this point is not a full-time job, although it was when we were still developing a lot of the basic material. The first thing we do is identify the audience, and what their needs are. We try to consider what that audience's relationship might be with our local affiliate. There is always the objective—sometimes subtle, sometimes spoken—that whatever I do will enhance the work of Planned Parenthood, even though there may be times when I never mention Planned Parenthood in my speech.

So we try to get the setting, get a sense of all of the factors with respect to the setting of the event. And then we develop [the speech] either from existing speeches that can be modified or tailored to that particular event, or develop an altogether new one. Since I am still fairly new in this position, I am still breaking ground with audiences to whom I haven't spoken, so we are still in the process of developing new material.

S.L. I've seen copies of some of the speeches you've delivered. Do you always read them word for word?

F.W. I almost never read them word for word, unless there are some really excellent lines that I don't want to muff. And I almost never do them extemporaneously. It's kind of a mixture. I try to digress from time to time and add comments that reflect my personal experience, because I think that gives a speech color. I think there is nothing more boring than for a person to stand up and read from a written page.

I also think it says a lot about how much that person cares about the audience. You should care enough to prepare well enough not to have to read from the written page. You should also prepare yourself in terms of skill, so that your delivery can be more conversational and intimate with the audience. I have a need when I'm speaking to really develop a very intimate kind of communication with the audience, and I find I can't do that if I'm reading a speech.

A lot of it has to do with the speech itself. What looks good on the written page can sound awful when you try to deliver it. It can be deadly boring, and vice-versa—things that sound good when they're spoken may appear illiterate to a reader. Many people fall into the fallacy of believing that if a speech reads great, it's going to make a great speech. You learn the hard way that's not always true.

Being prepared is just so important. Early on in this position, I went to a person who does speech training. She was very helpful in developing what she perceived as some already existing skills. She did not feel I was an altogether untrained student. I guess I went to her three or four times. She helped me develop a format, and techniques for delivery from a written text. She helped me understand that gestures can come across as being very warm and human, even when I may feel they're somewhat exaggerated. Being human is one of the things I feel is important in any delivery. I'm not there to mimic my male brethren or "one-up" anybody; I feel I have my own style. I'm a woman, with all that that implies, and while I feel I have a very strong message, I do not seek to deliver it through any medium other than my own.

S.L. I love everything you just said. These are important lessons for anyone who would be a good speaker. You brought up the issue of being a woman, and I'd like to discuss that. In the last several years in my business, we've had more and more women who are rising in their careers. They are concerned about projecting authority without losing their femininity. You are attractive, and you definitely exert the authority without losing the warmth. Are you struggling with this as an issue?

F.W. Not anymore. I believe that if there is any message that any person, but especially women, must convey, it is one of honesty. It would be very dishonest for me to take on a masculine aura; it would be perceived as a mechanism and not really a statement of me as a person. What that says is that I've got to act like a man to be as strong as a man. It denies that women can be strong, too. What I want to do is convey to the audience that I am who and what I am; I am a woman and proud to be a woman. I happen to feel that there are some characteristics that are specific to gender, and I'm very comfortable with that.

I really want to enhance that and to reflect it at its best, just as I want to reflect my other qualities at their best. So, I dress in a way that is me. I speak in a way that is me. I hope that what I say has enough substance to convince people that I am a person of substance and not of frivolity. I think my position reflects that. I have encountered from time to time around the country those who have said, "When one first sees you, they think they see a woman who has been put in your position for reasons other than your capabilities and your substance, but you tend to dispel that very quickly."

S.L. The minute you open your mouth.

F.W. I think that's the most profound compliment anyone can give me. No one will ever find me mimicking anyone as a way of affirming my own strength.

S.L. Back to speechwriting. I agree with what you said about the written word and the spoken word, that something that reads well may not sound great when it's delivered. In looking at your speeches, they seem to be exceptionally well edited for delivery. Your sentences are shorter and more direct than in many I've seen. Does this come with working together with your writer for several years, or are you still doing a lot of your own editing to get it the way you want it?

F.W. It's a breeze now to get it the way we want it. At first it was very traumatic for her. She would give me beautiful speeches that read like they deserved to be in the best professional journals. And I'd send them back saying they weren't speech material. Over the last couple of years, she's developed a sense of my style and its succinctness. I don't like to bore people with a lot of statistics, and a lot of high-sounding things that make people think I'm an intellectual.

I think it's more important to have people feel something in their gut about the issue on which I'm speaking. The best thing is to reach the audience emotionally. Because, after all, why are you speaking to them? When you're on the circuit speaking to people, they come to hear what you have to say about the issues. I feel that you must leave a profound impact, and you can't do that if you are reading endless sentences. I just don't think the human brain hears it that way, and certainly human emotions don't respond to it that way.

So my speeches reflect that part of my philosophy, and developing them is now at the point where I can basically say, "I want to put that speech, that speech, and elements of this third one together," and the result is pretty much the way I want it. Recently, because of a hectic travel schedule and meetings, I didn't see one of my speeches until the night before the event, and it just wasn't right. The next morning, with an hour and a half to go, I had to ask her for a rewrite. I told her why it wouldn't work and she gave me back a speech that was excellent. In an hour and a half!

S.L. So the bottom line is, you can't say to the speechwriter, "I've got to give a speech in two weeks. Come up with twenty minutes."

F.W. "Well, sometimes the schedule really gets jammed up. But they try to follow the rule that I get a speech at least a week before I'm to give it, so I have time to react. When we get to the last-minute crunches, we have more trouble getting it retyped than we do with preparing or revising it.

S.L. Looking at someone like you, there are two issues as far as power goes. One is position power—you're head of a large organization. The other is personal power. How much of Planned Parenthood's new, higher profile—in which you speak for personal freedom and against the views of the Moral Majority—has to do with you? By that I mean your image, style, personal power, and your willingness to stand up, commit yourself, use the pronoun "I" and, as you said a little while ago, to speak from your gut. How much have those parts of you gone into what Planned Parenthood is now?

F.W. I think a lot of it has to do with that. I think the events of the times are certainly a contributing factor. The leader of any organization has a profound impact on that organization, whether it's good or bad. I think that my personal qualities have been an asset. I think that my unwillingness to be compromising in what I say or in the programs I have built has created an image of the

organization that is very different from the image it may have had
several years ago. I do that with a recognition at all times that
there are always down sides to any gains that can be made when
we're speaking strongly and without compromise.

I realize that what I say in essence is the voice of the organization. That is a profound responsibility, and I see it as responsibility, not power. I recognize that if my words put the organization
in a position that is detrimental to it, it might damage the organization for years to come. By the same token, if I'm on target and
my position is correct, it enhances the organization for years to
come. The ultimate enhancement is for those who are served by
the organization, and in that I think I have been successful.

S.L. You face many different audiences. Some I would guess
are friendly—students, civil-liberties groups, women's groups.
But resistance is something that almost every speaker has to face,
and I certainly saw you facing it on the Phil Donahue show. When
you were preparing for that appearance with Representative
Henry Hyde, a leader in the anti-abortion movement, I'm sure you
thought about your content. Did you also think about your feelings
as you had to confront this person who was against most of what
you stand for?

F.W. With Mr. Hyde, I was prepared for the emotion of his
rhetoric, but not for the emotion of the person or my emotional
response. I think that what I was not prepared for was his failure
to use rules of politeness. I don't mean that I was looking to be
treated gently, but before the show, Phil suggested that we follow
a certain routine. Mr. Hyde completely ignored that. I went to the
show believing that I would really be dealing with this man on the
intellectual and emotional aspects of the issue. What I found is
that I had to adjust how I responded to him.

I learned a valuable lesson in how these events are used to really
win the audience. It didn't matter to me that I did not win over
Henry Hyde. What did matter to me at the time I got there and
saw what I was up against was that I did not want to alienate my
audience by becoming as strident as he did. Some people said that
I was really too soft, that I came across as not being as strong and
forthright as he was. But I picked up my vibes from the studio
audience; I felt had I been that way, I would have turned off a lot
of people. I would have lost something I feel is important to always

preserve—a sense of human caring and concern he clearly did not demonstrate. I was told it was an audience hostile to my point of view, but as it went on he became more strident and clearly more uncaring, outrageous, out of touch. I think they began to identify with my position and my persistence in stating it: "Mr. Hyde, I respect your point of view. However, there is another, and we must each be left to our own point of view and our own way." At the end, I would say that less than ten percent of the studio audience was on his side. There was a woman who said, "I may not be for abortion, but I sure don't want you telling me what to do."

S.L. Not only are you a woman talking about an emotional issue, but a black woman as well. That means that not everyone in your audiences will love you. No matter how articulate you are, there will be some who because of their own problems will not be able to accept you. You must be very comfortable with yourself to handle that with an audience.

F.W. We human beings all need to be stroked, and I need that as much as anyone. But if someone like me is not willing to confront these mean spirits, who will? I don't see it as personal even if I've been personally attacked. I see my role and position as being symbolic of many things that people hate a great deal. I also see my ability to nullify that somewhat.

I think that if you're in a position like this, and you take it as a personal attack every time you're confronted, then you're useless. You are quickly immobilized. It is the nature of human beings not to put themselves in that kind of vulnerable position, to be constantly affronted. You really have to have a sense of who you are and why you're here, particularly in a position as controversial as this one. You can't do it for the adulation. You've got to have a stronger motivation, or your statements will only reflect which way the wind is blowing.

S.L. I had assumed that some of your audiences would naturally be friendly. Is that an unfair assumption?

F.W. Anytime you have a public meeting, there are always people who will come to challenge you. So I am frequently confronted and challenged. The one time I was physically attacked was not at an unfriendly event; it was at a Planned Parenthood event. A gentleman in the audience was particularly unhappy that Planned Parenthood in New Jersey had given his daughter birth-control pills. He stood up and started ranting, saying I was a demon, that I needed to be destroyed and that he would do anything necessary to destroy me. With that, he went down into his pocket and I thought, "Now I've had it. If he comes out with a gun there's no way that I can live." What he came out with was a package of birth-control pills that had been dispensed from one of our clinics over two years earlier. He threw them at me, hit me with them, and yelled that he would stalk me all over the country until he stopped me.

That was probably the most sobering experience of my speaking career, and that was not an unfriendly event. So now I assume that in any audience, whether it's a public gathering or nonpublic, there is the likelihood that I'll be confronted by an unfriendly person.

S.L. I would imagine that like most speakers you have some churning in your gut, or a little bit of excitement, or something, before you speak or go on a TV show. Is that correct?

F.W. Well, the churning in my gut is when I think I'll have trouble establishing communication with the audience. That troubles me more than the size of the audience, or the nature of the presentation. I get particularly concerned when I'm speaking to groups like doctors, who tend not to be into the social issues. It takes more to get them hooked in and settled down until they're looking at you without blinking. I don't mean hooked in a manipulative sense, but that I'm really getting a message over to them.

S.L. Did you do anything when you realized that your appearance with Mr. Hyde was going to be more unpleasant than you thought?

F.W. Well, my message to myself was, "Watch it. Don't try to answer him word for word. Most assuredly, don't appear to be angry. (He angered me greatly.) You are on television and it's like a magnifying glass, so not only what you say but the way you look will be very important." That was what I said to myself over and over again, that I must not only suppress my emotions, but not give the appearance of those emotions, which is sometimes not easy. But I refused to be hooked into his game, into what he wanted to talk about, and I felt I really had exerted the authority over him. He was so upset that at the end of the program, he left the studio immediately.

S.L. In watching, I did not feel that you were consciously suppressing your emotions. You stated things in a firm way and you seemed in charge of yourself. He didn't. His emotions and energies were controlling him. You were controlling yours by making conscious choices. I think that's what true strength and authority are about—you make the choices. What do you feel as you look around and see more women today developing in roles similar to yours?

F.W. As I said before, if there is anything that I want to leave with an audience, whether they agree or disagree with me, it is a sense that I have presented myself as honestly as I possibly can, that I am believable. I am not a fabrication of some image. I think the greatest trap that any woman can fall into is to try and form herself in a manner that is inconsistent with her own being. Ultimately, that will not stand you well when things get tough; people tend to see through phoniness. They have a gut response to what is not real.

I suppose it takes a degree of comfort with yourself as a person, with who you are. That's not always so easy for women who are going through tremendous transitions, who are moving to the top and who may have had to make certain accommodations that were at odds with their own beliefs. That's one of the luxuries of being at the top—if you are not too vulnerable to criticism and if you pursue what you know is honestly you, if your positions are reasonable and responsible, you will be exonerated almost every time.

I don't mean to suggest that every time I speak my message is received with relish. When I first came to this position some of the strongest voices of dissent were within Planned Parenthood. I could have modified my position, but that's not really the quality that reflects leadership.

Tony O'Reilly

TONY O'REILLY is the President and chief executive officer of the H. J. Heinz Company. He is a native of Dublin, and was the youngest member of the Irish National Rugby Team. His reputation as an innovative manager dates to his leadership of the Irish Dairy Board from 1962 to 1966. He became joint managing director of Heinz-Erin, Ltd., in 1967, and came to the company's world headquarters four years later. He was the chief operating officer of Heinz for six years before being named to the top spot in June 1979. O'Reilly continues to commute between the United States and Ireland, where he retains business interests of his own. I asked him about the speaking skills he has developed during his active career in an interview at the Heinz Company's Pittsburgh headquarters.

S.L. Let's start at the beginning. Have you ever had any training in speaking or communication?

T.O. Most Irishmen's training in the art of speaking is a form of self-defense. Samuel Johnson once said that the Irish are a very fair people: They never speak well of one another. So it is an important part of your armament as a child to learn to express yourself. The Irish have a great facility for speech.

I went to a Jesuit school, which was noted for its competence. James Joyce went to the same school. The school was resolute in its determination that people should be able to write and speak clearly, and I think they have been successful. There were debating societies and there was a very stern attention to the essay as a form of communication. Apart from those two basic disciplines, I cannot say there has been any formal training. We did, of course, like most schools in Great Britain and Ireland, involve ourselves in some form of theater. In our case, it was Gilbert and Sullivan, and W. S. Gilbert requires very clear enunciation.

S.L. From what I have read about you, you were successful in the business world quite early on. Were you aware at that time of your skills in speaking and persuasion?

T.O. My first breakthrough was really as an athlete. I was what I suppose was the equivalent of your Heisman Trophy winner, and I played at eighteen for the National Rugby Football Team, and also for the touring team that represented Great Britain and Ireland. I was the youngest member of the team by six or seven years, and this thrust me into an early limelight in which I was forced to communicate very actively. We were all amateurs, and the tour was a singular event; it occurred once every five years. When we returned from the tour we gave countless talks about it, showing films and so on. So suddenly I found myself talking, lecturing, communicating.

I went from that to a job in England, then came back and taught at University College, in Cork, so I was communicating as a teacher.

S.L. But you were also trained in law.

T.O. Yes, I am a solicitor. My basic qualifications are a doctorate in marketing and economics. I have a solicitor's qualification and a bachelor's degree in civil law.

S.L. Does such a varied background help, or have an application, for the chief executive of an American corporation?

T.O. Yes. In fact, I think it is important to be an "all-rounder." I don't think you can be a specialist at the top of any American corporation which is concerned with the many constituencies that a chief executive has to be concerned with. With a single focus at the top, I'm afraid those particular prejudices would resonate throughout. You would exclude some very important talents and disciplines that would assist in communicating to your principal constituents: the shareholder, the customer, the public, legislatures, your own employees. All of these require high communication ability.

S.L. Tell me about your experience in Ireland with the Dairy Board. What communication abilities did that require?

T.O. I was for five years chief executive of the Dairy Board, which was a new creation, a form of armed truce between the government and the farmers. It was an extremely important role. With 112,000 milk farmers, at five or so members per farm, there were probably 600,000 members out of a population of three million, so this was the biggest single political lobby in the country. I was the spokesman for it. I had to draw the line between the natural need of the farmers and the natural frugality of the Finance Department and the Department of Agriculture. I believed profoundly in what I was doing, and the dairy farmers are now the most prosperous single sector of the farming community in Ireland.

S.L. In that situation, you were communicating with the government on one hand and with farmers on the other. I assume some of the farmers were sophisticated and some were not. What did that bring out in your speaking ability?

T.O. The basic skill you need in dealing with a job like that is knowing what's needed. I think the second thing is a belief in what you are doing and, thirdly, the capacity to communicate in very simple language to an audience that, as you say, is a combination of people who are quite sophisticated and those who are very innocent. It had to be relevant to them and, therefore, it had to have humor. My sporting background was helpful, because I was able to draw parallels and allegories from it. I had played in their village and remembered their local hero. It helped me identify with the audience. I wasn't an outsider.

S.L. So you were aware of the difference in style that you had to use with that audience. Skipping over some of your other positions in Ireland and the United Kingdom, where you joined the company that was purchased by Heinz, what about when you came here to take over the company? How has your style changed?

T.O. When I first came here, I was one of eight contenders. I became president and chief operating officer after about fourteen months and in 1978 I became the chief executive officer. I brought a reputation as someone who was a bit witty and flamboyant. I didn't think that helped very much, so I became grim-faced and boring in delivering a formal speech. Since then I have gained some tools in forms of communication. I still make the formal speech, but when I'm through I have a question-and-answer session. Then my natural good humor bubbles to the surface. I think when you are dealing with the financial community you have to be a bit stern, because these are serious business people with a serious business outlook. They demand a certain reverence.

You can be a little irreverent afterwards in the questions and answers.

S.L. Do you ever work with a speechwriter or do you always plan your own speeches?

T.O. I never work with a speechwriter. Our head of public relations will sit down with me and we'll talk about what theme to explore to get their attention. For example, most people nowadays are telling you what their company is doing and what it plans to do. Last year, we drafted a speech that told our shareholders what we won't do—six things that won't happen at Heinz. That gets a lot of attention.

S.L. So you are very much aware of the need to do something to make the audience sit up and listen, rather than just tell them how much you know.

T.O. Oh, absolutely. And in order to integrate yourself into their consciousness and ingratiate yourself into their understanding, you have to find humor or local color, or some kind of contact that is relevant to focus your topic down to the local level.

I also think one of the most important things to have in public speaking is a commanding presence. There are a lot of people who say the same things as others, and yet deliver it with the correct blend of menace or clarity or wit to make the same facts instantly recognizable and somehow more valuable.

S.L. In your position now, when you have to not only lead but also motivate and encourage people, have you had to work more on developing empathy and listening skills?

T.O. Well, although I do talk a lot I feel that a lot of people talk simply because they love the sound of their own voices. I would like to pride myself on being a good leader and also a good listener. I think the two are very important.

S.L. You've said that you think people are born speakers. My book is dedicated to the proposition that speakers are made, not born. I think their experiences make them.

T.O. I don't think that these are incompatible. When I say they are born, the athlete who thinks he can rely on natural ability alone is a fool. Coaching and the refinement of all these basic natural attributes are necessary to make him into a world-class competitor in whatever. The same is absolutely true in speaking; there are a great number of tricks and tools that you have to pick up on the way. When I say that a person is a natural speaker, I think that means a confluence of ease of manner, ease of personality; he speaks clearly and has a command of the language. All of these things make what I consider to be a natural speaker.

S.L. I agree.

T.O. And if you can graft humor onto that, then you've got somebody you would like to work with. But I believe, as you do— and I have reached it I suppose without the formal training that you are giving to a much wider audience—that there are a number of very important techniques to learn. The first one is the quelling of the audience.

S.L. Would you talk about that?

T.O. If an audience were impatient or rowdy when I stood to speak, I would stand there silent for ten minutes if necessary. There is no way I would rush into my speech.

S.L. So you are comfortable with pause when you are in front of a group. That is also a very important technique.

T.O. I also think that the joke is an extremely good point of assessment in a formal speech, and it is also a point of reengagement for the wandering mind. It enables you also, in giving a speech that is written down, to make better eye contact. It enables you to move freely on the platform, and that is why I hate a fixed mike. I much prefer a floating one.

S.L. I would like to talk about your style. You seem to be willing to let your personality come out, and not be just a cog in the wheel. I think that speaking style goes more with the entrepreneurial personality than with the corporate personality. From the companies and the people with whom you've interacted in this country, would you comment on that?

T.O. There is a great deal of sublimation of self in any large organization. The John DeLorean–type figure in a General Motors setting tends to act as an irritant on a great number of sensibilities and sensitivities, and probably the greatest group with the greatest number is served by the policy in which everyone sublimates themselves and conceals some of the more extreme qualities they have. We [at Heinz] try to encourage diversity. I like to see people express themselves in a literary sense and in a life-style sense.

S.L. It's very common for top executives and political candidates to get coaching on their style and image. What advice would you give to young people starting out in the business world who want to be a success in a big corporation?

T.O. Be yourself, but do not wear your own self-awareness on your sleeve, and be tolerant that other people want to also be themselves.

S.L. In preparing yourself for a speech, you apparently do a lot of thinking about where the audience is and how to connect with them.

T.O. I don't do that much public speaking outside the company. I find that in a position like mine, I'm often asked to speak more because of the position than what people think I really have to say. So unless it's a subject or a group that really interests me, I can get "spoken out" very easily. But when I'm committed to the subject and have an objective I want to reach, I really enjoy it. For example, I'm giving a speech soon in which I'll talk about Ireland. I plan to use slides. I will say, "This is Ireland," and there will be beautiful background music and slides of Ireland at its most beautiful. Then I will stop and say, "And this is Ireland." I will show them Belfast and the bombs and the destruction and the atrocities. "And this is also Ireland," and here I will show slides depicting the social and political history of Ireland from the tenth century to today. I think the slides will form the mood I want: the capacity for contradiction, a mosaic, the inability to be simplistic about Ireland, the romantic nature of the people, their aspirations, their current relationships with America and Europe. This I hope will connect.

S.L. And you will do the writing yourself?

T.O. Yes.

S.L. It's evident that you put a great deal of time and effort and thought into planning.

T.O. Yes, and I think that keys back to my belief that if you are a natural athlete, don't think you are automatically world class. If you are a natural speaker with a good educational background, don't think you can stand on your feet and spellbind people, particularly on a new topic or in a formal arena where people expect a high degree of new knowledge or existing knowledge, without adequate preparation.

Dean Rusk

DEAN RUSK was U.S. Secretary of State from 1961 to 1969, under Kennedy and Johnson. Since 1970, he has taught international law at the University of Georgia. He has been a popular speaker and lecturer outside as well as in the classroom. I interviewed him in his book-lined office on the university campus in Athens.

S.L. From our correspondence and from what others say who are familiar with your speaking, you have some very definite ideas on speaking and a reputation for doing it well.

D.R. Well, as LBJ used to say, even a blind hog can find a few acorns if he roots around long enough.

S.L. You've been in situations where speaking has been very important. But let's go back to your time in Washington.

D.R. I went into the State Department when [George C.] Marshall became Secretary of State. I served as president of the Rockefeller Foundation. In 1961, John Kennedy asked me to be Secretary of State.

You know, in Washington, they referred to me as "the quiet American." The most difficult thing for me, as far as speaking is concerned, was the necessity to adhere rigorously to a prepared text because of the importance of every word. This clearly had some negative effect on style. My wife said she would never let me speak from a prepared text again, and I have not. I speak simply from notes. You give a lot of thought to it in any case, but it takes eight to ten additional hours to put down on paper what you want to say.

Some people have developed a talent for it, though. Lord Hume [former British Prime Minister] could circulate the text of a speech in advance, then use two or three cards for his notes, and deliver it word for word! There is a rule in the House of Commons that you cannot read a speech.

S.L. There are times when using a manuscript speech is absolutely necessary.

D.R. . . . when the use of each word carries with it significant consequences. Sometimes now, people will ask me for a copy of my speech and, of course, I can't do that because I use notes. If the host wants to tape my speech and send me a transcript so I can tidy it up—there's a tremendous difference between written and spoken English—then I'll do that if they want me to.

S.L. One of the differences is that a speaker brings not only content but a tangible style to a speaking situation.

D.R. The most important thing, I think, is that if one speaks, one ought to understand fully what one is talking about. Nothing substitutes for your complete grasp of your subject and what you want to say. That's your insurance against your mind going blank and those embarrassing pauses. You can always move if you know where you're going and what you're talking about. Preparation and having something to say are most important. I never accept an invitation to speak on something I don't know anything about.

S.L. Have you found that too many speeches don't really say much of anything?

D.R. It's true. I get a good many invitations from people who don't give a hoot what I'm going to say. I tend to shy away from that sort of thing. Why should I go to that trouble and invest my time and energy just to help their publicity? When I go to another campus, I never just go to make a speech and go home. I always try to have a bull session with thirty to fifty students so that I can come home with an idea of what's on the students' minds.

Speeches need to be as short as one can reasonably make them in order to deal with the subject. My father used to say that you never save any souls after twenty minutes.

S.L. What do you do when people call you and say, "Can you come over and give us a forty-five-minute talk?"

D.R. I tell them I would rather speak for twenty minutes, and spend the rest of the time in a question-and-answer period.

S.L. Have diplomatic speeches been the most difficult challenges in your speaking career?

D.R. I have been before committees of the Congress hundreds of times. That's a real exercise in speaking! One learns from people like Harry Truman, George Marshall, John F. Kennedy, LBJ, and congressional committees to say what you have to say, as briefly as possible, and then shut up, because time is not to be wasted in those circumstances. It's funny, because now, coming back to the classroom, what I have to say is expected to last for fifty minutes.

S.L. Did your high school and college speaking coaches or teachers focus on style as well as content? When did you first become aware of style as a part of speaking?

D.R. I had some coaching in high school. I found that one can actually overdo the facial expressions, the smile and so forth, if they don't appear completely natural. Averell Harriman is an example. When he ran for governor of New York, he tended to put on an artificial face, smiling all the time. He was a good man, and if he had just been himself, he would have been much better.

It sometimes works the other way around. In a group of two hundred people having dinner at the White House, LBJ could be the most persuasive and eloquent individual one can imagine. But we could never get him simply to be himself before the TV camera. Of course, to follow Jack Kennedy was quite a job!

S.L. Having a style that's natural is important when so much communicating is done through television.

D.R. That's true. Reagan is doing very well with style. Of course, he's been doing it a lifetime. He's very comfortable with the camera. Jimmy Carter never did get comfortable with the camera.

Television has made a tremendous difference. The presence of the camera usually changes the scene. I am completely opposed to television cameras in legislative meetings or in courts. It simply transforms the scene!

S.L. During the time when you were Secretary of State, I know you had to deal with press conferences. How did you deal with them, and did you have any special training in the area?

D.R. No. I was pretty nervous in the first three or four . . . with twelve television cameras looking at you and hundreds of reporters. But then I began to realize that I knew more about what I was talking about than anybody else in the room, so I began to relax. The way you feel about your content, your confidence in your command of it, will affect your style.

S.L. You must have faced some pretty hostile audiences during that time. I'd like to know how you dealt with that—when you felt audience resistance, when they questioned what you were saying. I'd guess those times produced some of your toughest speaking situations.

D.R. In some respects, they did. But when you accept a high position in public life, that's part of the contract. There are going to be critics—people who are extreme left, fascists, extreme right, communists, and so forth. I have lived with that. It is very important for any person to learn to deal with a difference of view. If I were hiring somebody for a job, I would ask myself, "How does that person act in the presence of a difference of view?"

The most painful experience I had with speaking I had while Secretary of State. I went to Cornell at the height of the Vietnam controversy, and there were some law students there wearing death masks. This was particularly bad for me because my son was in the audience. Another time, I spoke at Indiana University, and about twenty young people made a noise. I didn't try to shout them down . . . I said, "Let them say what's on their minds." After I got back to Washington, I received a petition of apology from Indiana signed by twelve thousand students.

My practice has always been never to try to shout down anybody. If I'm invited to speak, I go to say what I have to say, and if they don't agree with it . . . well, the problem is theirs. I've never had to sit down, or walk off the platform. But if I know in advance that there's going to be a particularly hostile group in the audience, I try to go early and meet with them for a bull session before the meeting.

S.L. Do you have other ways of dealing with audience resistance?

D.R. Sometimes you can use humor, but you really have to be careful with that, because it can be offensive. Then, sometimes you just have to leave it that in our society, you can have your point of view and I can have mine. I got a question once . . . it was in a group of about six hundred people. After I finished and asked for questions, the first question was, "Some of my colleagues and I are convinced that the second coming of Christ is imminent. What is your view?" I said, "I'll have to leave that to the good Lord, and he has not taken me into his confidence." You mustn't make an enemy in these situations.

S.L. You seem to have a very warm and mellow approach to resistance from the audience. Were you quite as calm in the 1960s?

D.R. When you're before a congressional committee, your job is persuasion. But since I left the government in 1969, I have not set about to convince anybody of anything. If they want to hear my views, I'm willing to express them. I'm no longer out to sell anything.

S.L. What about your work with students here? Don't you find that many of them feel that in order to succeed, they have to persuade?

D.R. There may be distinctions between what you say to a diverse group where all points of view are present, and what you would say to individual senators or congressmen whose views you know. When you speak to a group, you must consider the matrix of that group.

When I held news conferences, my audience was not just the American people. You had potential adversaries listening. There were allies listening . . . Third World countries and so forth. If we could talk solely among ourselves as Americans, it would be quite different, but it has to be within earshot of those other groups, too.

S.L. Did you often give speeches that had to be either interpreted on the spot or translated? What restrictions did you find in such situations?

D.R. It means that you must speak very simply and accurately, and you must exercise great care in the use of idioms. For example, the saying "There are many ways to skin a cat" translates into no other language. One has to speak with great precision when it is to be interpreted into another language, because it is so easy to create misunderstandings.

S.L. Did you ever work with speechwriters?

D.R. Yes, but not all that successfully. It is extremely difficult to write a speech for someone else. Some have been very good at it. For example, Theodore Sorensen did a good job for JFK. But it is difficult to find someone who can prepare the right kinds of words for someone else. When distinguished foreign visitors came to Washington, the Secretary of State would give a formal luncheon or dinner, and it is his job to give a toast. Before the visitor arrives, the Secretary studies a briefing book, usually containing a proposed toast. . . . I was never able to use a single one of those, because the people who had written them never had taken the trouble to stand up and speak them and see how silly they sounded. That's again the difference between written and spoken English. I used to get background information from others, but I had to do all the writing myself.

S.L. Has it been your experience in Washington that the people who give the most effective presentations are also the most effective in one-on-one communication—that they can communicate with people, no matter how large or small the group?

D.R. Yes, by and large that's true. As I said earlier, LBJ was a fantastic persuader in a one-on-one situation. But he was not so good on television. A lot depends on your preparation. Before every presidential news conference, John Kennedy and a half-dozen of us would sit down and go over every possible question that he might be asked. When he went to a news conference, he had been briefed to the gills. So he almost never got a surprise question. LBJ did not prepare quite so thoroughly. It goes back to a command of your subject matter.

S.L. How much of it has to do with being comfortable with yourself and comfortable in the spotlight?

D.R. I suppose that has something to do with it. JFK was certainly more comfortable than Johnson. As majority leader of the Senate, LBJ did his most effective work not by speaking on the floor, but by talking individually with senators. The same thing would be true with visiting government officials or heads of state —he would be just superb! But when he had a state dinner for one of these people, and he would get up and give a toast, he always had a TelePrompTer there.

S.L. Did it ever occur to you, or did you ever think at any time during your career, "Maybe I need to work on polishing up my style"?

D.R. Not really, but there have been some advisers on that on the White House staff. LBJ had private coaching. For someone who is unfamiliar with the experience of speaking, I suppose words of advice or coaching might not be out of place. But one must realize above all, you must never lose your temper. Always keep in control.

I did notice that when we would replay meetings with the press or news conferences, there were times when I noticed I would let myself get into a "singsong" delivery. That puts people to sleep, you know. So I tried—still try—not to do that.

S.L. Do you have any special ways of dealing with stress in a speaking situation?

D.R. No way in particular. My wife used to tell me to have a drink of Scotch before I made a speech. She said it would always loosen my tongue!

S.L. Today there's a lot of emphasis on "packaging" people. Do you feel that success in law, in business, or in politics today is more affected by a person's speaking style than it might have been thirty or forty years ago?

D.R. I think it is possible. I think the first impression is more important than many people realize. There are lots of very competent, dedicated people who don't make good first impressions. You have to get to know them before you can appreciate them. We had in the law school here a very bright and able young woman who came from a rural area, and was self-conscious about that. I talked to her about it. I told her, "You have to overcome that. Don't appear to be fearful; speak directly to people; speak succinctly; realize that you are somebody." Lawyers are in the business of persuading. They have to persuade juries, judges, opposition counselors in negotiations, and so forth. These things are very important to a young lawyer.

Then, some people have a lot on top of the counter, and nothing underneath, so it can work both ways.

S.L. Would you say that your speaking ability has played a major role in your career?

D.R. Yes. By accident maybe, or chance. Luck plays a considerable role in what happens to any individual. But you can prepare yourself . . . prepare yourself to be lucky! The command of language, both written and spoken, is essential. And you must be able to develop your thoughts in a consequential fashion.

S.L. I've found that many good speakers were involved in debating in high school and college. Do you consider this essential training?

D.R. It certainly helps. In America, we learn English through description, as in "See the yellow ball." The British learn through debating, and arguing different points of view. And this produces different results: The English are very effective at debating, in the presentation and defense of points of view.

S.L. I have found that the people I've interviewed for this book are quite articulate about speaking, and advocate learning to do it well.

D.R. I agree. The principal difference between my recent experience and your book *Speak Easy,* which is very good incidentally, is that you are teaching people to produce a result. I went through that for eight years [as Secretary of State], but now that's not my target.

S.L. Ninety-five percent of the people we work with are business people and professionals . . . and sometimes politicians. At one time I had a bad attitude about selling. But a real estate person in one of my groups brought it to my attention that we're all selling. Most people have something to sell, whether it's a point of view or a product, and whether we're aware of it or not. As you said earlier, lawyers have to persuade juries, judges, other lawyers. Politicians have to take into account their audience. It's a luxury not to have to do that.

D.R. Well, you can't be what every audience wants, and one of the things I feel are most important is that one must never talk "down" to an audience. It's far better for a listener to think, "I wish I knew more about that." It's unforgivable for a speaker to talk "down" to his audience.

LBJ had a genius for working with a problem from the point of view of the other fellow. He could put himself in the other fellow's shoes. It gave him a considerable understanding of the nature of the problem. It's a real talent to be able to do that. In speaking, you always have to consider the other person's point of view without compromising what you have to say.

John deButts

JOHN DEBUTTS is the former chairman of American Telephone and Telegraph, the world's largest company. In more than thirty years with AT&T, deButts became known as an eloquent and versatile company spokesman. His appearances included business and diplomatic forums, charitable and civic events, and testimony before committees of the United States Congress. I interviewed him at his gracious country home in northern Virginia.

S.L. Do you feel that your role as a speaker and communicator played an important part in the advancement of your career?

J.D. If you're talking about just making speeches, no. But if you're including the ability to communicate with people in the organization—setting goals simply and clearly and giving people an opportunity to use their own initiative, encouraging, guiding, that kind of communication—yes. When I became president of Illinois Bell, I was active in many areas in which I made speeches, and that might have had something to do with my going on from there. And of course I was required to do more and more speaking from that point on.

S.L. Would you say communicating within the company is in any way different from giving speeches outside the company?

J.D. Well, it's been my experience that it's just as easy to talk to five thousand people as it is to five. You can still read your audience and you can tell whether your points are getting over or not. You can change your approach in the middle or stop and tell a story to regain their attention, or what-have-you. You always have to pay attention to the mood of the audience and what they seem to be looking for.

S.L. But many people are terrified of larger groups. They feel they have less control.

J.D. When I was running our annual stockholders' meetings, which had anywhere from two to seven thousand people, people would say to me, "My God, John! Running a stockholders' meeting with that many people?" I said, "I'd rather run mine than run a General Motors meeting that has two hundred." Of course, in that kind of meeting, you always have the hecklers and the gadflies, and you nearly always have some disgruntled employees. But the audience will stay with you if you handle them correctly —stay calm and courteous and let them speak their piece while at the same time not letting them disrupt the meeting. You have to be firm; you have to say what the rules are and you have to stick with them and make sure you apply them to everybody.

S.L. It lowers the tension level when you give them a chance to let it out.

J.D. That's true.

S.L. As your own career evolved, did you find that the need to be a good listener increased as your responsibilities increased? That you listened more and talked less?

J.D. Oh, yes. It's especially important when you've got a group of people together and you're attempting to analyze, evaluate various solutions to a problem . . . it's imperative that you listen to what those people have to say.

When I became chairman of AT&T, I tried to turn things around completely in that area. Morale problems existed because even in high management, there had been a period there when in several meetings, the speaker would get his head knocked off in trying to state an idea. I had mine knocked off! And I changed that. In the first big meeting I had with all the company presidents and AT&T officers, I told them that from now on I wanted to hear everything they had to say, and there would be no recriminations even if I disagreed with them. Because unless I knew all sides of every question, I couldn't make a final decision. And the first session we had was a five-day session and I think it's the greatest time they'd ever had. I followed that practice, and I used an "open door" policy—anybody could come to see me at any time about any problem they had, or any suggestion they had to solve a problem. Yes, the higher you go, the more important it is to listen.

S.L. Did you have any training in public speaking along the way?

J.D. I had one semester of public speaking while I was in college. And I had a superb professor. Incidentally, I think public speaking should be a required subject—that, and writing—in any business curriculum. The first major speech I made was a valedictory address. My professor did not believe in writing out a speech to read. He thought you should get it in your mind, but not memorize it. Well, I wrote the speech out and checked it and everything, but then I went over it so many times, looking in the mirror, going into the auditorium and getting up on the podium and speaking to the empty room, that I did memorize it; I didn't mean to; but I just went over it so many times that I did. When I got up to make it, I had a little piece of paper about so big that had about six key words on it, taken from the various parts of the speech in case I stumbled.

When I started working, my first job was supervising telephone operators. I found very quickly that you have to convince people of your point of view, that they should give it a chance and should listen to what you have to say. The need to communicate was brought home to me very quickly when I started working in business.

S.L. In the course of your career, particularly when you were president of Illinois Bell and later on with AT&T, did you ever use audio or videotape to look back at your speeches and analyze them for effectiveness?

J.D. Yes. They had training courses to teach people how to meet the press, how to be interviewed. Videotapes would be replayed to point out mistakes and areas for improvement. I had done I don't know how many interviews with the press up to that point, but it was still helpful to me. I think it was especially helpful when I started appearing on talk shows where you not only were dealing with the interviewers who were asking questions but were attempting to make contact with the entire television audience. It helped a great deal.

S.L. You mentioned your valedictory address. As your career progressed, did you tend to use more or fewer manuscript speeches as the speaking requirements of your job increased?

J.D. More, and for several reasons. When I became chairman, practically every speech I made went to the press, so I had to stick pretty close to the script. And even when I was talking to groups of management people, I wanted to be certain I made the points I wanted to make, so I used fairly detailed notes. Also, many of those talks were printed in company publications, so again I stayed close to the script. It was important to be able to stick close to the script without reading it.

S.L. How did you do that?

J.D. Practice, I guess. By the time I was ready to give a speech, I probably had been over it fifteen times. I knew what was in it, and only glanced at the manuscript to jog my memory or make sure I was still on track.

S.L. So the idea that a speechwriter just throws a speech at a top executive and he gets up and reads it without looking at it beforehand doesn't hold true.

J.D. Well, it does on occasion, but it's not very effective. I made a commencement address at Knox College years ago, and the president of the school laughingly told me about the commencement speaker the previous year. He got up and was obviously reading his speech and he read this one sentence and just stopped. He looked back down and seemed to be reading it to himself. Then he looked at the audience and said, "I don't believe that." It was obvious he had never seen the speech and was reading it word for word. And he was chairman of the board of a big company, too.

S.L. Obviously you feel that someone like yourself had an obligation to become involved in the preparation and content of a speech. Would you talk about what you went through in preparing speeches?

J.D. It depended on the occasion. For instance, if I was speaking to the Economic Club of New York, I knew the audience was the business community and the press. Then, I had to decide what I wanted to talk about . . . what message did I have? It usually was something to do with the company that they wanted to hear about, or more general governmental matters or the state of the economy. I would decide, and then von Auw [Alvin von Auw, who as AT&T's vice-president and assistant to the chairman is responsible for speechwriting] and I would sit down and chat about the approach. He would then prepare an outline and I would go over that . . . modify, edit, or delete . . . and he would come in and we'd go over it again. Then he would provide quotes, figures, and so forth, and I would take the speech home to work on it some more. I never could work on a speech at the office. There were too many interruptions. I'd go over it with some more editing. It would go back and forth like that, until I was satisfied with it. A speechwriter like [von Auw] is superb, by the way. He has splendid ideas, knew how I thought, and was familiar with the business; he knew the kinds of things we wanted to make a point about.

S.L. Would you comment on the fact that people in positions like yours are called on to speak not only about their company, but on a range of topics like government regulations and the world economy?

J.D. I've been called on to make speeches for the United Way, the Boy Scouts and Junior Achievement, the Salvation Army, B'nai Brith. Sometimes they expect you to just get up and speak extemporaneously, as I was once asked to do to a committee of the Egyptian parliament. I ran a national savings bond campaign and made over thirty speeches all over the United States about why people should buy savings bonds. That was in 1974, the year the Justice Department filed the antitrust suit against AT&T. When I called [then Treasury Secretary] Bill Simon to let him know we had topped our savings-bond goal two months early, he was ecstatic. He said, "John, that's just marvelous. Your country owes you so much for what you've done." I said, "You've got a hell of a way of showing it," and told him about the suit. I thought he was going to come right through the phone. But having to just stand up and start talking is the most difficult of all.

S.L. In a position like yours, executives are expected to have an incredibly broad range of interests. As you rose in your career, did you spend time making sure you didn't get too narrow?

J.D. Sure. I remember that when I finished my last examination before graduating from college, I told my roommate, "Thank God! No more studying." I didn't know what studying was! I studied more the last year I was chairman of AT&T than I did any year I was in college.

S.L. How do you go about finding common ground with your audience when you're speaking to a group that might disagree with you? You once spoke to the National Association of Manufacturers, for example. How did the chairman of AT&T, which is essentially a monopoly, find common ground with a group that would favor free enterprise?

J.D. Well, I'm a free-enterpriser myself. Years ago, we used to

be competitive, but the public recognized telephone service oper-
ated better as what's described as a natural monopoly, that today
is completely regulated. I knew they recognized the effects of
regulation, and I felt they didn't understand what was being done
to the telephone companies and how it would affect them.

S.L. Did you consciously put something in your speech that
would lower their natural resistance from the beginning?

J.D. In a speech like that, you have to recognize right away that
not everybody agrees with what you are saying. In one speech I
made, I said, "Some people are going to accuse me of self-interest.
There are going to be a lot of you who disagree with me, but I
believe this and therefore I have to say it. I have an obligation to
express my point of view."

S.L. That's laying the cards on the table. I happen to think that
it's an effective thing to do to lower resistance at the beginning of
any kind of presentation. But a lot of young business people seem
afraid to do that.

J.D. There are a couple of reasons for that. One is that the public
relations people are frightened to death to have their CEO say
anything controversial. And the other is the lawyers. They're
scared to death you're going to say something to provoke a law-
suit. But my feeling is, you have to make your position clear. If it
gets us in trouble, it's up to the public relations people and the
lawyers to get us out of trouble.

S.L. When you thought about content for a speech, did you
usually think in terms of main ideas, several big pictures, as opposed to a lot of detail?

J.D. I'd call them major points, I think, but I'd figure out the
main points that I wanted to make and then build around them. I
tried to make the major points clear. One of the best compliments
I've ever had was from a nun who had heard me speak at a meeting
of the American and Canadian Hospital Associations. She said,
"It was a great talk. I remember all six points you made." And
she had all of them. Too much detail loses them.

S.L. Even though you did a good deal of speaking, did you
experience any anxiety before you were to give a talk or appear
before an audience?

J.D. I was terrified of the camera when I first began having to
appear on television shows, interview shows, but after a while I

stopped noticing it. At luncheon and dinner talks, sitting up at the head table, I'd break out in profuse perspiration. I couldn't eat. I'd just sort of push the food around. But once I was on my feet, no problem. All that went away. I was perfectly comfortable, perfectly at ease . . . and ravenously hungry.

S.L. Did you do anything special when you got tight like that?

J.D. Yes. Breathe deeply, and look at the audience to get accustomed to looking at them, and try to spot people who are looking at me. I also talked to the people on either side of me to get my mind off of it. I could bank on being nervous. If I wasn't nervous before a speech, I was going to make a lousy speech. Helen Hayes told me once that after all the years, still the first night before she went on stage, she was sick at her stomach.

S.L. Do you feel that the pressure on someone in his thirties to develop communications skills in business today is different than it was twenty or thirty years ago?

J.D. Yes. It's much more important today because of the complexity of business.

S.L. You were once described in an article as "quiet, forthright, always smiling, eloquent." Do you feel that in talking to a group of company people, your style is as important as your content in indicating that you see them and care enough about them to reach out in the manner in which you address them?

J.D. I think that's always been true. You have to let people know that you're sincere in what you're saying. In order to have "believability," you've got to show warmth, you've got to be relaxed enough to smile and to gesture when it's appropriate.

S.L. Should young people in business develop a speaking style that sort of lets them fit in, versus finding a style that allows them to express their individuality? In a large corporation, which is more important?

J.D. I never did believe in the old saying "Don't rock the boat." I tried to encourage people to feel free to say what they thought. As long as you express yourself, and have logical reasons for the positions you take and the things you do, I don't see any problem with that. Of course, if your boss takes a different position, then you forget it and go ahead and do your best to follow orders. You can't go around with a chip on your shoulder just because somebody doesn't agree with you.

S.L. When you were in authority, did you have any special techniques to get people to open up and state their minds, talk about what needs to be said rather than what someone wants to hear?

J.D. I despise yes men. I would ask questions, find out what people really thought.

S.L. Honesty and directness would seem to be keys to being an effective speaker no matter what the situation.

J.D. I think you have to be direct, candid, forthright, honest, and sincere . . . and above all, I think you have to believe what you're saying. And another thing that I think is extremely important: You can never duck a question. If you don't know the answer you should say so. Evading a question is one of the biggest mistakes businessmen make, with an audience but especially with the media. Because, you know, they're not stupid. They'll read you like a book and then they'll close their ears. They won't hear anything good that you say.

I remember once I lectured at the Columbia University School of Business, and then took questions for about an hour and a half. At the end, one of the graduate students came up to me and at first I thought he was paying me a compliment. Then I realized that it was the greatest indictment of the business community that I had ever heard. He said, "You're the first businessman to appear here who has been willing to answer our questions." You know, that's shocking!

S.L. If you had to give advice to young executives, in your company or other large corporations, about considering or working on their speaking, are there any special things that you would say to them?

J.D. Yes. There are a number of good books, yours included, on public speaking. Read them, study them. Collect anecdotes that can be dropped in to illustrate a situation or use if you see your audience begin to wander; you need to have one that's appropriate for the occasion. And practice. My wife will tell you that, years ago, I'd come home and read speeches out loud to practice enunciation, timing. I practiced my gesturing in front of a mirror, although they have videotape today. And I worked hard at not being pompous, at not letting my position stand between me and the audience.

The most important thing I'd say, though, I've said many times before. I feel very strongly that although every employee really represents a company every time he speaks, the one person who *must* speak out for a corporation or an organization is the head of it. I think it's a real obligation on his or her shoulders to accept that challenge and to do something about it.

Don Baeder

DON BAEDER is executive vice-president–science and technology and chief environmental officer at Occidental Petroleum. But he is perhaps best known for his term as the president of Hooker Chemical Company, which is owned by Occidental, during a time of intense national media scrutiny over the chemical waste burial ground at Niagara Falls, N.Y., that was known as Love Canal. Interest focused on toxic chemical waste disposal in general, and on Love Canal in particular, beginning in 1977; in 1978, Baeder appeared on the CBS television news show *60 Minutes* in an interview with reporter Mike Wallace. Baeder's defense of Hooker Chemical's actions in chemical waste disposal lasted seven minutes when the show was aired; he had spent two and a half hours in his taping session with Wallace.

S.L. You had a real baptism by fire in a very short time. Tell me about your career in terms of the speaking that was required, that might have prepared you for *60 Minutes*.

D.B. I had been at Occidental just about a year, after twenty-five years with Exxon. During that time I rarely was called on to speak to groups larger than, say, twenty to fifty or sixty people.

S.L. At that time, as an engineer, did you feel that speaking, communicating, was particularly important to the progress of your career?

D.B. No, I really didn't, not then. I thought writing was much more important. Of course, writing and speaking do tend to flow together. Exxon was very good about preparing people to do a better job of communicating through writing. They also had some beginning speech courses where you had an opportunity to prepare a speech and deliver it, but these were very elemental.

S.L. Like Speech 101?

D.B. Yes, like a college course. Very few of the engineers ever took it.

S.L. So speaking wasn't a major issue during the first twenty-five years of your career. Was the situation pretty much the same at Occidental?

D.B. Yes.

S.L. You became president of Hooker Chemical in January 1977. You were thrown into the limelight shortly after that. Was *60 Minutes* the first program of that type that you had done?

D.B. It was, and it was quite an experience.

S.L. Did you prepare in any way to be on the show?

D.B. We did two things. First, we felt that we had to make our presidents of the various chemical divisions available to the press. So we looked for a simple program that would at least give them the rudiments of preparation and training to appear on camera. We contracted for a one-day program for our top executives. I took the program, so I had that kind of training. That was probably three or four months before the Mike Wallace show.

S.L. Just one day . . . ?

D.B. Just one day, and it was only for five hours. Basically what you learned was, don't react immediately. Think of what you want to say. Understand the question. If you don't, ask for clarity. Keep in mind that you don't necessarily have to answer the question in terms of specifics; you can use it to make a point. The instructor felt that with some training, you could go into an interview with three or four critical points you wanted to make, and with a little bit of practice and skill, you could get those across without looking like you are fuzzing the answer or dodging the question. He had some examples of politicians and others who really did a very skillful job of making their point while trying to answer a very difficult question.

At the end of the day, we were interviewed on camera. The questions covered some very sensitive areas, so you got a chance to literally see whether you would fluster, or crack. There were definitely some people in the group about whom I said, "Gee, I don't know if we want to put him on camera without more training." The instructor felt I had a good approach that he characterized as forthright and honest. He said, "Don, I think if the situation arises, you'll do well." But that was all of the training.

S.L. You said you did two things to prepare. Was there specific preparation on the Love Canal issue?

D.B. We spent about a day and a half going over the key issues on Love Canal that we thought [Wallace] would deal with. I felt very well prepared on the issues, and of course I had a few points that I wanted to make, such as the fact that no one had been hurt from emissions from that [chemical] plant. I was quite prepared to talk.

S.L. What was your reaction when you were actually called for the *60 Minutes* interview?

D.B. First, I think he was surprised that when he called, he was put through to me directly. I checked with the corporate office. We accepted readily, and I think that surprised him, too. I knew it would be an adversary situation and would be very difficult.

I did make one proviso with him, and that was that we had to meet the morning prior to the interview. I said I would buy him breakfast and he said, "Oh, no. We can't do that. Why would you want to do that?" I said, "I think it's important for you to know a little bit more about me, and me about you, before we face each other in this situation." He said, "I just don't do these things." I said I wouldn't do the interview any other way and he said, "Well, let's not be hasty." So we agreed to talk over a cup of coffee. I took an article my wife had cut out of the paper that said a person is a fool to subject himself to an interview with Mike Wallace. His comment was, "Look, if you've got nothing to be afraid of, you'll get a fair shake with Wallace."

Well, we went into the taping, and the first thing he saw was a TV monitor, our monitor. We had asked for a videotape of the interview and they had said it was against CBS policy to do that. So we wanted to tape it ourselves. The producer said, "This is highly irregular. We've been taped on audio before, but never on camera." Finally I said to Mike, "Look, we've just had a nice talk in the lobby and you told me that if I had nothing to hide . . . what have you got to hide? Why are you so concerned about our camera?" And he said, "Well, it's never happened."

S.L. How did you feel when it was over?

D.B. The way they set up the interview was kind of unnerving because they had me wired in such a way that I had to sit on the edge of my seat. And that was bothersome to me. I had to be in an awkward position while he sat very relaxed in a chair. And sitting right next to him was his producer, who was passing him documents which you couldn't see on camera.

But frankly, I felt fairly good about the interview when I finished. I was able to make the points I felt were important, and we had a chance to look at those in the context of the total situation, so I felt very comfortable with it.

At the end of the interview he said to me, "Mr. Baeder, I don't know whether this will get on the program or not, but I want to put it on tape. I've talked with a lot of executives. You could have run. You could have stonewalled me. You could have dodged my questions. But for two hours or more we've stood toe to toe here, and you've answered all the questions. I don't know what the outcome of all this will be, but I want to tell you, I have a tremendous amount of respect for you, and you're one fine person." So I felt pretty good about that.

S.L. How did you feel when you saw the program?

D.B. Shocked! I really, in all my expectations, never felt that they would be literally as unethical as they were.

S.L. Because of the way it was edited?

D.B. Yes, and because of the way they ignored information. We provided documents—facts—which were just totally ignored. He called me about two weeks after the program. I was so upset by the way he handled the main issues that I just refused to talk with him. He said to [a Hooker public relations man], "I don't understand what Mr. Baeder's so upset about." [Hooker's man] said, "Look, he *gave* you documentation. In addition to the letters we gave you, he sent you stuff special delivery, which you signed for and never used."

Wallace [offered explanations] and said, "Tell him if it makes him feel any better, my mail was all in his favor. There were two programs I felt bad about last year, and this is one of them." He said, "Tell Mr. Baeder he came across very well in my opinion." But I was very upset because what they did in my opinion was very unethical.

S.L. Would you put yourself in that situation again?

D.B. No. Not with Mike Wallace. Once you've been burned . . . I've been interviewed on many occasions since then, and we do ask for some degree of control. One practice we would insist on if we ever went back on *60 Minutes* is that my answers be handled in context—applied to the specific question that was asked.

S.L. So it's fair to say that no matter how honest an executive is or how skilled a speaker, where a great deal of editing is possible, he can come across in a distorted way.

D.B. Absolutely. I'll give you another example. Bruce Davis, who is the president of the Industrial Chemicals Group at Niagara Falls, and I spent half an hour with [CBS reporter] Gary Shepard. [Davis] answered every question that he had, and I thought it was a good interview. The questions that were asked were good, and Bruce handled himself well. On the Walter Cronkite show, the story came on and they used about fifteen seconds of it, and they used it in literally the worst possible way. It was totally out of context.

S.L. It's one thing to handle yourself in a live interview, or an interview where you're on for five or seven minutes, where whatever you do you can be responsible for. But once the editing takes place, you can be made to look any way at all.

D.B. What's happened as a result of that is that large corporations—I think General Motors is an example—have a policy where they will not allow any of their executives to subject themselves to that. There's got to be some way that they can have control. But even then . . . Kaiser Aluminum refused to come on a program with [ABC reporter] Geraldo Rivera without total editorial control. They said that if you'll send us several questions, we'll provide you with short, to-the-point answers, but you've got to run those answers in toto. He refused to do that, and he claimed they refused to come on the show.

It's not all bad, though. Ted Koppel dealt with the question in his program on ABC, where he pointed out industry's feeling that it had not been well handled by the media and made an attempt to look at both sides. That gave industry an opportunity to bring its viewpoint across on a number of critical stories, including Love Canal.

S.L. Is there anything you think you might have done differently in the *60 Minutes* interview?

D.B. No. As I said, I felt well prepared and believed I had handled it well.

S.L. Going into an interview like that, do you feel wound up or nervous?

D.B. Well, I generally feel just a little weak in the stomach.

S.L. Do you have anything special that you do?

D.B. No. The few times I've done it, I guess the adrenaline begins to flow when you get involved in a situation like that, and you just forget about it. Generally for me, it's the same way in a talk. Somehow, I get involved in a talk. It becomes a very personal thing with the audience.

S.L. Let's talk about a specific speech, the one you gave to the Commonwealth Club of San Francisco after you had been on *60 Minutes*. Did you stay word for word with the manuscript?

D.B. Only at times. Most of it I knew well enough that I didn't have to read it.

S.L. Did you work with a speechwriter on that speech?

D.B. For that speech we brought in a writer. That was the last time we ever did that. I probably ended up working twice as hard on that speech as the result of working with a professional writer.

S.L. Well, I thought it was very well organized, with the theme of facts versus perceptions.

D.B. That was a theme we had developed in the corporation, and that's probably why it was so hard to work with an outside writer. The theme really came about because after the initial onslaught from the media on Love Canal, I wrote to all the employees of the corporation, telling them that Hooker Chemical was a very responsible company, that you just don't stay in business seventy-five years without having highly responsible personnel. We just kept feeling that there were a tremendous number of perceptions that the public had that were wrong. You've got to get them the facts.

So the theme was a fairly logical extension. Each of the facts that we developed was based around erroneous perceptions.

S.L. In gathering material for this book, I was looking at the ways in which good speeches were organized. You used the theme that "things aren't always what they seem to be," starting with the seven minutes that people saw you on *60 Minutes* versus the two-and-a-half-hour interview. Then you used four arguments, giving perceptions and then facts to contradict them. I was very impressed with the logical organization.

D.B. I don't want to take a lot of credit, but that is a technique that I have tried to bring into every organization that I have been with. It really is an approach to effective writing, and is like a lawyer's approach to a jury. You start out with a very clear position. Then you bring out all the issues, favorable and unfavorable, and deal with them, one by one.

I told the speechwriter, "Don't write a speech. Write me some positions and issues, and just lay out what we want to leave the audience with. I don't care whether it's subtle or not, but you've got to take the position [in the speech] that a lot of things you've come to believe just aren't so. That's a good position, and now we can look at the key issues under each of those that will fortify that position." I was happy with the end product, but it really required a lot of work.

S.L. It was a much more logical approach than you'd have just sitting down and writing.

D.B. You're absolutely right. I spent a couple of hours recently with a young woman who was working on a major speech for an executive. I said, "If I were you I would write an outline for the speech, and give him an opportunity to make the fine points on key issues."

S.L. On your Commonwealth Club speech, did you then, and do you usually, spend time analyzing the audience?

D.B. Yes. It was one of the reasons I accepted that one, although I must tell you that I refuse very few opportunities. It is a more conservative group, and I really got a very warm reception.

S.L. Would you modify the speech if you were giving it to a different audience?

D.B. To some extent, yes. For example, I have given a similar talk at the University of Vermont, and I did take a different approach to the audience.

S.L. So you now do all of your own speechwriting?

D.B. I do get help from the public relations department for facts and research. My best speeches, in terms of audience interaction, are when I don't have a written document, where I can speak from a mental outline.

S.L. So you think in terms of three or four or five big ideas or main points?

D.B. Yes, main positions that I want to get across. I take each one of those and deal with them separately.

S.L. In the last several years, have you done more thinking about your speaking and about your style?

D.B. I'm certainly more conscious of it. For example, I'm very conscious that I have a tendency to lower my voice. My wife watches this . . . she'll raise her hand like this, and I'll say, "Oh-oh." But I haven't really tried to become a polished speaker. I guess my goal has been to be an effective communicator on what I know and what I can speak on . . . on various points and positions I want to get across.

S.L. I notice you're not afraid to be vulnerable. In your speech to the Commonwealth Club, you told your audience that you were a father and you didn't want your children or grandchildren exposed to unnecessary hazards any more than they did. Is that something you are usually willing to do, to talk about your feelings even when you are in front of a large group?

D.B. Yes. You see, I have a feeling that too often, young people have stereotyped big business. They don't realize that business people are human and large corporations are human.

S.L. Would you say that with the public scrutiny directed at business today, speaking plays a more important role? At Occidental, for example, even with people who are engineers, should part of their training be in communication?

D.B. Oh, yes. One of the reasons that U.S. business is not held in as warm respect as I think it should be is that we've been too private. We've got to be more public. When an executive from this company or that gets up in a public situation, there's just no way that they're not representing the company. And the audience associates them with the company. It's important for them to be good representatives.

S.L. Would you give any particular advice to young people starting out in a company like yours as you think about the speaking and communication experiences you've had in the last four or five years?

D.B. Yes. To me, communication is extremely important to almost any career, and yet we spend probably the least amount of time in college or school really developing effective communication. I look on a lot of my success in moving forward within the company as part of being able to effectively communicate. Even one-on-one . . . if what you're saying isn't organized, and you really haven't thought it through to make your point, you're going to have a hard time succeeding in your situation.

Conclusion

NOW THAT you've finished this book, what have you learned?

You haven't learned formulas that will guarantee an effective content and style every time you make a presentation. There are no pat formulas and there are no guarantees, because each speaker is an individual and each speaking occasion is unique.

Your audience's needs and your own needs will change from situation to situation. The approach to content planning that I've outlined in this book is aimed at helping you put together the most effective presentation for each particular occasion. You can use this approach for every presentation only because the approach itself won't allow you to treat every presentation the same way. The questions stay the same, but the answers keep changing.

So too with the techniques for effective delivery in this book: They are not meant to produce perfect, polished robots. All of them have the speaker as their basis—and every speaker is an individual. I strongly believe that no speaker can be really effective unless he is being himself. The techniques are just ways to help each individual express the best of what he or she is. Just as the content of your presentation should take full account of the uniqueness of the occasion, so too your style should express the uniqueness of you.

No, you haven't learned rules or formulas. Instead you've learned some questions to ask, steps to follow, some techniques to explore and adapt. But they all have one and the same objective: to help you get results whenever you speak. The goal is not to have the perfect stance or absolutely the best main ideas—it's to make something happen. I wouldn't have written this book if my years of experience with business people had not convinced me that my approach to style and content can make a big difference to a speaker's effectiveness. But this same experience convinces me that all techniques are only a means to an end—to have style and content working together to reach out and connect with your audience. When you make that connection, and get the results you want, then you experience the real reward of careful planning and personal risk-taking. It's the exhilaration that comes not from "getting it right," but from *making it happen*.

ABOUT THE AUTHOR

SANDY LINVER, president of the Atlanta-based consulting firm Speakeasy, Inc., is the nation's leading expert on spoken communication in business.

Speakeasy's seminars on content, style, and media are considered by many major corporations to be an essential part of their executive training. The firm now counts among its clients the Coca-Cola Company, IBM, AT&T, Arthur Andersen & Company, and Martin Marietta Data Systems, as well as various government agencies, law firms, and thousands of business executives and politicians who have used Speakeasy privately.

For more information on courses, books, and tapes, please contact Speakeasy, Inc., 400 Colony Square, Atlanta, Georgia 30361; telephone: 404-892-0889.